AF506006

Social Economies of Fear and Desire

Social Economies of Fear and Desire

Emotional Regulation, Emotion Management, and Embodied Autonomy

Valérie de Courville Nicol

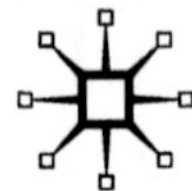

SOCIAL ECONOMIES OF FEAR AND DESIRE
Copyright © Valérie de Courville Nicol, 2011.

First published in 2011 by PALGRAVE MACMILLAN®
in the United States—a division of St. Martin's Press
LLC, 175 Fifth Avenue, New York, NY 10010.

Where this book is distributed in the UK, Europe and the rest of
the world, this is by Palgrave Macmillan, a division of Macmillan
Publishers Limited, registered in England, company number 785998,
of Houndmills, Basingstoke, Hampshire RG21 6XS.

Palgrave Macmillan is the global academic imprint of the above
companies and has companies and representatives throughout the
world.

Palgrave® and Macmillan® are registered trademarks in the United
States, the United Kingdom, Europe and other countries.

ISBN: 978-0-230-33868-5

Library of Congress Cataloging-in-Publication Data

Courville Nicol, Valérie de, 1969-
    Social economies of fear and desire : emotional regulation, emotion
management, and embodied autonomy / Valérie de Courville Nicol.
        p. cm.
    Includes bibliographical references.
    ISBN 978-0-230-33868-5
    1. Fear. 2. Desire. 3. Emotions. I. Title.

    BF575.F2C58 2011
    152.4'6—dc23   2011023724

A catalogue record of the book is available from the British Library.

Design by Scribe Inc.

First edition: December 2011

10 9 8 7 6 5 4 3 2 1

Transferred to Digital Printing in 2012

CONTENTS

ACKNOWLEDGMENTS

I would like to thank the Social Sciences and Humanities Research Council of Canada (SSHRC) and the Fonds de recherche sur la société et la culture (FQRSC) for funding the research that aided in the writing of this book; the research assistants who devoted time to this project: Tara Lyons, Daniel Trottier, Sheila Oakley, Lisa Smith, Kristy Heeren, Brandi Heeren, Julie Blais, Sandra Smele, Jodie Allen, Joan Donovan, Nathalie Reid, and Steve Richter; and my colleagues in the Department of Sociology and Anthropology at Concordia University, especially Marc Lafrance, Beverley Best, and Bart Simon, for their help and encouragement along the way. A special thank you to Shelley Z. Reuter, with whom I shared many different emotions in the course of our respective maternity leaves, for reading some of my work and for her suggestions. I am also grateful for the efforts of two anonymous reviewers, one in particular for the judicious and insightful suggestions that provided me with the guidance I needed. For their ongoing support and friendship, I also thank Bruce Curtis and Alan Hunt at Carleton University; Diane Pacom and Julie Laplante at the University of Ottawa; Anouk Bélanger, Marie Nathalie LeBlanc, and Jean-François Côté at the Université du Québec à Montréal; and Heidi M. Rimke at the University of Winnipeg. For his generosity, thanks go to Kevin Walby at the University of Victoria. For inspiration and for her commitment to a very important field, I thank Lisa Blackman at Goldsmiths College. Thanks also go to Nikolas Rose at LSE, who helped me realize I needed to write this book, and for his stimulating scholarship.

I presented different portions of this book in draft form at the Laboratoire Ville et Espaces Politiques (VESPA), directed by Julie-Anne Boudreau at l'Institut national de la recherche scientifique; at colloquiums organized by Magali Uhl, Shirley Roy, Johanne Collin, and Marcelo Otero during the annual meetings of the Association francophone pour le savoir; and in the "Culture, Power and Everyday Life" sessions of the Canadian Cultural Studies Association, chaired by Bart Simon, Marc Lafrance, Beverley Best, Anouk Bélanger, and myself.

I am grateful for these opportunities. In particular, I thank Marcelo Otero from the Université du Québec à Montréal and Johanne Collin from the Université de Montréal for inviting me into their network and for their generosity. Thank you to Jon Claytor who generously agreed to contribute the cover art. For his kindness and for believing in this project, I am grateful to my editor at Palgrave Macmillan, Burke Gerstenschlager; to Kaylan Connally, editorial assistant, for her support and diligence; and to the rest of the editorial team.

I wish to thank Didier Fayon for a useful reference, Rachel Lefebvre for her unfailing insight, Serge Tremblay for his support, Frédérique Jacoby-Boissy for her help in watching over my youngest son over the past few months, my mother, Michelle de Courville Nicol, for her life-saving editorial and maternal support, and the rest of my family and friends for being in my life. For taking on Sundays with our three very energetic children during the final months of revision, and for going through the various ups and downs of book writing with me, I am especially grateful to my partner, Pascal Harvey. I dedicate this book to our children, Romane, Florian, and Arnaud, because I love them.

INTRODUCTION
ANALYZING EMOTIONAL SELVES

Is it morally dubious for a child to learn to use caution in the handling of sharp objects, or for a social group to feel guilt at the thought of harming others? This book took shape as an attempt to move beyond the common approach to fear as an undifferentiated emotion tied to irrational, morally, or ideologically suspect effects that thwart the exercise of autonomy. It was also developed in an effort to counter the lack of nuanced attention paid to emotional experience—its modalities, its relational content, its triggers, and the agential forms to which it gives rise—in the contemporary analysis of social–emotional configurations. On the one hand, emotional experience is viewed as a structured form of felt in/capacity—as an emotional perspective—through which subjects exercise subjective and moral forms of autonomy. On the other hand, agency is conceived of as the outcome of embodied self-regulation in the course of subjects' interactions or co-constitutive relations with forces they experience as dangerous or as securing. When agency is fear-driven, emotional experience is structured by felt powerlessness in the face of forces that are anticipated to produce pain. When agency is desire-driven, emotional experience is structured by felt powerfulness in the face of forces that are anticipated to produce pleasure. The collective forms taken by these felt in/capacities make up the emotional norms on whose basis subjects interact with the world, much as these norms are understood to emerge through subjects' embodied interactions with the various forces that surround them.

There is a great deal of interest among scholars today in the emotional and affective dimensions of human, social, cultural, and political life—interest in an "affective turn"[1] that rivals the earlier "cultural," "linguistic," or "discursive turn." The increase in the widespread experience of fear as a result of global social transformations decried by "risk society" analysts like Ulrich Beck, Anthony Giddens, and Zygmunt Bauman; the increase in the widespread manufacturing of fear for less than noble purposes that preoccupies "culture-of-fear" analysts like Barry Glassner, Peter N. Stearns, and Michael Moore; and the growing number of products and approaches promoting individuals' management of their fearful selves (from psychological therapeutics to psychopharmaceuticals to scholarly perspectives to security systems) that have been identified by various other critics—all testify to the fact that there is a great deal of fear about fear in late modernity. A driving concern of this book is the current collective desire to take charge of felt incapacity. How and to what effect has fear become a moral problem in late modern societies—a dangerous force for which we feel responsible and upon which we feel compelled to act? This question raises quite a few others, which I address through three sets of queries.

A first set of issues has to do with the interactive and relational processes that govern embodied emotional experience. In what way is affect at the core of the logic of emotional experience? Why are all emotions either painful or pleasurable? How is it that all emotional experiences express either relational threat or relational promise and all are structured by hope? What is the nature of emotions' relationship to danger and security? Why can we not make sense of fear without making sense of desire?

A second set of questions pertains to the relationship between emotional experience and agency. How do emotions fuel and structure agency, and more particularly the exercise of power? Why should all emotions be thought of in pairs? How and why do distinct emotions develop? In what ways are emotions tied not only to behavioral agency but to biological, sensory, emotional, cognitive, and moral forms of agency as well? Why is it useful to distinguish between the subjective and moral experience of emotions? How do emotions promote social conformity and condition social change?

A third and final set of questions involves the features of the emotional economies that structure emotional experience in their relation to the dynamics of emotion management.

What is the nature of the relationship between emotions and moral self-control? What is the difference between suffering and moral suffering, well-being and moral well-being? How do these structure emotional experience and agency? How do emotional norms, as normative structures of felt in/capacity, encourage the development of specific types of emotional experience?

Contemporary subjects are governed through their capacity for autonomy (Rose 1999), but how is this capacity structured and what does it feel like? And how might we identify the socially rewarding actions that produce heteronomy? Conceptualizing the exercise of autonomy as an embodied process enables me to explore the ways in which subjects self-regulate within felt structures of in/capacity. Fear forms are structures of felt incapacity that determine desire forms, while desire forms are structures of felt capacity that promote the exercise of power via various forms of agency.

The conventional association of emotions with "irrational," "excessive," "impulsive," "feminine," or "self-destructive" forms of agency[2] obscures the fundamental involvement of emotions in all forms of agency, including those we might think of as "rational." As Jack Barbalet (2002a) argues, while Weberian and other approaches in sociology have been based on the premise that effective social action is achieved through self-control and against impulses and emotions, all behaviors must be accompanied by emotions that facilitate them, whether confidence in the resolution of a problem, trust in the helping of others, or dissatisfaction in the achievement of success. Emotions act as a bridge between structure and agency, and are, one might add, normative forces in their own right.

Emotional norms of incapacity and of capacity designate the forms of subjects' felt perceptions of problems in the overcoming of danger and in the implementation of security. Emotions motivate us and help us in the resolution of problems, and they do so because they are the felt forms of those problems. I have given the name "fear" to the urge that prompts subjects to overcome danger. In turn, "desire" is the name I give to the urge that prompts subjects to implement security. I conceive of this emotional energy as structured by three basic strategic orientations to problems: terror/courage, phobia/escape, and worry/safety. Emotions consist of the structured urges to confront, to avoid, or to prevent problems and can constitute a mix of these orientations. I think of them as felt perceptions and embodied knowledge.

It is my hope that embodied in/capacity theory provides a viable alternative to the dominant perspective that actions are either informed by reason or malformed by emotion. I understand emotions as a structuring energy that grounds all subjective and moral actions in the process of moving from incapacity to capacity. Fear emotions, as felt incapacities, should not be thought of outside of their relationship to desire emotions, or felt capacities, toward which they tend. For instance, outrage is the fear-based urge to move from the perceived lack of ability to confront another's illegitimate hurting of oneself. Its experience should be made sense of in relation to the feeling of vindication, the desire resulting from the perception that one possesses the ability to do so. The feeling of frustration is a felt incapacity having to do with the inability to confront the forces that stand in the way of one's goals, and the feeling of sadness a felt incapacity having to do with one's inability to prevent the loss of a force to which the self is attached. In turn, these experiences move us to implement security-driven satisfaction and happiness.

All feelings of emotional incapacity can be paired with the feelings of capacity to which they correspond, such as oppression with emancipation (the felt in/ability to confront forces that illegitimately constrain one's freedom) or alarm with reassurance (the felt in/ability to avoid the sudden emergence of an adverse force). Emotional-norm pairs name the problem and the solution orientations that guide agency. If meaning economies tell us about how subjects make sense of the world and are made sense of in this world in ways that inform their actions, emotional economies tell us about the kinds of in/capacities that subjects experience in particular settings, and about the felt strategic orientations that inform their actions.

I define the feeling of incapacity as a felt lack of ability to move away from the anticipated pain that forms the experience of danger, and the feeling of capacity as the felt ability to move toward the anticipated pleasure that forms the experience of security. On the one hand, when an emotional experience is the expression of a subject's felt powerlessness or incapacity in the face of a pain-producing force, it is structured by a lack that is given its form by the fear-based urge to overcome danger. Fear is the hope-based quest to determine the form of in/capacity and the experience of this form. On the other hand, when an emotional experience is the expression of a subject's felt powerfulness or capacity in the face of a pleasure-producing force, it is structured by a lack that is given its form by the desire-based urge to implement security. Desire is at once the hope-based quest to determine the form of power and the experience of the urge to exercise that power.

The irrational effects of agential spontaneity are frequently invoked to explain the tie between emotions and ineffectual or self-destructive actions. I develop three modalities of emotional experience that allow us to account for the relationship between emotions and agential outcomes and provide an alternative to this view. The panic/excitement modality of emotional experience implies that an agent knows of and has access to an adequate means of power to respond to a threat, such as when a subject runs in a marathon with confidence in his or her ability to complete it or to do well. The anxiety/interest modality of emotional experience implies that an agent's knowledge of and access to means of power to respond to a threat are inadequate, such as when a subject runs in a marathon with ambivalent feelings about his or her ability to complete it or to do well. The distress/relief modality of emotional experience implies that an agent's knowledge of the means of power to respond to a threat is nonexistent, such as when a subject doubts his or her ability to run in a marathon at all.

While agential responses to threats governed by the panic/excitement-driven modality of fear and desire tend to be more spontaneous, they should not be thought of as inherently irrational or destructive. Spontaneous forms of agency can be highly rational and protective, such as when a terrified subject who desires to go on living spontaneously jumps out of the way of a rapidly approaching vehicle. Similarly, the traditional or habitual forms of behavior associated with spontaneity should be thought of as effective and protective in the overcoming of danger and in the implementation of security in contexts where innovative forms of behavior would be ineffectual in allowing a subject to do so. The rationality or irrationality of an action should therefore be determined on grounds other than whether or not it is spontaneous.

The three modalities of emotional experience represent agents' sense of being able to exercise power over a problem, and the modalities qualify all emotional experiences. Thus the quality of the experience of disgust/purging or of guilt/innocence will vary, depending on whether an agent feels capable of moving from incapacity to capacity in a satisfactory manner, in an unsatisfactory manner, or not at all.

While various means (cognitive, behavioral, moral, sensory, emotional) could be invoked in order to transform a currently perceived modality of emotional experience, when emotional means are employed, they involve the transformation of a current emotional experience into an alternative one. I develop the concepts of emotional blending and differentiation to account for the processes through which alternative or new emotions come into being as a result of subjects' anxiety/interest-driven or distress/relief-driven interactions with the various forces that surround them. Emotional blending designates the process through which an already existing alternative emotional-norm pair experience is invoked as a means to deal with the inadequacy of means to problem resolution, while emotional differentiation refers to the process through which a new emotional-norm pair experience is created as a means to deal with the absence of existing emotional or other means.

The embodied in/capacity theory developed here is an attempt to move beyond the opposition between emotions as either biological and natural or social and constructed that has animated much scholarship on the emotions. While a biologically reductionist view of emotions has caused some analysts to ignore emotional life forces based on the perspective that they are unalterable phenomena that are not amenable to sociological investigation and are unrelated to social change, by contrast the biological and other embodied features of emotions have been denied or glossed over by others taking a socially reductionist position. In their appeal for a medical sociology that makes use of interactive approaches to emotions, Williams and Bendelow (1996) suggest we can overcome the discursive essentialism that has ensued from the exclusion of the biological by viewing subjects as embodied and emotions as a bridge between the private and the public. The concept of "emotives" developed by Reddy (1999, 1997) similarly seeks to move beyond the shortcomings of social constructionism. With a growing list of others who seek to offer complex accounts of embodied subjectivity,[3] I take the position that emotions have an affective basis and are experienced biographically through embodied subjects' interactions with social and other forces.

Beyond producing a model for the understanding of felt forms of subjective in/capacity, on whose basis agents seek to overcome danger and implement security, this work produces a model for the understanding of felt forms of moral in/capacity, on whose basis subjects seek to overcome moral danger and implement moral security. Experiences of self-fear and of self-desire result from a process of "responsibilization," in which subjects become morally responsible for their suffering and well-being, and on whose basis they become compelled to exercise power over themselves through efforts at moral self-control.

While there is increasing recognition of the fact that emotional expression is largely mediated by agents' interactions with social norms, when accounting for the self's emotion management efforts upon itself, emphasis is usually placed on the repressive form of this control rather than on its expressive form. However, agents meet the requirements of morally normative and more idiosyncratic social expectations not only through the repression and correction of their desires but also through their activation and formation. As such, some social groups may be said to favor morally expressive over morally repressive means of emotional self-transformation. For instance, in the contemporary Western context, agents' moral conformity is increasingly based on the ability to achieve normative forms of selfhood through the proper expression of desire rather than through its negation. This logic, which I refer to as the logic of healthy self-realization, can be contrasted with and has developed in opposition to the logic of rational self-discipline that characterizes an earlier modern emotional economy.

I pay particular attention to the exercise of moral power, which I understand as the affectively motivated, deliberate transformation of the self as a force in the fulfillment of an imperative or of an ideal, in the moving away from suffering and toward well-being. I identify two modes in the exercise of moral power. Where the exercise of moral power is structured by a subject's relation of compliance with a command, moral danger is produced by a transgressive desire and is an expression of immoral powerfulness. Here, illegitimate and erroneous desires must be repressed and corrected in the production of moral security. I argue that this mode of moral power is dominant in the modern repressive discipline-based society. Where the exercise of moral power is structured by a subject's relation of measurement to an ideal, moral danger is produced by an inadequate desire and is an expression of immoral powerlessness. Here, inactive and immature desires must be activated and formed in the production of moral security. I argue that this mode of moral power is dominant in the expressive late modern society that is realization based.

In the moral exercise of power, the emotional management of self and other is accomplished through the wielding of hedonic power, which compels agents to seek the avoidance of pain and the pursuit of pleasure. More specifically, emotion management is achieved by initiating the mechanism of emotional regulation. By triggering a particular emotional experience, emotion management makes use of the structured urge to overcome danger and implement security that characterizes emotional regulation, and through this means it succeeds in directing the course of agency. Emotion management is exercised in the expectation that the eliciting of a particular emotional experience will generate other actions, for instance particular behaviors, or will generate a subject's desire to engage in behaviors or other actions that it is the emotional manager's desire to activate and whose salience ought therefore to be produced in the effort at emotion management.

When successfully performed upon the self, emotion management is referred to as moral self-control. When successfully performed upon others, emotion management can either trigger effective moral self-control efforts on the part of these others or simply have an emotional regulation effect. Whether it aims to transform the self (as an other) or another self, emotion management should be understood here as a form of social control that I refer to as "emotional socialization." I account for the exercise of moral self-control through four principal means of self-transformation in modern and late modern societies: the self's repression of illegitimate desire, the self's correction of erroneous desire, the self's activation of latent desire, and the self's formation of immature desire. Emotional campaigns, whether of fear or of desire, use rhetorical means in an effort to emotionally manage subjects. Campaigns of fear deploy a rhetoric of fear to prompt the repression or correction of destructive and norm-transgressing desires, while campaigns of desire deploy a rhetoric of desire to prompt the activation or formation of constructive and norm-enhancing desires.

The approach I develop allows social analysts to delineate the features of distinct emotional economies on the basis of various features, including the frequency, intensity, and scope of the experience of specific emotional-norm pairs, of the actions and objects of fear and desire to which they are tied, and of the signs of danger and security that trigger them; the prevalence of emotional-norm pairs tied to any of the three strategic orientations, whether confrontation, avoidance, or prevention; the prevalence of any of the three modalities of emotional experience, whether the subjective panic/excitement, the moral anxiety/interest, or the moral distress/relief; the prevalence of either or both processes of emotional blending and differentiation, through which culturally specific emotional-norm pairs develop; the scope of the exercise of moral autonomy and of the experience of responsibilization; the extent to which subjects remain caught in experiences of emotional pain; the extent to which experiences of emotional pleasure promote structural powerlessness; the incidence of social emotions and of their political forms, as well as their relationship to social change; the dominant mode of emotion management, whether self-discipline or self-realization; the extent to which agents are morally acted upon by others or by themselves; and the logic of master emotional-norm pairs.

In the first part of this book, which includes Chapters 1 through 3, I outline the premises and principles of the approach to emotional life and agency that I develop and call "embodied in/capacity" theory. I begin by arguing that the commonly held notion that dangers can be real or threatened, unreal or imagined, on whose grounds a distinction between fear and anxiety is often made, should be rejected. I propose alternative definitions of fear and desire and maintain that they both involve hope. I explore the relationship between fear and pain, desire and pleasure. I make a case for how fear and desire are forms of remembering. I develop a formal definition of emotions and of emotional norms and tie them to three basic strategic orientations (confrontation, avoidance, and prevention). I provide definitions of a series of emotional-norm pairs to illustrate how they are emotional perspectives that inform attempts to exercise power in the overcoming of danger and the implementation of security.

In Chapter 2, I introduce the concepts of affective, agential, and symbolic attunement in order to explain how objects of fear and desire are attached to emotional orientations, means of exercising power, and signs of danger and security. I produce an account of three modalities of fear and desire—panic/excitement, anxiety/ interest, and distress/relief—that are governed by subjects' relationship to the means of exercising power. I conclude this chapter with an examination of how new emotional-norm pairs can be thought of as coming into being through the moral processes of emotional blending and emotional differentiation.

In Chapter 3 I begin by critically engaging with the work of the philosopher Ian Hacking (1999) on interactive and indifferent kinds. This serves as a point of entry into my conceptualization of three distinct and interacting modes of embodied autonomy—biological, subjective, and moral—on whose basis I seek to account for the affect-bound nature of embodied interaction. To this end, I propose novel definitions of key concepts in sociocultural analysis that I think through in their relation to emotional experience and agency. Finally, I distinguish between subjective, moral, and social emotional experiences based on whether the self feels compelled to exercise power over external forces, over internal forces, or over the quality of self–other relations as external or internal forces. I also differentiate between subjective, moral, and social emotions, where the latter two are structured by the unsuccessful resolution of an objectified emotional problem, and provide definitions and examples of political emotions as well.

In the second part of this book, which includes chapters 4 through 8, I explore how we might make sense of the distinct social configurations of emotional life that I refer to as emotional economies. In Chapter 4, I produce a critical reading of the late sociologist Norbert Elias's contribution to the analysis of differing emotional economies and of the types of suffering and forms of self-fear they engender (1978, 1982). I explore the process through which individuals develop a moral relationship to danger and security—a process defined as "responsibilization"—on whose basis they are prompted to engage in moral self-transformation efforts, or to exercise moral self-control. I discuss some of the ways in which self-fear may be said to be on the rise. I distinguish between discipline-based means of moral self-control—self-repression and self-correction—which are tied to individuals' experience of immoral capacity or powerfulness, and realization-based means of moral self-control—self-activation and self-formation—which are associated with individuals' experience of immoral incapacity or powerlessness. I suggest that collective differences in the quantity and quality of experiences of moral in/capacity constitute grounds for elucidating the dynamics of distinct emotional economies.

In Chapter 5 I discuss the importance of social norms in emotional experience and develop the concepts of emotional regulation, hedonic power, and emotion management in order to account for the role of moral action in the exercise of power over and by way of emotional selves. I argue that emotional regulation is the outcome of emotional socialization, while emotion management constitutes the means of this socialization. I explore the significance of shame/pride and personal insecurity/self-esteem as feelings governed by agents' sense of responsibility for social approval. I build upon Mary Douglas's concept of the danger ritual (1966) in order to explain how the practices of inclusion, of exclusion, and of expulsion of socially disruptive forces promote agents' attempts to resolve shame and personal insecurity, and also I explore how these emotions are related to activist forms of social change.

In Chapter 6 I critically engage with the pioneering work of sociologist Arlie R. Hochschild (1983) on emotion management in order to increase the scope and coherence of this concept. I make a case for the concept of heteronomy in lieu of the concept of self-estrangement as a means of accounting for self-destructive efforts at emotion management, and I explore the significance of lying and acting in their relation to distinct forms of moral self-control. I conclude this chapter with an exploration of William Reddy's concept of "emotives" in its relation to the modalities of fear and desire and moral self-control (1999, 1997).

In Chapter 7 I develop the concept of the master emotional-norm pair as a means to make sense of the different logics that govern distinct emotional economies and the emotional-norm pairs that develop within them, and as a means of explaining the way in which social emotional change emerges as a result of an antagonism between rival forms of capacity that benefit some agents and not others. I refer to the logic of late eighteenth and nineteenth century gothic[4] and late twentieth century self-help discourses to provide examples of discipline and realization-based emotional norms, which I situate within modern and late modern emotional structures. I argue that the first is characterized by a repressive logic grounded in reason and the second by an expressive logic grounded in health. I also introduce a distinction between campaigns of fear and campaigns of desire based on a reformulation of Brian P. Bloomfield's and Theo Vurdubakis's work on emotion management (1995). I compare and contrast two contemporary emotion management campaigns and further develop the distinction between discipline-based and realization-based approaches to moral self-control.

In the concluding chapter, I analyze the structural differences between the modern fear of desire and the late modern fear of fear itself. While the former favors the disciplining of irrational desire, the latter favors the realization of healthy desire. I critically engage with the culture-of-fear approach and hold that it is based on an overly narrow understanding of danger and is a powerful rhetoric that must be situated in its normative context. Finally, I develop Noël Carroll's concept of "situation assimilation" (1990) in order to account for some of the ways in which the mass media achieve emotional effects on their audiences.

Emotions are felt incapacities and capacities that structure agency. Painful fear emotions express a relation of threat that motivates the search for the form of in/capacity through which to overcome danger, whereas pleasurable desire emotions express a relation of promise that motivates the search for the form of power through which to implement security. Emotional experience motivates human agents' fear and desire-driven exercise of power over their selves, over other selves, and over internal and external forces more generally, as means to move from painful incapacity to pleasurable capacity. In short, emotions affect us because we experience them as either painful or pleasurable. Their embodied nature is therefore of consequence, in the general sense that they prompt us to move away from pain-producing danger and to move toward pleasure-producing security.

Embodied in/capacity theory encourages us to consider that the effects of discursive and other social practices on agency are governed by emotional perspectives experienced through social interaction and by emotional norms acquired through emotional socialization. In this view, the effects of regimes of power/knowledge (Foucault 1979) need to be rethought in order to include the affective effects of emotional knowledge in the workings of social orders—affective effects that ought not to be thought of as inherently irrational. Subjects are not only constituted through their interactions with socially produced cognitive perspectives (ways of thinking) and truths (collectively held beliefs about what reality is); they are also constituted through their interactions with socially produced emotional perspectives (ways of feeling) and emotional norms (collectively held feelings of how to act and of orientation.)

"Emotional analysis" (or "discursive emotional analysis," as the case may be) could consist of the examination of the agential and power effects of the emotional perspectives (which may or may not be emotional norms) produced through discursive and other social practices (e.g., spatial arrangements, governmental programs, advertising, conversations, financial systems, popular literature, and the like) as effects that might bypass what agents consider to be true from a cognitive perspective (e.g., crying at the thought of the loss of a loved one whose death I imagine or purchasing a product that makes me feel youthful even though I do not believe it to be effective at reducing the signs or process of aging). In short, embodied in/capacity theory allows us to explore the dynamics and effects of emotional relations so that we might cease to dismiss as irrational the expressions of agency that are in conflict with our beliefs about reality and instead consider how they involve our feelings of orientation, where these form a part of a complex web of interactions.

Part I

Embodied In/Capacity Theory

CHAPTER 1

ANALYZING FEAR AND DESIRE

RELATIONAL THREAT AND RELATIONAL PROMISE: THE ANTICIPATION OF PAIN AND PLEASURE

To start, I shall briefly comment upon the distinction between fear and anxiety often associated with Freud, where fear is understood as "a reaction to a real or threatened danger," and anxiety as "a reaction to an unreal or imagined danger."[1]

This definition of fear rests on what I consider to be a misleading opposition between real and threatened danger. The experience of fear is always the experience of being in danger—of painfully anticipating pain. Thus even while one might be said to be already in pain, it is the threat of this pain's continuation that constitutes the fear relation, which is a relation of avoidance to pain.

Because a danger can no longer be said to be a danger once its painful consequences are realized[2] and are no longer expected to realize themselves, it is in the nature of danger to be an anticipation of unrealized or imagined pain, which is itself painful. In sum, it does not make much sense to speak of a danger as real, since it is in its nature to be unrealized. And since the notion of threat grounds that of danger, it is equally unhelpful to distinguish between types of dangers on the basis of whether they constitute a threat. Danger, or anticipated pain, is by its very nature a threat. It suffices to say that one is in danger, or that one is threatened, or that one is afraid. It is certainly unnecessary to explain that one is threatened by a danger, endangered by a threat, or afraid of a danger, unless of course one is designating the experience of fear as a moral danger. To the extent that it can be treated as a moral danger—as a force that ought not to be as it is and about which one ought to do something—it is true that fear, as the painful urge to overcome danger, can itself become an object of fear, or a danger.

This means that an anticipated painful outcome, whether the chances it will become realized are high or low, remains a danger and prompts the urge to overcome it. Relational threat constitutes danger, even if the realization of the pain with which it is associated is unlikely. This is why potential painful outcomes that are made salient are more likely to be feared than those that are not, irrespective of the likelihood of their occurrence.[3]

If it is in the nature of fear to involve the painful anticipation of unrealized pain, then one should not make a distinction between fear and anxiety on the basis of their opposing relations to some unrealized pain, or on the grounds that in the one the danger that is anticipated is real and in the other it is not. The moral relation to fear that governs experiences of anxiety or of distress, which I later discuss,[4] produces a quality of fear, but does not make these experiences species that are distinct from it. Fear requires that subjects experience, through the painfully felt anticipation of pain, the painful outcome of the realization of pain. It is the painful expectation that relational effects will be painful that makes the fear experience. And it is the *felt* nature of this expectation that makes this experience affective.

Fear is a painfully felt anticipation of pain that is also a relation of avoidance to unrealized pain. Fear is the felt urge to avoid anticipated pain. This unrealized pain exists by virtue of an anticipated and therefore imagined (remembered) relation to a force that it is felt will cause it and that I call "danger." The threat posed by a force is always imagined, since a force cannot be said to be dangerous in and of itself, or to contain danger. Fear is not an unmediated reaction to an inherently dangerous force. It is triggered by the perception that a particular kind of relation will engender pain. Fear is both anticipatory and a form of remembering.

Much of what I have been saying about fear can be also said about desire. Desire is a pleasurably felt anticipation of pleasure that is also a relation of pursuit to unrealized pleasure. Desire is the felt urge to seek anticipated pleasure. This unrealized pleasure exists by virtue of an anticipated and therefore imagined (remembered) relation to a force that it is felt will cause it and that I call "security." The promise posed by a force is always imagined, since a force cannot be said to be securing in and of itself, or to contain security. Desire is not an unmediated reaction to an inherently securing force. It is triggered by the perception than a particular kind of relation will engender pleasure. Desire is both anticipatory and a form of remembering.

Simply put, fear is the painful anticipation of pain that produces the urge to overcome danger, while desire is the pleasurable anticipation of pleasure that produces the urge to implement security.

Pain is a subjective experience individuals move to avoid through fear-driven anticipation.[5] Pleasure is a subjective experience that individuals move to pursue through desire-driven anticipation. Inasmuch as pain is a force from which we seek to move away, and pleasure a force toward which we seek to move, our experience of pain and pleasure is always governed by anticipation. We know that an experience is painful because we are driven to move away from it. We know that an experience is pleasurable because we are driven to move toward it. The fear experience is an experience of emotional pain in its most general form, while the desire experience is an experience of emotional pleasure in its most general form.

Objects of fear and desire are problem and solution contents. The object of fear is the problem content of the object of desire, while the object of desire is the solved content[6] of the object of fear. To illustrate, let us say that I perceive the presence of smoke produced by cigarettes as dangerous, in which case I may be said to fear the presence of smoke produced by cigarettes. This is the problem content. I shall also perceive the absence of smoke produced by cigarettes as securing, in which case I may be said to desire the absence of smoke produced by cigarettes. This is the solved content. Or let us say that I perceive the lack of equity in the sharing of domestic tasks as dangerous, in which case I may be said to fear the lack of equity in the sharing of domestic tasks. This is the problem content. I shall also perceive the presence of this equity as securing, in which case I may be said to desire the presence of equity in the sharing of domestic tasks. This is the solved content. In these examples, the objects of fear (the presence of smoke produced by cigarettes, the lack of equity in the sharing of domestic tasks) are constituted by the association of a particular force—the presence of cigarette smoke or the lack of equity in the sharing of domestic tasks—with a painful outcome. And the objects of desire (the absence of smoke produced by cigarettes, the presence of equity in the sharing of domestic tasks) are constituted by the association of a particular force—the absence of smoke produced by cigarettes or the presence of equity in the sharing of domestic tasks—with a pleasurable outcome.

This means that objects of fear and desire share the same solution. For instance, the problem of the presence of smoke produced by cigarettes can be resolved by insisting that those who smoke refrain from doing so, by avoiding places where individuals smoke, or by preventing the sale of cigarettes. These same means are the means through which the absence of smoke produced by cigarettes is brought about. Similarly, the problem of the absence of equity in the sharing of domestic tasks can be resolved by confronting the issue through heated discussions, by a less productive partner's repair of the situation through an increased contribution, or by preventing the absence of equity by working out an equitable agreement. Again, these same means are the means through which the presence of equity in the sharing of domestic tasks is brought about.

In sum, the object of fear is produced by the prior embodied association (whether inborn and previously embodied or more recently embodied) between a force and a painful outcome that constitutes it as a pain relation one can anticipate, or, in short, as a relational threat. The object of fear is the content of danger.

Fear is a self-driven urge to avoid anticipated pain, or to overcome danger. The experience of relational threat is therefore a painful experience of danger, and danger is a force whose content is an object of fear constituted in the past. Fear's effect is to move subjects to avoid the painful outcome this object represents by constituting a felt identification with this outcome—by making subjects feel what they anticipate this pain will be like. Thus fear is a painful felt perception of anticipated pain.

In sum, the object of desire is produced by the prior embodied association (whether inborn and previously embodied or more recently embodied) between a force and a pleasurable outcome that constitutes it as a pleasure relation one can anticipate, or, in short, as a relational promise. The object of desire is the content of security.

Desire is a self-driven urge to seek pleasure, or to implement security. The experience of relational promise is therefore a pleasurable experience of security, and security is a force whose content is an object of desire constituted in the past. Desire's effect is to move subjects to pursue the pleasurable outcome this object represents by constituting a felt identification with its outcome—by making subjects feel what they anticipate this pleasure will be like. Thus desire is a pleasurable felt perception of anticipated pleasure.

The form and relational content of emotional experience can become attached to signs that trigger this experience. I call these signs, signs of danger and of security. The experience of fear occurs as a result of a prior association between a force (signifier) and a painful outcome (signified) that come to constitute a threat relation that I have called the object of fear. This threat relation becomes tied to a sign of danger that can then trigger specific forms of emotional experience.[7] Similarly, the experience of desire occurs as a result of a prior association between a force (signifier) and a pleasurable outcome (signified) that come to constitute a promise relation that I have called the object of desire. This promise relation becomes tied to a sign of security that can then trigger specific forms of emotional experience.

A sign of danger or security may be identical to or obviously related to the objects of fear and desire to which it is tied. For instance, if the presence of cigarette smoke constitutes an object of fear, the presence of cigarette smoke might also act as a sign of danger and trigger the experience of fear. Here the sign of danger is identical to the object of fear. The sight of a cigarette or the smell of smoke produced by other matter might also trigger the experience of this object of fear. Here the sign of danger remains obviously related to the object of fear. The same is true of signs of security. For instance, if the absence of cigarette smoke constitutes an object of desire, the absence of cigarette smoke might also act as a sign of security and trigger the experience of desire. Here the sign of danger is identical to the object of desire. "No smoking" signs or the smell of fresh air after leaving a smoke-filled environment might also act to trigger the experience of this object of desire. Here also the sign of security remains obviously related to the object of desire.

However, a sign of danger or security may be related to objects of fear and desire in ways that are much less obvious or not obvious at all. In other words, the sign of danger or security does not necessarily contain any clues about the perceptual process that led to its association with an object of fear or desire. For instance, a subject may have an intense fear of bearded men or of spiders but may not be able to recall the processing that led to the association of this sign of danger with an object of fear. Similarly, a subject may have an intense desire for curly hair or frog paintings but may not be able to recall the processing that led to the association of this sign of security with an object of desire.

This explains why subjects do not always know why they are afraid or why they desire, even though they may know what they are afraid of or what they desire. In other words, subjects are not always aware of the relational threats and promises that ground their fears and desires, and may take signs of danger and security for their cause. To know why one fears bearded men or spiders, or why one desires curly hair or frog paintings, one would have to know to which objects of fear and desire these signs are attached. In some instances, we can remember or reconstruct the perceptual processes through which objects of fear and desire became associated with particular signs of danger and security. In less obvious cases, various techniques may be used or developed to try to reconstruct these associations if need be. Other than the examination of biography where idiosyncratic signs are concerned, the careful examination of social forces is also of use in making sense of a connection.[8]

The process through which a sign of danger or of security dissimulates the objects of fear and desire they represent can be referred to as displacement.[9] In his analysis of why Americans have become so fearful and often misplace their fears, Barry Glassner (1999) argues that the fear triggered by problems whose solutions are complex and challenging, and whose solutions pose a threat to the interests of those in authority or who stand to profit from the provision of "symbolic substitutes" for "moral insecurities" (xxviii), is often displaced onto other targets. Fearmongering involves "the tendency to trivialize legitimate concerns even while aggrandizing questionable ones" (9). Thus a common form of displacement involves shifting the focus from "disturbing shortcomings in society" to "disturbed individuals" (6). For instance, Glassner holds that Americans' feelings of guilt over their recent failure to properly care for the nation's children through adequate nutrition, education, and housing is projected onto moral deviants like "preschool teachers, preteen mass murderers, and homicidal au pairs" (xxvi).

The process of displacement is understood by Glassner as resulting from two main causes: manipulation and powerlessness. For instance, he discusses (66) a marketing ploy in which postcards that are sent to potential consumers feature a picture and information about a missing child on one side, and an advertisement for a business on the other. The question "Have you seen me?" featured above the picture of the missing child manipulates the consumer into looking to the services of the business featured on the reverse side of the card as a solution to their powerlessness with regard to the problem of the missing child. Various corporate brands can in this way come to act as triggers for forms of powerlessness or of endangerment, and can serve to promote the consumption of their commodities as a means of becoming powerful or secure. This is a compelling example of how signs of danger and security that have no obvious relation to the underlying relational threats and promises they trigger can serve to manipulate embodied subjects. I now turn to a discussion of the relationship between fear, hope, and desire.

FEAR, DESIRE, AND THE HOPE RESPONSE

Fear is the outcome of the embodied perception of anticipated pain that is danger. It is the felt, relationally governed emotional urge and stance that orients subjects in the avoidance of pain. Desire is the embodied perception of anticipated pleasure that is security. It is the felt, relationally governed emotional urge and stance that orients subjects in the pursuit of pleasure.

In short, fear is the painfully felt urge to overcome danger in order to avoid pain, while desire is the pleasurably felt urge to implement security in order to pursue pleasure. Together fear and desire constitute the most basic forms of subjective motivation to act. To understand how fear and desire become translated into action, we need to examine what I have chosen to call the hope response.

As the urge to act that grows out of the painful anticipation of pain, fear implies the hope that pain can be avoided. As the urge to act that grows out of the pleasurable anticipation of pleasure, desire implies the hope that pleasure can be pursued. As such, fear and desire are constituted through both lack and hope—the lack of an orientation to pain avoidance that motivates the hopeful quest for its discovery, and the lack of an orientation to pleasure seeking that stimulates the hopeful quest for its discovery. Fear entails the painful perception that one lacks but might obtain the means of avoiding anticipated pain (or of overcoming danger), while desire entails the pleasurable perception that one lacks but might obtain the means of pursuing anticipated pleasure (or of implementing security).

Fear and desire are structured by hope. Fear is structured by the hope that is implied by the anticipated and therefore uncertain nature of the pain outcome that engenders fear, and therefore by the hope of moving away from pain, while desire is structured by the hope that is implied by the anticipated and therefore uncertain nature of the pleasure outcome that engenders desire, and therefore by the hope of moving toward pleasure.

The hope response to the problem of relational threat involves the successful determination of the form of incapacity through which one might overcome the power of a dangerous force. Fear is therefore the urge that prompts the subject to seek and identify the form of incapacity to which a threat corresponds, as well as the experience of this form. Because the form of incapacity contains the form of capacity toward which it tends, this moment in the overcoming of danger allows the subject to move into the experience of relational promise, or of felt capacity. The subject now desires anticipated pleasure, or security, rather than fears anticipated pain, or danger. The hope response to the problem of relational promise involves the successful determination of the means of power required for the implementation of a securing force. Desire is therefore the urge that prompts the subject to seek, identify, and implement the means of power to which a promise corresponds, as well as the experience of a form of capacity.

Strictly speaking, the only actions we can properly tie to fear are the pursuit and identification of the form of incapacity (of powerlessness) whose transformation into capacity is the basis of the overcoming of danger, as well as the move into desire. By contrast, desire is tied to the pursuit and identification of the means of power through which security can be implemented, as well as to the exercise of these means. This signifies that actions that are commonly associated with fear-driven emotions, such as defense mechanisms and aggressive types of behavior, as well as actions that are commonly associated with desire-driven emotions, such as physical arousal and sexual types of behavior, are generally understood here to be the outcome of the successful resolution of fear and desire-driven lacks, but are more precisely understood to be the outcome of the desire-driven implementation of security. In other words, projection, rioting, and dressing appealingly, for instance, are tied to fear in the sense that they are conditioned by its setting the stage for the desire to engage in these particular actions, but should ultimately be understood as means of power in the actualization of desire—as means through which security is implemented—and therefore as actions that are tied to desire.

Subjects' knowledge of the means of averting pain (the determination of the form of in/capacity) and of seeking pleasure (the determination of the means of power) may be inborn or embodied more recently, but, like their knowledge of the forces that cause painful and pleasurable consequences—like their knowledge of objects of fear and desire—it is in any event a result of prior interactions with their environment. As such, subjects may be born with the previously developed ability to respond through a particular fear form to specific objects of fear or the signs of danger that trigger their experience, such as with terror to unknown sounds in the darkness, or to respond through a particular desire form to specific objects of desire or the signs of security that trigger their experience, such as responding with courage to light. In the first case, a form of incapacity has previously been tied to a particular object of fear and sign of danger, such that the experience of unknown sounds in the darkness triggers terror, while in the second case, a means of power has previously been tied to a particular desire form and sign of security, such that light triggers courage.

Evolutionary and functionalist thinkers have called something akin to the hope response "adaptation." And because the hope response favors conformity to social norms as a means of avoiding the pain of social disapproval and of seeking the pleasure of social approval, social construction theorists more generally have viewed it as a form of social control. However, I prefer the concept of embodied interaction (in the context of the exercise of embodied autonomy) to that of adaptation.

First, the concept of embodied interaction suggests that all the forces involved in a relation are transformed, whereas the concept of adaptation usually implies the one-sided transformation of passive forces in their dealings with immutable forces. Used in this way, the concept of adaptation fails to account for the very real effects of individual and collective forms of agency on the world.

Second, the concept of embodied interaction accounts for the purpose-driven affective basis of auto-transformation when it involves subjectively embodied agents, rather than presuming that this transformation is purely arbitrary or accidental, or that the effective transformation of other forces is best achieved through the absence of feeling.

And third, the concept of embodied interaction allows for the possibility that different relations involve different ratios of force, whereas the concept of adaptation makes it seem as though individual and collective agents are simply or mostly powerless in the face of larger structures, such as social, physical, and biological structures. This is clearly not the case, whether or not agential power is conceived of as drive based, will based, or intention based. I later define the feeling of adaptation that corresponds to the force of adaptation as the felt capacity to prevent self-destruction by conforming to a more powerful force's logic. My point is that not all embodied interactions involve this particular power dynamic.

I am also interested in an inclusive understanding of the hope response in recognition of the principle that the lack that is its basis is the outcome of embodied subjects' conflicts with all the forces with which they interact, not just social ones. Hope is the expression of the potential for a solution to a lack of power, and it is as such that it motivates the actions of subjectively embodied agents. Hope is made manifest in the felt quest for and identification of solutions to lacks caused by all types of embodied conflicts, such as the conflict between a self and the physical force that causes it to experience pain when it is struck by hard objects, the conflict between a self and the social force that causes it to experience pain when it violates or falls short of a social expectation, or the conflict between a self and its biological being that causes it to experience pain when it fails to align itself with its requirement for oxygen or nourishment.

Fear and desire are distinct yet interdependent motivational forces whose purpose is pain avoidance and pleasure seeking. We may think of painful and pleasurable emotional states as existing on a continuum with varying degrees of intensity, such that one is never on neutral emotional territory. Fear is always a moving toward desire that is motivated by pain, and desire a moving away from fear that is motivated by pleasure. The more intense the anticipated pain, the more forceful the fear; the more forceful the fear, the more forceful the threat-driven hope response; the more forceful the threat-driven hope response, the more forceful the desire; the more forceful the desire, the more forceful the promise-driven hope response; the more forceful the promise-driven hope response, the more intense the anticipated pleasure, whose intensity should equal that of the initial anticipated pain, or that of the accumulated effects of the historical failure to move away from it.

The view of fear as a felt means of orienting self-driven agency in the avoidance of pain means that all negatively valenced emotions can be included in its scope, including emotions we more typically associate with fear, such as terror, horror, shame, and guilt, as well as emotions we may not associate with fear, such as sadness, anger, hatred, and regret. On the other hand, the view of desire as a felt means of orienting self-driven agency in the pursuit of pleasure means that all positively valenced emotions can be included in its scope, including emotions we might more typically associate with desire, such as order, love, and happiness, as well as emotions we may not associate with desire, such as courage, trust, innocence, and vindication.

I am proposing that fear emotions are those emotions that emerge from the painful experience of relational threat and that objects of fear are dangers we seek to overcome. I am also proposing that desire emotions are those emotions that emerge from the pleasurable experience of relational promise and that objects of desire are securities we seek to implement. All forms of fear entail an anticipatory dimension by virtue of the fact that fear is the painful anticipation of pain that motivates a self-driven hope response geared toward pain avoidance. Similarly, all forms of desire entail an anticipatory dimension by virtue of the fact that desire is the pleasurable anticipation of pleasure that motivates a self-driven hope response geared toward pleasure seeking.

While the object of fear that is danger is constituted by the previously embodied association between a force and a painful outcome, the object of desire that is security is constituted by the previously embodied association between a force and a pleasurable outcome. The overcoming of danger is therefore a moving away from the pain associated with an object of fear and toward the pleasure associated with an object of desire, whereas the implementation of security is a moving toward the pleasure associated with an object of desire and a moving away from the pain associated with an object of fear.

Emotional experience is generated by the embodied perception of relations as danger-producing or security-producing forces. It arises from the memory-bound anticipation of the painful or pleasurable consequences of interactions. I divide all emotional experience into two main relational agential stances: relational threat (fear-driven, painful emotions) and relational promise (desire-driven, pleasurable emotions). On the one hand, fear emotions promote the embodied quest for the means of avoiding pain in the form of an emotional orientation. On the other hand, desire emotions promote the embodied quest for the means of pursuing pleasure in the form of a means of power. In this view, emotional experience is a structured experience of agential incapacity, in the case of fear-driven emotions, and a structured experience of agential capacity, in the case of desire-driven emotions.

Now that I have explained what it is that I mean by fear and desire as general felt orientations to danger and security, it is time to discuss their specific forms, which I call emotional norms. As we shall see, all emotional norms exist in pairs.

EMOTIONAL NORMS: FEAR AND DESIRE FORMS IN RELATIONAL CONTEXT

We have seen that when an emotion is the product of relational threat, it constitutes a painful source of information that motivates the search for means to overcome danger. Fear motivates the search for the means to overcome the threat of pain. When, on the other hand, an emotion is the product of relational promise, it constitutes a pleasurable source of information that motivates the search for means to implement security. Desire motivates the search for the means to implement the promise of pleasure.

Painful and pleasurable emotions are structured along agential lack. Once filled, the agential lack that is the source of the negative emotion leads to the experience of the positive emotion. In turn, once filled, the agential lack that is the source of the positive emotion leads to the self's exercise of power, should the means of exercising power be accessible and should the subject choose to make use of them.

Three distinct agential steps are involved in the process of emotional resolution and in the self's exercise of power.

Fear is triggered by the perception of the inability to avoid anticipated pain. To move from this perception into the perception of the ability to seek pleasure instead, the self must determine the form of in/capacity on whose basis it can direct its action in problem resolution. The form of in/capacity gives a shape to the lack that structures fear and therefore also produces the form of desire. This is the first agential step.

Desire is triggered by the perception of the ability to pursue anticipated pleasure. To actualize this perception, the self must identify the means through which it can exercise power. The power form gives a shape to the lack that structures desire and therefore also produces the means of power. This is the second agential step.

Once the means through which it can exercise power have been identified, the self can then implement security. This is the third and final agential step, provided the means of exercising power that were identified are accessible and provided the subject chooses to exercise power through these means.

Let me now offer the following definitions of emotion and of emotional norms.

Emotion designates the painful or pleasurable anticipation of pain or pleasure that motivates a self's directive action and whose specific form depends on the perceived nature of the lack of ability to overcome the forces that are anticipated to cause painful consequences, on the basis of which a first hope response achieves its motivation, and desire its direction in the form of a new hope to implement the forces that are anticipated to cause pleasurable consequences, and where the forms taken by both hope responses are conditioned by the self's interactions with other forces.

Emotional norms[10] are the collective patterns of pain-producing incapacity and of pleasure-producing capacity that develop through individuals' embodied interactions with other forces. Emotional norms are normative structures of felt in/capacity that both enable and constrain emotional differentiation and expression. Emotional norms condition emotional forms. They condition the kinds of emotions that embodied subjects use to orient themselves within the world in order to move away from pain and toward pleasure through fear-driven and desire-driven forms of agency.

Given that the effect of painful emotions is to motivate the search for the means of overcoming danger, and that pleasurable emotions motivate the search for the means of implementing security, emotional differentiation may be said to occur as a result of the interaction between the basic stance of relational threat (pain avoidance), the basic stance of relational promise (pleasure seeking), and the specific demands of one's environment, including one's body. Emotional-norm pairs are the forms of felt incapacity and of felt capacity through which danger and security are experienced and managed.

The form taken by the lack of ability to overcome danger (the fear-driven type of problem or the formlessness of in/capacity), and by the lack of ability to implement security (the desire-driven type of problem, or the formlessness of the means of power), emerges through subjects' felt interactions with other forces. We can classify various forms of fear on the basis of the type of lack that structures their transformation into forms of desire. As we shall have the opportunity to discuss in following sections and chapters, these desires may be channeled into forms of directive action (means of power) that become associated with them or that come to be through more current exercises in self-driven agency. And while they all have in common the hope that security can be implemented, the means through which power is exercised are varied. They can, however, all be seen to be structured by one of three basic emotional-norm pairs: terror/courage, phobia/escape, and worry/safety. These basic emotional orientations can themselves be thought of as differentiated expressions of the even more basic feelings of powerlessness/powerfulness, unfreedom/freedom, and hopelessness/hopefulness.

We have seen that fear involves the search for and determination of the form of incapacity to which a threat corresponds, as well as the urge to move into the feeling of capacity that is desire. The feeling of **powerlessness** or of **incapacity** is the fear associated with the perception that one lacks the capacity to overcome danger, whose pair is the feeling of **powerfulness** or of **capacity**, which is the perception of the capacity to implement security.[11]

The feeling of powerlessness can be said to accompany the force of powerlessness, which is the lack of ability to exercise power, while the feeling of powerfulness can be said to accompany the force of powerfulness, which is the ability to exercise power. In other words, the inability to exercise power implies a threat relation, while the felt inability to overcome danger implies knowledge of this inability through the feeling of powerlessness. And the ability to exercise power implies a promise relation, while the felt ability to implement security implies knowledge of this ability through the feeling of powerfulness.

To illustrate: Like all fears, anger is a form of felt incapacity—the form of an insufficient quantity of force. Anger grounds action in designating felt powerlessness in the face of another's denial of one's desires. Its pair, assertiveness, is, like all desires, a form of felt capacity—the form of a sufficient quantity of force. Assertiveness grounds action in designating felt powerfulness in the face of another's hurting of oneself.

We have also seen that desire involves the search for and determination of the means of power, as well as the urge to exercise power in the implementation of security. The powerlessness/powerfulness emotional-norm pair structures the feeling of **unfreedom,** which is the fear associated with the perception that one lacks the capacity to access the means of exercising power, whose pair is the feeling of **freedom,** the desire associated with the perception that one has the capacity to do so. Unfreedom/freedom is experienced in the desire phase of problem resolution, which, since it is structured by lack, also entails the hope-based experience of powerlessness/powerfulness.

The feeling of unfreedom can be said to accompany the force of unfreedom, which is the lack of ability to access the means through which power can be exercised, while the feeling of freedom can be said to accompany the force of freedom, which is the ability to access to the means through which power can be exercised. In other words, the inability to exercise freedom implies a threat relation, while the felt inability to resolve this problem implies knowledge of this inability through the feeling of unfreedom. And the ability to exercise freedom implies a promise relation, while the felt ability to implement security implies knowledge of this ability through the feeling of freedom.

Finally, we have seen that fear and desire are urges that are structured by a lack of capacity to overcome a threat or to implement a promise. The subjective motivation to act, whether in the move from fear to desire or from desire to the exercise of power, rests upon the feeling of hope. The feeling of **hopelessness** is the fear associated with the perception that one lacks the capacity to improve one's situation, whose pair is the feeling of **hopefulness,** the desire associated with the perception that one has the capacity to do so.

The feeling of hopelessness can be said to accompany the force of incapacity to augment one's capacity, or the inability to improve one's situation, while the feeling of hopefulness can be said to accompany the force of capacity to augment one's capacity, or the ability to improve one's situation. In other words, the inability to augment one's capacity implies a threat relation, while the felt inability to resolve this problem implies knowledge of this inability through the feeling of hopelessness. And the ability to augment capacity implies a promise relation, while the felt ability to implement security implies knowledge of this ability through the feeling of hopefulness.

Beyond these three most essential emotional-norm pairs, which can be understood as forming the basis of the distinct yet complementary fear-driven and desire-driven hope responses, emotional norms can be classified in terms of three general strategic orientations to problems: *confrontation*, *avoidance*, and *prevention*.

Terror designates the fear associated with the perception that one lacks the capacity to overcome danger through *confrontation*, with **courage** as its pair. Terror/courage may be thought of as the emotional-norm pair to which the fight response best corresponds when experienced through the modality of panic/excitement.[12]

Phobia names the fear associated with the perception that one lacks the capacity to overcome danger through *avoidance*, while **escape** is the desire triggered by the perception that one is able to do so. Phobia/escape may be thought of as the emotional-norm pair to which the flight response best corresponds when experienced through the modality of panic/excitement.

Worry refers to the fear associated with the perception that one lacks the capacity to overcome danger through *prevention*, while **safety** names its pair. Worry/safety may be thought of as the emotional-norm pair to which the freeze response best corresponds when experienced through the modality of panic/excitement.

Terror/courage, phobia/escape, and worry/safety are structured by another basic emotional-norm pair: self-doubt/self-confidence. The feeling of **self-doubt** is the fear associated with the perception that one lacks the capacity to implement security effectively, whose pair is the feeling of **self-confidence**, which is the perception of the capacity to do so. The feeling of self-doubt can be said to accompany the force of the self's lack of ability to exercise effective agency in the overcoming of danger, while the feeling of self-confidence can be said to accompany the force of the self's ability to do so.

The emotions that are structured by the confrontational strategic orientation imply that, in the course of interaction, an agent is able to wield an amount of power that is sufficient to overturn an adversarial force. The fight response suggests one's confidence in one's ability to squash one's adversary and ought therefore to engage them in battle. In the emotional-norm pairs that are structured by terror/courage, the form of capacity is the binary opposite of the form of incapacity it overturns. The confrontational structure can be understood as revolutionary, and its temporality is the present.

While confrontation implies an agent's sense of confidence in one's ability to radically transform one's adversary, avoidance implies that an agent would be better off counterbalancing its force. The flight response suggests that one has little confidence in one's ability to overturn one's adversary and ought therefore to run away. In the emotional-norm pairs that are structured by phobia/escape, the form of capacity mitigates the force of the form of incapacity. The avoidant structure can be understood as compensatory, and its temporality is the past.

Prevention is the strategic orientation that implies the agent's least amount of direct power over an adversarial force, such that the agent should avoid coming into contact with it altogether. The freeze response suggests that one has little or no confidence in one's ability to overturn or mitigate the power of one's adversary and ought therefore to circumvent it. In the emotional-norm pairs that are structured by worry/safety, the form of capacity precludes the force of the form of incapacity. The prevention structure can be understood as anticipatory, and its temporality is the future.

The most basic emotional norms are those that motivate us to find and implement solutions to the most basic problems we are faced with as rule-bound beings, and whose recurring forms have caused us to develop deeply ingrained strategic orientations to problems. Terror/courage, phobia/escape, and worry/safety all structure the means of dealing with a great variety of relational threats and promises, and as such they may be said to constitute basic means of exercising subjectively embodied autonomy.[13] Unlike the more basic feeling forms that structure them (powerlessness/powerfulness, unfreedom/freedom, hopelessness/hopefulness, self-doubt/self-confidence), they are tied to strategic agential orientations that increase agential efficacy. Together with two emotional-norm pairs (alexithymia/empathy and indifference/sympathy) that condition emotional socialization through situation assimilation,[14] I consider these three pairs to be the basis for socially driven emotional differentiation and blending.[15]

We will see in later sections that various factors can impact the development of new emotional-norm pairs, as well as the manner in which and the frequency with which such pairs are experienced. For instance, we might find that the emotional norms that stem from any one of the terror/courage, phobia/escape, or worry/safety pairs are more frequently experienced in some groups than in others. It is the group specificity of these emotional processes that conditions our ability to speak of distinct emotional economies.

EMOTIONAL-NORM PAIRS

I now provide examples of emotional-norm pairs that are structured by terror/courage, worry/safety, and phobia/escape. This means that their agential orientation is based on the parent pair from which they differentiate themselves through a more specific agential content. My choice of examples and their definitions are informed by my own, group-bound emotional subjectivity—for instance, I am socially positioned as Western, white, female, mother, university professor, heterosexual—as well as by my reading and experience of late eighteenth century gothic novels and late twentieth century self-help books. These are useful sites for the identification of key emotional experiences in discipline-based and realization-based societies, which I discuss later on.

I stress that the examples of emotional-norm pairs I provide are preliminary attempts at defining felt forms of in/capacity that emerge in relational context. Some were produced here mostly for heuristic purposes, while others were developed with greater care. Many come up in examples or in lengthier discussions later on in this book. Defining specific emotions is a task that ought to benefit from the collaborative work of scholars across disciplines. Furthermore, their actualizations are not static. In an effort to make them as analytically relevant as possible, I expect that I (and perhaps others) will continue to refashion these definitions so that they better perform the work of helping to make sense of how our feelings are dynamic, relational, and interactive structured urges orienting our actions as embodied autonomous beings.

Finally, while the emotional-norm pairs I discuss are likely to find some resonance with Western subjects, more context-specific, Western-based, emotional-norm pairs should also be considered, as well as non-Western ones.[16] The approach of embodied in/capacity theory is one that allows for a great diversity of emotional-norm pairs, to the extent that all actions are thought of as being prompted by structured forms of in/capacity that impel them.

To avoid any confusion, I emphasize that emotional norms designate the feelings of in/capacity that condition the development of capacity (e.g., the feeling of dishonesty, the feeling of self-restraint, the feeling of insignificance, the feeling of patience), not the in/capacity itself (e.g., being dishonest, exercising self-restraint, being insignificant, being patient). As such, it might help the reader to add "the feeling of" before each feeling. Also, rather than list the emotional-norm pairs in alphabetical order, I have grouped them in ways that correspond to discussions of them throughout this book (e.g., social emotions are grouped together, pairs belonging to emotional economies that are contrasted are grouped together). Otherwise, they appear in an arbitrary order.

Confrontation-Based Emotional-Norm Pairs

Here are examples of emotional norms I view as being structured by terror/courage, whose strategic orientation is present-directed *confrontation*.

Uncertainty names the fear produced by the perception that one lacks the ability to confront the forces that cause inconstant effects, while **certainty** names the desire produced by the perception that one has the ability to do so.

Distrust is the fear associated with the perception that one lacks the capacity to confront the lack of honesty of another self, whose pair is **trust**.

Dishonesty is the fear associated with the perception that one lacks the capacity to confront one's lack of truthfulness with others, whose pair is **honesty**.

Irrationality names the fear produced by the perception that one lacks the ability to confront the forces that impede cognitive fluidity, while **rationality** names the desire produced by the perception that one has the ability to do so.[17]

Mystery names the fear produced by the perception that one lacks the ability to confront the forces of cause and effect that elude one's understanding, whose pair is **elucidation**.

Confusion names the fear that one lacks the ability to confront forces that cloud one's understanding, whose pair is **clarity**.

Ignorance is the fear associated with the perception that one is incapable of confronting one's lack of understanding through learning, with **knowledge** as its pair.

Disagreement is the fear triggered by the perception that one lacks the capacity to confront the continuation of a conflict based on a divergence of views, with **reconciliation** as its pair.

Alexithymia names the fear that one lacks the ability to confront one's lack of understanding of what others feel. Its pair is **empathy**.

Indifference is the fear triggered by the perception that one lacks the ability to confront one's lack of care for what others feel. Its pair is **sympathy**.

Frustration is the fear triggered by the perception that one lacks the ability to confront the forces that stand in the way of one's goals, whose pair is **satisfaction.**

Ingratitude is a fear prompted by the perception that one lacks the ability to confront the self's lack of appreciation for the gifts bestowed upon it. Its pair is **gratitude.**

Selfishness is the felt incapacity to confront the self's unappealing consideration of its own needs over and above the needs of a deserving other, with **self-sacrifice** as its pair.

Envy is the fear associated with the perception that one lacks the ability to confront one's lack of command over the resources required to take pleasure in forces that others are believed to enjoy, while **contentment** is its pair.

Failure is the fear that names the perceived lack of ability to confront the forces that put the self at a disadvantage, with **success** as its pair.

Anger is the fear associated with the perception that one lacks the ability to confront another's hurting of oneself. Its pair is **assertiveness**, the desire associated with the perception that one possesses the ability to do so.

Outrage is the fear triggered by the perception that one lacks the ability to confront another's illegitimate hurting of oneself. Its pair is **vindication**, the desire associated with the perception that one possesses the ability to do so.

Rage is triggered by the perception that one lacks the ability to confront one's victimhood through the causing of retaliatory hurt to one's victimizer. Its pair is **revenge.**[18]

Resentment is the fear triggered by the perception that one lacks the ability to confront another's illegitimate advantage over oneself.[19] Its pair is **fairness.**

Spite is triggered by the perception that one lacks the ability to confront one's treatment of another with illegitimate will, while **kindness** is its pair.

Oppression is the fear triggered by the perception that one lacks the ability to confront forces that illegitimately constrain one's freedom. Its pair is **emancipation.**

Stinginess is a fear prompted by the perception that one lacks the ability to confront the self's illegitimate hoarding of resources. Its pair is **generosity.**

Social disapproval is the fear prompted by the perception that one lacks the ability to confront others as disruptive forces. Its pair is **social approval.**

Embarrassment is a fear prompted by the perception that one lacks the ability to confront the self's improper behavior. Its pair is **politeness**.

Dislike names the fear triggered by the perception that one lacks the capacity to confront disruptive forces, whose pair is the feeling of **like**.

Self-dislike is the fear prompted by the perception that one lacks the ability to confront one's self as a disruptive force. Its pair is **self-like**.

Shame[20] is the fear prompted by the perception that one lacks the ability to confront one's self as a disruptive force through self-discipline. Its pair is **pride**.

Personal insecurity is the fear prompted by the perception that one lacks the ability to confront one's self as a disruptive force through self-realization. Its pair is **self-esteem**.

Being ignored is the fear associated with the perception that one is incapable of confronting another's disregard for oneself, with **being noticed** as its pair.

Insignificance is the fear associated with the perception that one is incapable of confronting one's lack of feeling special in the eyes of another, with **importance** as its pair.

Anonymity is the fear associated with the perception that one is incapable of confronting the lack of widespread acknowledgment by others, with **being famous** as its pair.

Grief names the fear produced by the perception that one lacks the ability to confront the loss of a cherished force through the integration of this loss, while **mourning** names the desire triggered by the perception that one has the ability to do so.

Misery names the fear produced by the perception that one lacks the ability to confront burdensome forces, with **joy** as its pair.

Exclusion is the fear triggered by the perception that one lacks the capacity to confront one's marginalization by others, with the feeling of **inclusion** as its pair.

Isolation is the fear triggered by the perception that one lacks the ability to confront the absence of familiar contact with others, with **connection** as its pair.[21]

Artificiality names the fear produced by the perception that one lacks the ability to confront the forces that taint one's essence. Its pair is **authenticity**.

Impatience is triggered by the perception that one lacks the ability to confront the forces that cause the self to suffer without complaint. **Patience** is its pair.

Irritation is the fear associated with the perception that one lacks the capacity to confront a minor or banal form of suffering. Its pair is **tranquility**.

Tension names the fear produced by the perception that one lacks the ability to confront strain by releasing it, while **relaxation** names the desire triggered by the perception that one has the ability to do so.

Unfamiliarity is the fear produced by the perception that one lacks the ability to confront forces with which one is unacquainted. **Familiarity** is its pair.

Alienation is the fear triggered by the perception that one lacks the ability to confront one's separation from a valuable part of oneself. Its pair is **wholeness**.

Immorality is the fear triggered by the perception that one lacks the capacity to confront one's failure to adhere to moral imperatives or standards. Its pair is **morality.**

Evil names the fear that one lacks the ability to confront one's lack of rational adherence to moral imperatives, whose pair is **righteousness**.

Irresponsibility names the fear that one lacks the ability to confront one's lack of healthy adherence to moral standards, whose pair is **responsibility**.

Submission is the fear associated with the perception that one is incapable of confronting one's failure to conquer one's adversary through self-realization, with the feeling of **domination** as its pair.

Dishonor is the fear associated with the perception that one is incapable of confronting one's failure to win the respect of others, with the feeling of **honor** as its pair.

Battle is the fear associated with the perception that one is incapable of confronting one's failure to comply with imperatives in the context of a competition, with the feeling of **command** as its pair.

Rivalry is the fear associated with the perception that one is incapable of confronting one's failure to measure up to standards in the context of a competition, with the feeling of **advantage** as its pair.

Incivility is the fear associated with the perception that one is incapable of confronting the primitive, animalistic, or bodily impulses that hold one's reason hostage through self-discipline, with the feeling of **civility** as its pair.

Disempowerment is the fear prompted by the perception that one lacks the ability to confront the personal shortcomings that compromise one's healthy desire through self-realization. Its pair is **empowerment.**

Impulsivity is the fear triggered by the perception that one lacks the capacity to confront one's irrational failure to delay gratification, with **self-restraint** as its pair.

Passivity is the fear triggered by the perception that one lacks the ability to confront one's unhealthy failure to take command of one's life. Its pair is **proactivity**.

Negativity is the fear triggered by the perception that one lacks the ability to confront one's unhealthy negative thinking in the improvement of one's life. Its pair is **positivity**.

Self-stagnation is the fear triggered by the perception that one lacks the ability to confront one's unhealthy failure to take risks. Its pair is **self-growth**.

Emotional stress is the fear resulting from the self's perceived inability to confront the demands of everyday life in ways that promote health, with **resilience** as its pair.

Dependence is the fear triggered by the perception that one lacks the capacity to confront one's unhealthy reliance on another force to be happy; **independence** is its pair.

Procrastination is the fear triggered by the perception that one lacks the capacity to confront one's unhealthy wasting of one's time, with **accomplishment** as its pair.

Underachievement is the fear triggered by the perception that one lacks the ability to confront the forces standing in the way of the healthy realization of one's goals, with **achievement** as its pair.

Prejudice names the fear that one lacks the ability to confront one's preconceived irrational beliefs, whose pair is **enlightenment**.

Arbitrariness names the fear that one lacks the ability to confront another's irrational exercise of power, with **impartiality** as its pair.

Denial names the fear that one lacks the ability to confront the forces that cause one to fail to recognize the truth, with **acknowledgment** as its pair.

Backwardness names the fear that one lacks the ability to confront the forces that impede the achievement of a superior moral state, with **progress** as its pair.

Degeneration names the fear that one lacks the ability to confront the forces that cause one to regress toward one's animal nature, with **evolution** as its pair.

Disenchantment names the emotion triggered by the perception that one lacks the capacity to confront the loss of moral certainty by perceiving beyond the ordinary range of perception; its pair is **transcendence**.[22]

Nostalgia is the fear triggered by the perception that one lacks the capacity to confront one's failure to move beyond one's longing for past circumstances through the longing for new ones. Its pair is **utopia**.

Dystopia is the fear triggered by the perception that one lacks the capacity to confront one's failure to move beyond one's rejection of past circumstances through the creation of new ones. Its pair is **revolution**.

Heartlessness is the fear triggered by the perception that one lacks the capacity to confront one's lack of support for those who have been victimized; its pair is **compassion**.[23]

Angst names the fear that one lacks the ability to confront the loss of moral certainty, whose pair is **faith**.

Faithlessness is the fear that results from the lack of ability to confront angst, whose pair is **agnosticism**.

Avoidance-Based Emotional-Norm Pairs

Next are examples of emotional-norm pairs that are structured by the basic phobia/escape pair, whose strategic orientation is past-directed *avoidance*.

Disappointment names the emotion triggered by the perception that one lacks the ability to avoid feeling the absence of a desired outcome, while **reparation** names the perception that one has the ability to do so.

Unpreparedness is the fear triggered by the perception that one lacks the ability to avoid unexpected challenges, with **adjustment** as its pair.

Annoyance is triggered by the perception that one lacks the ability to avoid a source of irritation, with **acceptance** as its pair.

Disruption is triggered by the perception that one lacks the ability to avoid disorder, with **comfort** as its pair.

Intransigence is triggered by the perception that one lacks the ability to avoid being permanently caught up in conflict, with **compromise** as its pair.

Regret is the fear triggered by the perception that one lacks the ability to avoid having been the cause of hurt to oneself or to another, with **self-forgiveness** as its pair.

Remorse is the fear triggered by the perception that one lacks the ability to avoid having been the cause of hurt to another, with **atonement** as its pair.

Disgust names the emotion triggered by the perception that one lacks the capacity to avoid further contact with disruptive forces;[24] its pair is **purging**.

Self-disgust names the emotion triggered by the perception that one lacks the capacity to avoid further contact with one's self as a disruptive force; its pair is **self-purging**.

Victimization is a fear that is triggered by the perception that one lacks the capacity to avoid being the object of an illegitimate exercise of power. Its pair is **survival**.

Victimhood is triggered by the perception that one lacks the ability to avoid being the systematic object of an illegitimate exercise of power. Its pair is **surrender**.

Alarm is the fear triggered by the perception that one lacks the capacity to avoid the sudden emergence of an adverse force, with **reassurance** as its pair.

Unprofessional involvement is the fear triggered by the perception that one lacks the ability to avoid experiencing undesired emotions as a result of their unwanted emotive outcomes in the context of the requirements of one's service-oriented work, with **professional detachment** as its pair.

Being overwhelmed is the self's perceived inability to avoid the pressures of everyday life, with **coping** as its pair.

Torment is the fear triggered by the perception that one lacks the capacity to avoid extreme hardship, with **resignation** as its pair.

Doom is the fear triggered by the perception that one lacks the capacity to avoid the self's lack of control over an unfavorable destiny. Its pair is **fate.**

Prevention-Based Emotional-Norm Pairs

Here are some examples of emotional norms I view as being structured by worry/safety, whose strategic orientation is future-directed *prevention.*

Tardiness is the fear triggered by the perception that one lacks the capacity to prevent one's failure to arrive on time through self-discipline. **Punctuality** is its pair.

Separation worry is the fear associated with the perception that one lacks the ability to prevent the disappearance of the force on which our vitality and integrity depends; its pair is **attachment**.[25]

Sadness is the fear associated with the perception that one lacks the capacity to prevent the loss of a force to which the self is attached, and it is paired with **happiness**.[26]

Betrayal names the felt in/capacity to prevent another self's violation of their vows of allegiance. Its pair is **loyalty**.

Jealousy names the fear triggered by the perception that one lacks the ability to prevent another's appropriation of a force the self would like to keep for itself, while **possession** is its pair.

Injustice is a fear that is prompted by the perception that one lacks the ability to prevent being the victim of an illegitimate exercise of power; its pair is **justice**.

Withdrawal is the fear triggered by the perception that one lacks the ability to prevent the loss of familiar contact with others, with **involvement** as its pair.

Defeat is the fear associated with the perception that one is incapable of preventing one's failure to conquer one's adversary, with the feeling of **victory** as its pair.

Guilt names the fear that results from the perception that one lacks the capacity to prevent having to hold oneself responsible for causing another hurt. **Innocence** is its pair.

Humiliation is a fear that is prompted by the perception that one lacks the ability to prevent being treated with contempt by others. Its pair is **dignity**, the perception of the ability to prevent such treatment.

Inferiority is the fear triggered by the perception that one lacks the ability to prevent being of lesser value by devaluing others, with **contempt** as its pair.

Dysfunction is the fear triggered by the perception that one lacks the ability to prevent self-destruction by conforming to a more powerful force's logic; its pair is **adaptation**.

Hate names the emotion triggered by the perception that one lacks the capacity to prevent one's interactions with disruptive forces, whose pair is the feeling of **love**.

Self-hate names the emotion triggered by the perception that one lacks the capacity to prevent one's interactions with one's self as a disruptive force, whose pair is the feeling of **self-love**.

Abnormality names the fear that one lacks the ability to prevent one's empirically determined moral deviance, with **normality** as its pair.

Clinical depression names the fear that one lacks the ability to prevent one's empirically determined moral deviance through observable depressive symptoms, with **being oneself** as its pair.

Difference is the fear triggered by the perception that one lacks the ability to prevent being unlike others, with **integration** as its pair.

Rejection is the fear triggered by the perception that one lacks the capacity to prevent being marginalized by others, with the feeling of **belonging** as its pair.

Stigmatization is the fear triggered by the perception that one lacks the ability to prevent being marginalized by others as a result of being visibly disturbing, whose pair is **attractiveness.**

Ugliness is the fear triggered by the perception that one lacks the ability to prevent being physically disturbing, whose pair is **beautifulness.**

Surprise refers to the fear associated with the perceived lack of capacity to prevent unexpected occurrences, with **predictability** as its pair.

Corruption names the fear that one lacks the ability to prevent immoral temptation through self-discipline, with **virtue** as its pair.

Gullibility is the fear triggered by the perception that one lacks the ability to prevent being misled by one's irrational beliefs; its pair is **skepticism.**

Weakness is the fear stemming from the perceived lack of ability to prevent being controlled by other forces through self-discipline, with **strength** as its pair.

Vulnerability is the fear stemming from the perceived lack of ability to prevent being controlled by other forces through self-realization, with **invulnerability** as its pair.

Disobedience is the fear associated with the perception that one is incapable of preventing one's failure to comply with imperatives through self-discipline, with **obedience** as its pair.

Incompetence is the fear associated with the perception that one is incapable of preventing one's failure to measure up to standards through self-realization, with **competence** as its pair.

Madness names the fear that one lacks the ability to prevent one's irrational transgression of moral boundaries, whose pair is **sanity.**

Mental illness names the fear that one lacks the ability to prevent one's unhealthy failure to measure up to moral standards, whose pair is **mental health.**

Being emotional is the fear triggered by the perception that one lacks the capacity to prevent the hold that one's illegitimate or incorrect desires have over one's reason, with **being rational** as its pair.

Being repressed is the fear triggered by the perception that one lacks the capacity to prevent one's healthy impulses from being blocked or impaired by unhealthy forces, while **being liberated** is its pair.

Risk can be defined as the fear triggered by the perception that one lacks the capacity to prevent a harmful outcome based on a calculation of its probabilities, whatever the form taken by this estimation, with **precaution** as its pair.[27]

Negligence is the fear triggered by the perception that one lacks the ability to prevent causing hurt to oneself or others through risk management, with **accountability** as its pair.

Boredom is the fear triggered by the perception that one lacks the ability to prevent the absence of pleasurable stimulation, with **amusement** as its pair.

Weariness is the fear triggered by the perception that one lacks the ability to prevent being consumed by the experience of routine troubles, with **entertainment** as its pair.

Addiction is the fear triggered by the perception that one lacks the capacity to prevent relying on a self-destructive force to cope with everyday life, with **abstinence** as its pair.

Craving is the fear triggered by the perception that one lacks the capacity to prevent one's unhealthy hunger for a pleasurable stimulant, with **indulgence** as its pair.

Horror names the fear triggered by the perception that one lacks the capacity to prevent the shocking appearance of disruptive forces, with the feeling of **order** as its pair.

Being harmed names the emotion triggered by the perception that one lacks the capacity to prevent engaging with forces that are injurious to the self, while **being cared for** is its pair.

Shock is the fear triggered by the perception that one lacks the capacity to prevent being violently unsettled by a surprise, with **forewarning** as its pair.

Disorientation is triggered by the perception that one lacks the ability to prevent one's loss of direction in the face of adversity, with **guidance** as its pair.

Emotional blends

Beyond being structured by emotional-norm pairs that logically precede them and from which they differentiate themselves through the production of a novel agential content that implies the parent content, some emotional-norm pairs can be thought of as coming into being through a process of emotional blending, in which existing emotional-norms pairs that may belong to different strategic orientations are combined.[28] The experience of another emotional-norm pair can be and often is a means through which power is exercised and security implemented. Thus while guilt/innocence may be said to derive from the more primary worry/safety emotional-norm pair in expressing a form of incapacity to *prevent* danger, the means to alleviate it might ultimately entail the *confrontation* or the *avoidance* of danger if an emotional-norm pair from a parent belonging to another strategic orientation is turned to as a means to implement security.

For instance, remorse/atonement is a potential means through which guilt/innocence is resolved and it is structured by phobia/escape rather than by the worry/safety that structures guilt/innocence. We have seen that remorse is the felt in/capacity to avoid having been the cause of hurt to another, with atonement as its pair. By blinding himself, Oedipus may be said to have expiated his guilt at having murdered his father and wed his mother through remorse/atonement. In the Western contemporary context, remorse/atonement continues to be a common emotional means through which guilt/innocence are resolved, though self-blinding is not usually the means through which this objective is achieved.

While some of the emotional-norm pairs that I have already discussed can be shown to result from emotional blending (for instance, horror/order is a blend of shock/forewarning and of hate/love), in order to further explain the process of emotional blending, I follow Jesse J. Prinz's (2004) lead in discussing jealousy.

Prinz seeks to explain the development of complex and culturally specific emotions through the blending of more basic emotions. For instance, upon discovering the infidelity of one's partner, jealousy could be formed through the perception of loss, offense, and contamination leading to the experience of a blend of sadness, anger, and disgust. Thoughts of infidelity might later serve as a trigger for this particular emotional blend.

Translated into the terms of embodied in/capacity theory, emotional blending gives rise to a new emotional experience as a solution to the subject's dissatisfaction with his or her initial emotional response and with the means of implementing security that are attached to it. The feelings of jealousy/possession emerge as means of structuring in/capacity in response to the kinds of problems that arise as a result of another self's actions in a particular normative context. The perception of another self's actions as a form of infidelity warranting the experience of jealousy structures one's ability to implement security. Thus if sadness/happiness forms part of jealousy, it is because the attempt to prevent the loss of a force to which one is attached through holding onto it is useful in dealing with the implications of one's partner's actions. And if anger/assertiveness forms part of jealousy, it is because the attempt to assert one's needs in the face of another's hurtful denial of these is equally useful in dealing with the implications of one's partner's actions.[29] And if disgust/purging forms part of jealousy, it is because the attempt to expulse a disruptive force is also useful in dealing with the implications of one's partner's actions. To these emotional norms we might also, in the case of infidelity, add betrayal/loyalty, which conditions the attempt to prevent another self's violation of their vows of allegiance.

I have attempted to illustrate the manner in which emotional norms are differentiated from a set of three basic strategic forms of felt in/ capacity, and have shown that these differentiated emotional norms can also be combined through emotional blending. Whether through emotional differentiation or emotional blending, subjects can be said to move from the feeling of powerlessness to that of powerfulness, from the feeling of unfreedom to that of freedom, and from the feeling of hopelessness to that of hopefulness, as they engage with the world emotionally. I begin the next chapter by considering Prinz's work further as a means of thinking through the interactive relationship between emotional-norm pairs, objects of fear and desire, signs of danger and security, and embodied means of power.

C H A P T E R   2

ANALYZING EMOTIONAL INTERACTION

AFFECTIVE, AGENTIAL, AND SYMBOLIC ATTUNEMENT

Jesse J. Prinz (2004) uses the concept of calibration to designate the process through which beliefs are set up in memory files as triggers for certain emotions. In basic emotions, these files are genetically determined. In derived emotions, the genetically determined files are supplanted, or recalibrated, based on cultural imperatives. Along with calibration files, argues Prinz, emotions may also have behavioral files—cultural scripts that regulate our behavior when we experience a particular emotion. According to Prinz, calibration allows us to make the case for the existence of culturally unique affective states. For example, the *p'a-leng* disorder in China is an extreme fear of the cold that causes its victims to wrap themselves up in blankets even when it is quite warm.

Prinz reasons that while one could argue at a general level that this experience is one of fear and that it is no different, physiologically, from other fear experiences, one could also argue that it is a distinct emotion elicited by a calibration file associating fear with coldness, such that its real content is not physical dangers in general, but fear of the cold.

Prinz holds that this view allows us to explain how high cognition can be involved in triggering emotions without forming part of the emotion itself. For instance, the emotion known as *Schadenfreude*, which is a feeling of joy triggered by the perceived suffering of others, can be explained through the constitution of a calibration file that rests on the belief that the suffering of others allows the self to achieve its goals, the perception of which results in joy. While initially *Schadenfreude* might only be triggered when one has the cognition that one's goals have been satisfied through the suffering of others, it is conceivable that eventually the mere perception of suffering others, such as hearing a scream, might bring on the emotion. It is in this sense, for Prinz, that feeling can replace cognition.

According to Prinz, emotions are made up of two kinds of contents, both of which are subject to cultural influence. "Nominal content" refers to somatic changes associated with emotions, such as heartbeat frequency or facial expressions, whereas "real content" refers to the relational themes they evoke, such as danger or loss. Breathing patterns are an example of a nominal content that can be affected by culture and may in turn produce unique, culturally driven emotional experiences. When bodily practices such as respiration are influenced by culture, Prinz holds that they give rise to what Marcel Mauss called "habits of the body." Similarly, display rules that govern the way in which an emotion is expressed on one's face affect its nominal content and therefore its experience. For example, the repression of the facial display of negative emotions in Japanese culture has been shown to lead to its subjects' less intense experience of these emotions in comparison with that of American subjects.[1]

While there are notable differences between Prinz's approach and my own, his invites us to think about the nature of the relationship between the form of relational threats and promises (emotional-norm pairs), the content of relational threats and promises (objects of fear and desire), the signs that trigger their experience (signs of danger and security), and the means of exercising power (of implementing security). I develop the concepts of affective, agential, and symbolic attunement in order to account for the associative process through which emotional-norm pairs become interactively bound to objects of fear and desire, signs of danger and security, and means of power.

Affective attunement designates the process through which the pain- or pleasure-producing nature of a force is associated with a structured emotional response and embodied. Affective attunement is a process through which objects of fear and desire (problem and solution contents) come into being in their interactive relation to emotional-norm pairs. Thus an embodied affective memory might cause someone to react with terror/courage to an interaction with an aggressive bull/a contained bull or with worry/safety to an interaction with an empty refrigerator/replenished refrigerator.

In other words, encounters with objects of fear and desire cause us to react with a certain kind of fear or of desire. Should encounters with snakes in the wild form the content of a problem (an object of fear) that is associated with a phobic type of fear, one should expect an agent to respond to the sight of a snake in the wild with the avoidant feeling of escape and with the escape-driven desire to implement security through means of power that correspond to escape as a desire orientation, such as fleeing. Or should encounters with freshly baked chocolate cake form the content of a solution (an object of desire) that is associated with an indulgence type of desire, one should expect an agent to respond to encounters with freshly baked chocolate cake with the prevention-based feeling of craving and with the indulgence-driven desire to implement security through means of power that correspond to indulgence as a desire orientation, such as consuming freshly baked chocolate cake.

Objects of fear and desire come into being in the process of becoming attached to emotional norms. The fear form, or form of incapacity, through which I overcome a dangerous force, or object of fear, determines the desire form, or form of capacity, through which I implement a security force, or object of desire.

For instance, I am terrified (fear form) of exams because they are painful forces (objects of fear) that I can confront through courage (desire form). I therefore desire time to study (means of power) as a means of implementing the pleasurable force that is the successful exam (object of desire). Or I have a phobia (fear form) of exams because they are painful forces (objects of fear) I can avoid through escape (desire form). I therefore desire a good excuse (means of power) as a means of implementing the pleasurable force that is the missed exam (object of desire). Or I am worried (fear form) about exams because they are painful forces (objects of fear) I can prevent through safety (desire form). I therefore desire dropping out of school (means of power) as a means of implementing the pleasurable force that is the inexistence of the need to take exams (object of desire).

Our ability to experience anticipated pain and pleasure is an ability to experience life emotionally. We embody the affective knowledge of a force we can then anticipate once our interaction with it causes some painful or pleasurable effect upon us. This embodied knowledge is the basis of the coming into being of objects of fear and desire.

It is important not to confuse agents' attempts to move away from the pain associated with objects of fear with the avoidance of either objects of fear or of pain-producing forces. One must necessarily interact with problems (objects of fear) to produce their solutions (objects of desire). This is true for all three strategic orientations. For instance, what one seeks to avoid when one uses a confrontational orientation to deal with problems is the pain associated with these problems, not the problems themselves. Here, one seeks to overturn a force's painful effects. Similarly, what one seeks to avoid when one uses an avoidant orientation to deal with problems is the pain associated with these problems, not the problems themselves. Here, one seeks to temper a force's painful effects. Finally, what one seeks to avoid when one uses a preventative orientation to deal with problems is the pain associated with these problems, not the problems themselves. Here, one seeks to circumvent a force's painful effects.

Moreover, while the avoidance of pain-producing forces may be a solution for some problems, it is certainly not a solution for all problems. Avoiding interactions with forces that are anticipated to produce pain may be the solution to one's problem in some cases (e.g., avoiding illness-causing bacteria to confront, avoid, or prevent an anticipated pain outcome), while, in other cases, promoting inter-actions with forces that are anticipated to produce pain is the solution (e.g., coming into contact with or searching for illness-causing bacteria to confront, avoid, or prevent an anticipated pain outcome).

In short, the overcoming of danger and the implementation of security involve the avoidance of the pain effects of objects of fear, not the avoidance of problems per se, and they may but do not necessarily involve the avoidance of pain-producing forces.

Agential attunement designates the process through which specific means of power are associated with a structured emotional response and embodied. It is a process through which means of exercising power come into being in their interactive relation to emotional-norm pairs and their objects of fear and desire. Such an embodied memory might cause someone to experience the desire to call a friend as a means to implement the security of connection, or to experience the desire to break all ties with others who have treated one with contempt as a means to implement the security of dignity.

Means of power come into being in the process of becoming attached to emotional norms. The fear and desire orientation helps determine the means of power through which security is implemented. For instance, if I am terrified of exams because they are painful forces that I can confront through courage, the means of power through which I deal with my problem implies confrontation. It would not do for me to desire a good excuse or to desire dropping out of school as a means of implementing the pleasurable force, which is the nonter-rifying (in this example successful) exam. In other words, the manner in which I implement security is attuned to the structure of a felt in/capacity and may also be said to interact with it.

Agential responses may involve many embodied dimensions. I view the forms of agency that can be attuned to emotional-norm pairs as including at least six forms of interactive embodied action, of which subjects are not necessarily conscious: the biological (e.g., heartbeat frequency, hormonal fluctuation), the sensorial (e.g., seeing, hearing), the cognitive (e.g., thought processes, forms of remembering), the emotional (e.g., emotional blending, emotional differentiation), the moral (e.g., self-repression, self-formation), and the behavioral (e.g., running, speaking, body language). The diversity of the potential means that may be enlisted in the implementation of security speak to the highly interactive nature of emotional experiences, which seem to be particularly subject to the influence of social norms and of personal biography.

Finally, *symbolic attunement* is the process through which the charging bull or empty refrigerator becomes attached to a sign of danger, or through which the charging bull that one has managed to avoid, or the refrigerator that one has managed to replenish, becomes attached to a sign of security. In other words, it is the process through which problems and solutions become attached to symbols that may trigger their experience. When this sign bears no obvious relationship to the object of fear or desire it represents and may therefore be said to dissimulate it, displacement[2] may be said to have occurred.

For instance, one might encounter a sign of danger that triggers one's experience of a terror/courage-driven encounter with an aggressive bull, where this sign is an actual aggressive bull or an image of it, or encounter a sign of security that triggers one's experience of a terror/courage-driven encounter with a contained bull, where this sign is an actual contained bull or an image of it. One might also encounter a sign of danger that triggers one's experience of a worry/safety-driven encounter with an empty refrigerator, where this sign is a check one has forgotten to cash at the bank, or encounter a sign of security that triggers one's experience of a worry/safety-driven encounter with a replenished refrigerator, where this sign is the smell of something cooking as one walks through the door. In all these examples, there is an obvious relationship between the sign and the object of fear or desire it represents. But were the terror/courage-driven encounter with an aggressive bull to be triggered by one's encounter with a particular category of people, or were the worry/safety-driven encounter with a replenished refrigerator be triggered by one's encounter with commercial fried chicken, the sign could be said to bear no obvious relationship to the object of fear or desire it represents and be the consequence of displacement.

I now turn to a discussion of the different modalities of fear and desire that are thought to govern the transition from emotional incapacity to emotional capacity in embodied in/capacity theory, followed by a more detailed discussion of the processes of emotional blending and emotional differentiation as they pertain to these modalities.

THREE MODALITIES OF FEAR AND DESIRE: PANIC/EXCITEMENT, ANXIETY/INTEREST, AND DISTRESS/RELIEF

It is relatively common to think of the emotional experiences that are triggered by popular entertainment forms as inauthentic or artificial, yet the emotions that result from these types of interactions are just as real as others.[3] The fear I experience when I watch a horror movie is just as real as the fear I experience when I hear a suspicious noise, prepare for a demanding exam, come across an enigma, think of being contaminated by a virus, or face a bear cub with his protective mother. The quality of these emotional experiences will be affected by the intensity of the anticipated pain or pleasure I associate with their outcomes. And as I shall now argue, their quality will also be affected by the modality of fear and desire through which pain and pleasure are anticipated.

I have been using the concept of fear to designate the painful experience of incapacity that motivates subjects to search for and identify a form of in/capacity, and that of desire to designate the pleasurable experience of capacity that motivates subjects to search for a means of power. The experience of fear and desire can be further delineated on the basis of the quality of their relationship to the means of overcoming danger (the form of in/capacity) and of implementing security (the means of power).

The three modalities of fear and desire that I refer to as panic/excitement, anxiety/interest, and distress/relief respectively correspond to the perceived knowledge of and access to adequate means of power for responding to a threat/promise, the perceived inadequacy of existing means of power for responding to a threat/promise, and the perceived absence of means of power for responding to a threat/promise. Panic/excitement, anxiety/interest, and distress/relief may have distinct physiological features.[4]

Panic/excitement designates the modality of fear and desire within which pain and pleasure are anticipated through the perceived adequacy of existing means of power for implementing security. The panic/excitement relation prompts the attempt to overcome danger and implement security through a previously worked out satisfactory solution, whether inborn or more recently embodied. "I am afraid that this is going to hurt. I feel I am in/capable of dealing with this threat/promise. I feel I know of and have access to the means of power to do something about it. Therefore I shall do what I feel I should do to overcome danger/implement security."

The panic/excitement modality corresponds to the perception of a threat/promise, for which satisfactory means of threat/promise resolution are already in place. For instance, I may feel angry about a driver's failure to signal his or her intention to turn left and satisfactorily implement assertiveness-based security by honking my horn. In this modality, the moment of fear is more likely to be experienced as partly pleasurable since the pleasurable means of implementing security are implied in its experience. Should a threat/promise not be resolved in the manner one had expected, the panic/excitement modality might give way to either the anxiety/interest or the distress/relief modality of fear and desire. But should it be adequately resolved, the emotional experience would remain one that is experienced through the modality of panic/excitement.

Anxiety/interest designates the modality of fear and desire within which pain and pleasure are anticipated through the perceived inadequacy of existing means of power for implementing security. The anxiety/interest modality prompts the attempt to develop more satisfactory means of implementing security. "I am afraid that this is going to hurt. I feel I am in/capable of dealing with this threat/promise. I feel I lack the knowledge of or access to the means of power to do something satisfactory about it. Therefore I shall search for alternative means of overcoming danger/implementing security."

Much as in the panic/excitement modality, the anxiety/interest relation corresponds to the perception of a usual threat/promise for which means of power in the implementation of security are already known. However, in this latter case the means of power are felt to be unsatisfactory. For instance, I may feel angry about a driver's failure to signal his or her intention to turn left as well as dissatisfied with the implementation of assertiveness-based security produced through the honking of my horn. Perhaps I feel irritated by the horn's noise or embarrassed about the attention the noise attracts to me. In short I feel conflicted. In the anxiety/interest modality, in order to regain the capacity for the exercise of power, new means of power would have to be identified. Should a threat/promise be satisfactorily resolved through new means, such as through moving into tension/relaxation, associated with the practice of deep breathing, rather than honking, the emotional experience would be resolved, but would remain one of anxiety/interest up until the time at which this new means no longer requires an emotion management effort. Should improved means of power not be found and action be frozen, anxiety/interest would be transformed into distress/relief.

Distress/relief designates the modality of fear and desire within which pain and pleasure are anticipated through the absence of an effective form of in/capacity through which to move into desire, or, should a form be known, through the inability to identify or access means of power for implementing security. The distress/relief modality prompts the attempt to develop a new form of in/capacity, or new means of implementing security. "I am afraid this is going to hurt. I feel I am incapable of dealing with this threat, or that I am in/capable of dealing with this threat/promise but lack knowledge of or access to the means of power to do anything about it. Therefore I must produce new means of overcoming danger/implementing security."

The distress/relief modality of fear and desire may correspond to the experience of a new threat that lacks a form of in/capacity, in which case the subject is caught in incapacity, or to the experience of a threat that belongs to a form of in/capacity but that lacks means of power for implementing security, in which case desire becomes painful. For distress to move into relief, a form of in/capacity must be produced if it is a threat with no corresponding effective form, or a new means of power for implementing security must be identified if it is a threat with a corresponding emotional orientation but where knowledge of or access to an adequate means of power for implementing security is lacking.

In the panic/excitement modality, the quality of the control subjects experience is such that they simultaneously experience threat, promise, and their resolution. The fear moment of the emotional experience is therefore tainted by pleasure and the move into self-confidence requires little effort. In the anxiety/interest modality, subjects experience a measure of control over the threat, the promise, and their resolution, but feel this control is inadequate. The desire moment in this emotional experience is therefore tainted by pain. The move into self-confidence requires some effort. In the distress/relief modality, subjects experience very little or no control over the threat, the promise, and their resolution. In some cases promise is not experienced at all. Subjects are therefore caught in painful fear. It is a modality in the experience of emotions that is very unpleasant for this very reason, and it may cause those who experience it to come to lack the hope response that motivates will-based and intention-based subjective and moral actions, while potentially affecting drive-based biological actions as well. Here the move into self-confidence requires the greatest emotional effort and may not happen at all.

I now attempt to think through subjects' pleasurable, ambivalent, and painful experiences of horror film consumption, based on the three modalities of fear and desire I have been discussing. If we assume that watching a given horror movie triggers the experience of horror/order, subjects for whom the negative affect engendered by horror is satisfactorily transformed into the positive affect engendered by order during the cinematographic event might be said to experience the horror movie through the modality of panic/excitement. In this modality, even the experience of horror is tainted by pleasure, since satisfactory means of threat/promise resolution are already felt to be in place during the moment of felt incapacity. In subjects whose horror film experience is anxiety/interest-driven, during the course of watching the film, horror may give way to order, but through unsatisfactory means, such that a surplus of negative affect remains and the experience is one of ambivalence. Finally, in subjects whose horror movie experience is distress/relief-driven, either the means to implement the security of order remain unavailable, such that the order-driven experience of desire is painful, or fear remains a formless incapacity, such that negative affect characterizes the whole experience.

Several avenues can be explored in order to account for a subject's experience of horror films through one or the other of these modalities. Horror films are obviously diverse and the same subject may interact in one way with one genre and in another way with another. Subjects may have inborn propensities to experience certain kinds of interactions as painful, and come to fear them, and others as pleasurable, and come to desire them. But subjects may also develop these propensities through situation assimilation and based on their social positioning.[5] As a consequence, different modalities of felt in/capacity may be triggered by horror movie watching based on socially defined experience. One's perception of the physical sensations triggered by horror films, if such sensations are experienced, can also be transformed through various means, such that an initially painful experience can be transformed into a pleasurable one, or vice versa.[6]

What determines the extent to which either one of these modalities will be operative in emotional experience? Here are three possibilities in the form of very general hypotheses that are by no means exhaustive.

First, the more a social group is formed of subjects whose experience of habitual forms of agency is pleasurable, the more that members' emotional experiences are likely to belong to the panic/excitement modality. This happens with subjects who seek to reproduce ingrained or habitual solutions to recurring problems (e.g., resolving the problem of hunger through traditional means). We might say that this modality is typical of what are sometimes called traditional societies.

Second, the more a social group is formed of subjects whose experience of habitual forms of agency is dissatisfying, the more that members' emotional experiences are likely to belong to the anxiety/interest modality. This happens with subjects who seek to transform ingrained or habitual solutions to recurring problems (e.g., resolving the problem of hunger through novel means). We might say that this modality is typical of what are sometimes called modern societies.

Third, the more a social group is formed of subjects who experience fear and desire through the modality of anxiety/interest, the more it produces new kinds of problems to be resolved, and the more likely it is that new means to overcome danger/implement security will be required. Here, emotions may often be experienced through the distress/relief modality. This happens with subjects who seek to produce novel solutions to novel problems (e.g., resolving the problem of hunger through new means produces a series of new problems for which new solutions are required but not necessarily forthcoming). We might say that this modality is typical of what are sometimes called late modern societies.

There are a number of other possibilities. For instance, the anxiety/interest modality of fear and desire might predominate in social groups that promote constant self-improvement, or that value scientific discovery and innovation more generally, whereas the distress/relief modality of fear and desire might prevail in social groups that make hard-to-achieve goals salient, such as placing the burden of responsibility for culturally valued goals on individuals who lack access to the means of exercising it.

The three modalities of emotional experience under discussion can be found in all social groups, and the types of societies I am identifying as traditional, modern, and late modern are by no means representative of all types of societies or of the nuances that exist among them. However, whether and on what grounds a society promotes one or the other of these modalities can help us make sense of its emotional economy.

FEARING FEAR AND DESIRING DESIRE: THE EMERGENCE OF INTERNAL (MORAL) CONFLICT

Let me now use the emotional-norm pair of sadness/happiness to briefly illustrate the way in which anxiety/interest and distress/relief involve internal conflict, where panic/excitement does not.

I have defined sadness as the fear associated with the perception that one lacks the capacity to prevent the loss of a force to which the self is attached, and happiness as the desire associated with the perception that one has the capacity to prevent this loss.

I have lost my glasses numerous times before and feel that I can resolve this problem in a satisfactory manner. I feel a panicked sadness and an excited happiness when I lose my glasses.

In panic/excitement there is one object of fear and one object of desire: the anticipated pain produced by the problem (the lost glasses) and the anticipated pleasure produced by the resolved problem (the found glasses).[7] In this modality subjects do not experience internal conflict.

I have lost my glasses numerous times before and feel that I cannot resolve this problem in a satisfactory manner. I feel an anxious sadness when I lose my glasses. I will remain caught in anxious sadness until I find alternative means of dealing with my problem. I feel an interested happiness when I identify an alternative means of resolving my problem.

In anxiety/interest there are two objects of fear and two objects of desire: the anticipated pain produced by the initial problem (the lost glasses), the anticipated pain produced by the related problem (the inadequate means), the anticipated pleasure produced by the resolved initial problem (the found glasses), and the anticipated pleasure produced by the identification of more adequate means. In this modality subjects experience internal conflict. In the anxiety/interest experience, agential inadequacy becomes a second object of fear, such that one can be said to be afraid of fear, or to fear felt incapacity, while agential adequacy becomes a second object of desire, such that one can be said to desire desire, or to desire felt capacity.

I have never lost my glasses before and feel that I cannot resolve this problem; or I have lost my glasses before and feel that I have not been able to find a means of resolving this problem. I feel a distressed sadness when I lose my glasses. I will remain caught in distressed sadness until I find new means of dealing with my new problem, or new means of dealing with my old problem, which I have exhausted all the means I know of to resolve.

In distress/relief, there are also two objects of fear and two objects of desire: the anticipated pain produced by the initial problem (the lost glasses), the anticipated pain produced by the related problem (the absence of means), the anticipated pleasure produced by the resolved initial problem (the found glasses), and the anticipated pleasure produced by the identification of new means. In this modality also, subjects experience internal conflict. In the distress/relief experience, agential inadequacy becomes a second object of fear, such that one can also be said to fear fear, or to fear felt incapacity, while agential adequacy becomes a second object of desire, such that one can also be said to desire desire, or to desire felt capacity.

No matter the basic emotional orientation that structures them, all emotional-norm pairs can be experienced through either one of these modalities. Thus I might experience terror/courage, phobia/escape, or worry/safety, as well as any other emotional-norm pair, through the modality of panic/excitement, anxiety/interest, or distress/relief.

To further clarify, let me say a little more about each modality of emotional experience with respect to agential spontaneity.

The panic/excitement modality is governed by the feeling that the adequacy of the means of resolving a problem is not at issue. This relation gives rise to embodied, spontaneous forms of agency—means of responding to threat and promise that have already been determined to resolve the type of problem with which the subject perceives they are being faced, whether these means are inborn or acquired during their lifetime. While means of responding to threat entail the determination of the form of in/capacity and the move into desire, means of responding to promise entail the determination of the means of power and its exercise.

If we take anger/assertiveness as an example, means of power may range from more spontaneous forms of agency such as increased blood pressure, to somewhat less spontaneous forms of agency such as hitting behavior or aggressive talk.

In the panic/excitement modality of emotional experience, agential responses to threat and promise can be rapidly produced since they are readily available. These agential responses are the embodied produce of past emotional exercises to which little or no energy is afforded in the present.

In a panic/excitement experience, the painful anticipation of pain is mixed with the pleasurable anticipation of pleasure. An emotional response associated with specific means of power is triggered. This could be the felt form of in/capacity engendered by an approaching grizzly bear, in response to which a subject might take flight in an ingrained, desire-driven effort to implement security. This could be the felt form of in/capacity induced by a nonreceptive crowd at a music performance, in response to which a subject might become more energetic in a habituated, desire-driven effort to implement security. Or this could be a felt form of in/capacity brought on by the loss of a loved one, in which case a subject might become more watchful of other loved ones as an ingrained, desire-driven means of implementing security.

The panic/excitement modality of fear and desire involves a response to the threat of pain and the promise of pleasure that does not question the adequacy of the means to relieve and achieve these. In contrast, the anxiety/interest modality involves a response to the threat of pain and the promise of pleasure that does. It emerges as a result of the pain-producing perception of agential inadequacy in the face of ongoing experiences of relational threat. In other words, the anxiety/interest modality of threat perception is a response to the perceived inadequacy of responses to in/capacity produced through either the panic/excitement or the distress/relief modality. Thus while the panic/excitement modality's object of fear is solely the force with which a pain outcome is associated, the anxiety/interest modality's object of fear is both the inadequate nature of the older panic/excitement-driven or a newer distress/relief-driven response to its object of fear, such that a reconsideration of this response through a renewed emotional exercise is required, and the panic/excitement or distress/relief modality's initial object of fear as well, whose danger it is the anxiety/interest modality's ultimate goal to overcome.

In an anxiety/interest emotional experience, as the painful anticipation of pain moves into the pleasurable anticipation of pleasure, an emotional exercise whose aim is to implement security through the identification of a more adequate means of power is triggered. This could be the felt in/capacity engendered by the perception of the inadequacy of an existing solution to an approaching grizzly bear, by the perception of the inadequacy of an existing solution to a nonreceptive crowd at a music performance, or by the perception of the inadequacy of a known solution to the loss of a loved one. In the panic/excitement modality, the attempt to move away from pain and toward pleasure is the result of a prior emotional exercise. In the anxiety/interest modality, the attempt to move away from pain and toward pleasure is governed by a new emotional exercise that, if successful, will result in newly embodied agential responses that are not likely to be highly spontaneous, at least not initially, but that may become so with time.

To be clear, while the anxiety/interest modality of emotional experience may lead to the exercise of innovative or unusual means of power in response to old problems, these means are not necessarily innovative or unusual when placed in a larger context. They may only be novel or unusual as solutions to previously experienced in/capacities for that individual. Thus it may not be unusual for a given individual to experience boredom/amusement or to drink a cup of coffee as a means to resolve the threat/promise of morning fatigue, but it may be unusual for this subject to do so as a means to resolve the threat/promise posed by an oncoming migraine, or as a means of resolving the threat/promise posed by social isolation.

The modern Western societies with which I am most familiar have tended to promote an anxious relationship to numerous existing solutions to relational threat/promise by associating spontaneous agency in general, and especially some of its forms such as particular expressions of sexual and aggressive urges, with painful outcomes. It is therefore no surprise to see that these societies also promote individual self-transformation through the repression or correction of forms of agency that are associated with these urges. However, I insist on the fact that particular expressions of these urges, rather than the urges per se, are problematized in Western societies, inasmuch as aggressive urges can be understood to form the basis of a great many forms of agency, and may also be taken to form the basis of confrontation-based fear and desire orientations to problems. As such, confrontation-based emotional-norm pairs and agential responses are operative in and valued by Western groups even though some of their expressions are subject to condemnation.

On the other hand, it should also be clear that panic/excitement-driven forms of agency remain of great importance to Western societies as the product or end result of earlier moral self-transformation efforts, such as the capacity to read and write, or to resolve conflicts through legal means rather than through physical ones. Because modern, discipline-based societies have associated spontaneous forms of agency in general with a dangerous expression of irrationality, it is easy to neglect the fact not only that spontaneous actions are inevitable in the everyday life of agents in all societies, but also that some agential forms of spontaneity are highly valued in the very societies that tend to condemn them (or a certain idea of them). Indeed, both discipline-based and realization-based societies have the habit I associate with the panic/excitement modality of fear and desire as a goal where numerous forms of agency are concerned.

Spontaneous action can be of great use in the overcoming of danger and implementation of security in a wide range of circumstances. Thus it is thanks to the panic/excitement modality of emotional experience that a person trained in cardiopulmonary resuscitation is able to perform a series of timely lifesaving gestures on the problem that is cardiac arrest, or that the overwhelmed parent of young children is able to perform a series of timely practical gestures on the problem that is getting through the day with all clothed, fed, washed, and unharmed (though admittedly the contemporary upbringing of children requires a great deal of anxiety/interest-driven moral self-transformation, as testified by the unrelenting popularity of self-help parenting guides). More basically, it is thanks to the panic/excitement modality of emotional experience that we accomplish many of the day-to-day things we are compelled or required to do, with very little emotional effort (though not without emotion).

Unlike the panic/excitement-driven fear and desire response, in which the adequacy of the means of resolving in/capacity is not a problem, and unlike the anxiety/interest-driven fear and desire response, in which the existing means of resolving in/capacity produce ambivalence, in the distress/relief-driven fear and desire response, the means of resolving in/capacity are absent. This modality emerges as a result of the painful perception of agential incapacity in the face of nonresolvable experiences of relational threat/promise. As such, it promotes and thrives upon creativity.

The distress/relief modality's object of fear is the lack of knowledge of the means to respond to a threat/promise, whether because of a form of in/capacity that is lacking or because of a means of power that is lacking because the subject fails to identify such a means or to achieve access to it. This lack can result from the threat's unusual nature or from the subject's problematic relationship to the means of resolving it or the promise with which it is associated.

The unusual nature of a threat can lead to the inability to develop a structured emotional perspective on it, and this perspective is required to allow the determination of means to implement security. In this type of distress/relief experience, the painful anticipation of pain is triggered by the inability to know how to feel about a danger and therefore what to do about it. It triggers emotional efforts whose aim is to gain a sense of the nature of the threat that is required in the defensive agential positioning of oneself toward it and for the move into desire.

When it is the subject's lack of knowledge or of access to means of implementing security that triggers a distress/relief modality of emotional experience, the aim of emotional efforts is to produce new means of implementing security through the production of a new form of in/capacity and of a means of power through which security can be implemented, or of a new means of power within the existing form of in/capacity. The distress/relief modality of emotional experience may therefore lead to already known or habitual forms of agency previously deployed as solutions to other problems in response to new problems, but it may also lead to innovative or unusual forms of agency in response to new or old problems.

In the following section, I explain how moral power can be exercised through emotional means in experiences of anxiety/interest and of distress/relief. In doing so, I begin to account for the moral mechanisms of self-objectification and self-transformation through which new emotional-norm pairs come into being.

EMOTIONAL BLENDING AND EMOTIONAL DIFFERENTIATION

Emotional-norm pairs are forms of orientation to the world. When I experience sadness, I experience the embodied knowledge that I presently lack the agential means to achieve happiness. Dealing with a relational threat/promise that may come to be embodied as sadness/happiness first requires the identification of the form of my incapacity as one that can be effectively overcome through the form of lack that is sadness, thereby prompting me to move into the form of lack that structures happiness. Once I experience the desire form of happiness, I am compelled to search for and identify the means of power through which I can fill the lack that structures it, and through which I can implement security.

Should I not be able to identify satisfactory means of resolving sadness/happiness through the panic/excitement modality of emotional agency, I may begin to perceive my sadness/happiness as a problem in itself. This self-objectification conditions the emergence of the anxiety/interest modality of emotional agency, on whose basis one may move into another emotional experience in an attempt to make alternative means of power available for dealing with anxiety/interest's two objects of fear and desire: the anticipated pain produced by the initial cause of one's sadness, the anticipated pain produced by the related problem of the inadequate means of overcoming it, the anticipated pleasure produced by the overcoming of the initial cause of one's sadness, and the anticipated pleasure produced by the identification of more adequate means of doing so. I shall call this anxiety/interest-driven embodied means of exercising moral power *emotional blending*.

A few examples should help illustrate the principle of emotional blending associated with the anxiety/interest modality of fear and desire.

While sadness/happiness is an emotional-norm pair that is structured by the more basic worry/safety pair associated with a prevention strategic orientation, because the determination of the agential means through which to resolve sadness/happiness may be made on the basis of another emotional-norm pair, resolving sadness/happiness may also involve an alternative strategic orientation, such as confrontation or avoidance.

I could therefore confront my sadness/happiness by perceiving my loss as a form of gain through the triggering of failure/success (the felt in/capacity to confront the forces that put the self at a disadvantage). Resolving sadness/happiness through failure/success might also lead to the actualization of thoughts having to do with the ways in which loss has allowed me to grow, or to behaviors that involve helping others through their own loss, for instance. Should this emotional blend of sadness/happiness and failure/success become a common cultural means of producing solutions to the problem of sadness/happiness, one might speak of an emotional-norm pair produced through blending within the anxiety/interest modality of fear and desire, and with which habitual means of threat/promise resolution may eventually become associated.

I could alternatively prevent my sadness by perceiving the object of my loss as no longer desirable through the feeling of vulnerability/invulnerability (the felt in/capacity to prevent being controlled by other forces through self-realization). Resolving sadness/happiness through vulnerability/invulnerability might also lead to the actualization of various prevention strategies, whether biological, sensorial, cognitive, behavioral, or moral. For instance, triggers that produce painful memories of the lost object could be avoided in order to prevent the experience of sadness. Should this emotional blend of sadness/happiness and vulnerability/invulnerability become a common cultural means of producing solutions to the problem of sadness/happiness, one might speak here also of an emotional-norm pair produced through blending within the anxiety/interest modality of fear and desire, and with which habitual means of threat/promise resolution may eventually become associated.

Finally, I could avoid my sadness by perceiving my loss as an impediment to amusement through the feeling of boredom/amusement (the felt in/capacity to prevent the absence of pleasurable stimulation). Resolving sadness/happiness through emotional boredom/amusement might also lead to the actualization of a behavior such as the consumption of entertaining media or of another pleasurable stimulant. Should this emotional blend of sadness/happiness and boredom/amusement become a common cultural means of producing solutions to the problem of sadness/happiness, one might speak here too of an emotional-norm pair produced within the anxiety/interest modality of fear and desire, and with which habitual means of threat/promise resolution may eventually become associated.

What we can gather from this is that the quest for the determination of more adequate means of power through which to implement security can lead us into another emotional experience that may become blended with the first. But what if alternative means of power are not found on the basis of a blended emotional experience, or in other words through resorting to the experience of known emotional-norm pairs? Another possibility is the agential course produced through the process of *emotional differentiation*.

Emotions represent the various forms of orientation to overcoming danger and implementing security. It is through the distress/relief modality of emotional experience that new emotional perspectives for dealing with in/capacities are produced. In a word, the distress/relief modality of emotional experience is responsible for the creation of new emotional-norm pairs.

Once fear takes on the form of an in/capacity, a particular means of exercising power may become associated with the form of capacity. We have seen that this is the case in the panic/excitement modality of emotional experience. This may cause us to think that specific means of exercising power are implied by the nature of the lack that characterizes fear emotions, or by the nature of the lack that characterizes desire emotions, but this is not the case. As we have already seen in our discussion of agential attunement, emotional orientations determine the strategic orientation of means of power, but do not usually determine the specific means of power through which security is implemented.[8]

The potential means through which power is exercised in the implementation of security can be quite varied. In the case of the panic/excitement modality of emotional experience, specific means are more likely to have been previously determined and associated with the emotional experience, whereas in the distress/relief and anxiety/interest modalities of emotional experience a new or more adequate course in the exercise of power remains to be produced or identified. As such, it is important that we distinguish between the social norms and other forces that help determine the form of lack or incapacity that is the basis of emotional differentiation, as well as the social norms and other forces that help determine the means of power for filling this lack, since it is easy to confuse them.

For instance, if angst names the fear that one lacks the ability to confront the loss of moral certainty, the quest that is implied by this lack is the identification of and move into the desire form (the form of capacity) with which this incapacity is associated. Let us say that faith is the appropriate name for the desire emotion invoked by the perception that one is capable of confronting the loss of moral certainty. The means to implement faith remain to be found in the determination of a specific means of exercising power. Religious or scientific practice might constitute examples of directive agency in this particular case. In other words, emotional forms direct actions like the move into a particular form of desire and the quest for and identification of means of power, but they do not necessarily determine the specific means through which one might exercise power. More specifically, the form of desire is distinct from the means of power through which the security to which it is tied is implemented. This leads us to consider the differing ways in which subjects relate to the means of power based on the modality of their emotional experience.

In the panic/excitement modality of angst/faith, a means of power has already been identified and motivates the faith-driven implementation of security. In the anxiety/interest modality of angst/faith, a previously identified means of power is judged to be inadequate and impedes the faith-driven implementation of security. Should an alternative and more adequate means of power be found, the faith-driven implementation of security could take place and might eventually form the basis of its expression in a panic/excitement modality. Should it not be found, it might give way to the distress/relief modality of angst/faith.

To make sense of the distress/relief modality in the experience of angst/faith, we might ask why the angst/faith emotional-norm pair arose in the first place. Angst/faith is itself a response to an experience of in/capacity that is structured by terror/courage and that emerged through the distress/relief modality of emotion. The distress/relief modality of angst/faith may similarly lead to the production of a new emotional-norm pair. This process of emotional differentiation is a means of overcoming the danger of remaining caught in distress/relief-driven incapacity.

In other words, should it not be possible to resolve an in/capacity through either panic/excitement or anxiety/interest, the distress/relief modality of fear and desire may spur the production of a new emotional-norm pair that corresponds to the need to overcome this danger and allow the move into desire. And should this process occur collectively or come to be disseminated within a social group, its members would embody a new emotional-norm pair.

For instance, let us speculate that the distress/relief-driven incapacity to move into faith, or to identify a means of implementing faith-driven security, or to access means of implementing faith-driven security prompts subjects to experience a new form of in/capacity that results from this incapacity. They might then come to experience the fear that results from the lack of ability to confront angst, which we might call faithlessness, whose pair is agnosticism.

The emotional-norm pair of angst/faith may be said to develop in contexts where a degree of relativism and of moral self-determination are social norms that exist alongside other forces and norms with which they are in conflict and where angst/faith is a solution to another emotional problem. Emotional norms develop as means to promote the search for, identification of, and actualization of agential solutions to relational threats and promises, though further interaction with the environment is necessary to identify or produce the means of power through which security is implemented.

Another, simpler example of an emotional-norm pair produced through emotional differentiation is that of tardiness/punctuality, which might be said to come into dominance during the industrial era, when the urge to move from the inability to arrive on time through self-discipline toward the ability to do so becomes a moral imperative for both workers and their bosses.[9] As such, a useful method in the tracking of the rise of differentiated emotional norms is to identify contexts of significant social change.

In emotional experiences governed by the modality of panic/excitement, the satisfactory results of a prior search for means of power have become attached to the emotional experience. But in emotional experiences governed by the anxiety/interest-driven and distress/relief-driven modalities, a further effort is required in the search for means of power. Interaction with the current environment is the basis of their determination.

Emotional norms that are experienced through panic/excitement are not likely to favor the overcoming of danger and the implementation of security in rapidly changing environments that consistently produce new problems requiring new solutions, because these experiences are accompanied by ingrained, routine solutions. Unlike the emotional norms that are experienced through panic/excitement, the emotional norms that develop through the modalities of anxiety/interest and of distress/relief are an expression of internal conflicts that bring about a current, moral search for solutions to problems. Emotional blending may result from the anxiety/interest-driven quest for more satisfactory means of power, while emotional differentiation may result from the distress/relief-driven quest for new means of power, should anxiety/interest fail to deliver adequate results. Were either of these processes to take on a collective existence, a blended or a differentiated emotional-norm pair might then be said to emerge.

In sum, the process of emotional differentiation is one in which the development of a new emotional-norm pair constitutes the specific means through which a persistent incapacity can be overcome and the security that it implies implemented. The process of emotional blending, by contrast, is one in which turning to an existing emotional-norm pair constitutes the specific means through which an inadequately resolved incapacity can be overcome and the capacity that it implies implemented. Thus while emotional blending belongs to the modality of anxiety/interest, emotional differentiation belongs to that of distress/relief.

Emotional norms and the means of power to which they may become tied through earlier emotional efforts, or through more contemporary ones, are the product of subjects' embodied interactions with their environment. In panic/excitement, agential responses may be highly spontaneous, but even these originate in prior interactions. Whatever the in/capacity and its modality, its embodied experience motivates a hope response whose goal is to avoid pain and move in the direction of pleasure. Should the hope response be successful in finding means to achieve this through the determination of the form of in/capacity, relational threat gives way to relational promise and the anticipation of pleasure drives agency in the direction of its realization.

Emotional blending and differentiation are conditioned by the feelings of in/capacity that inform the practice of embodied autonomy. Emotional-norm pairs can be understood as the collective blends and differentiations that act as solutions to the basic problems posed by powerlessness/powerfulness, unfreedom/freedom, hopelessness/hopefulness, and self-doubt/self-confidence: How can I most effectively direct other forces or my own forces so that pain is decreased and pleasure is increased?

The forms in the exercise of in/capacity therefore correspond to subjects' environment and ought to increase their ability to exercise power within it. Some emotional norms may be inborn rules that were embodied earlier on,[10] while others are embodied and become rules during one's lifetime.

As discussed earlier, the perception of danger is governed by the anticipation of a previously constituted association between a particular force and a painful outcome, while the perception of security is governed by the anticipation of a previously constituted association between a particular force and a pleasurable outcome. Various forces are involved in the constitution of these associations and of responses to them. I consider the role of social forces in these processes more closely in later chapters. As feelings relating to forms of in/capacity that motivate the exercise of power, emotions are embodied urges to exercise autonomy, while also informing its practice. The feeling of powerlessness or incapacity is an expression of embodied, autonomous agency that motivates agents to transform it into a form of felt capacity, while the feeling of capacity or powerfulness is an expression of embodied, autonomous agency that motivates agents to transform it into the exercise of capacity.

We have also seen that in contrast with the panic/excitement modality of emotional experience, in the anxiety/interest and distress/relief modalities of emotional experience, emotional experience is directed not only toward dealing with the problem produced by the self's conflict with an external force but also toward dealing with the problem produced by the self's conflict with itself. In other words, unlike the subjective emotional experience, which only involves objects of fear and desire constituted through the self's interactions with the external world, the moral emotional experience involves objects of fear and desire constituted through the self's interactions with the internal world. These objects are made up of the self's positive and negative emotional experience. The difference between the subjective and the moral experience of emotions appears in the distinction I draw between the subjective and the moral exercise of embodied autonomy in the following chapter.

It is useful to conclude this early part of the discussion of the subjective and moral experience of emotions with a brief overview of Roy Baumeister and others' (2007) affective feedback perspective on the relationship between emotions and behavior, which can be set in contrast to embodied in/capacity theory. The authors posit that one of the main ways in which emotions influence behavior is through their anticipation. When making a decision about whether to suffer through the pain and risk of vaccination, for instance, the anticipation of regret at having failed to protect oneself in the event of serious disease, or the anticipation of regret toward as grave a vaccination-adverse effect as death, are both extremely powerful agents of persuasion that increase the likelihood of either behavioral course.

To uphold the notion that emotions play an adaptive feedback role on behavior, the authors argue that emotions occur after behaviors rather than during or prior to them. They draw a distinction between "emotions themselves" and "anticipated emotions," and maintain that emotions inform future behavior by way of painful "affective residue" that helps subjects avoid behaviors likely to bring on painful emotional outcomes. This view rests on a distinction between emotions and their affective anticipation, where the latter gives rise to the "ubiquitous emotion regulation" that is understood to guide behavior.

Baumeister and his fellow authors argue that painful emotional states do not cause behavior, because in experiments, subjects who are led to believe that nothing can be done about their pain fail to engage in the behaviors that are usually associated with the alleviation of this pain. They further argue in support of the notion that emotions do not cause behavior (e.g., that aggression is not directly caused by anger, or that alcohol consumption is not directly caused by distress) since behavior is merely a means through which subjects seek to deal with a painful emotional state.

Embodied in/capacity theory takes anticipation to be a key aspect of all emotional experience. All emotions are felt and structured anticipations of pain or pleasure tied to behaviors and other forms of embodied action through which agents seek to move away from painful emotional states and toward pleasurable ones. Painful states constitute motivations to find the means of moving away from pain through the identification and move into a pleasurable form of capacity, while pleasurable states constitute motivations to find the means of moving toward pleasure through the identification and implementation of means of power. As such, emotional experience is ubiquitous and is a condition of various forms of agency, including behavior.

Embodied in/capacity theory is based on a distinction between the subjective and the moral experience of emotions. If a subject perceives that an existing agential response to the overcoming of danger and to the implementation of security, such as helping behavior, is satisfactory, then this form of agency is likely to be engaged in without further agential intervention. But should this prove not to be the case, to explicate the process through which agents move from consciousness-bound outer transformation to self-consciousness-bound self-transformation in responding to threats, I draw a distinction between emotional experiences that involve the anticipation of pain or pleasure through the exercise of subjective autonomy, and emotional experiences that involve the anticipated anticipation of pain or pleasure, or moral pain and moral pleasure, through the exercise of moral autonomy.

In sum, the three modalities of fear and desire I have been discussing are means through which individuals exercise embodied forms of autonomy. It is to the issue of this autonomy and of its biological, subjective, and moral forms that I now turn.

Chapter 3

Analyzing Autonomous Selves

Biological, Subjective, and Moral Autonomy: Unindividuated, Self-Involved, and Other-Directed Kinds

In his book *The Social Construction of What?*, social philosopher Ian Hacking (1999) proposes a distinction between interactive and indifferent kinds. Interactive kinds, such as people, are aware of and care about how they are classified, whereas indifferent kinds, such as rocks, are unaware of and do not care about how they are classified. As Hacking is careful to point out, indifference does not preclude interaction and does not imply passivity. There is no denying that horses and humans interact, for instance, yet horses are an indifferent kind in the sense that they are not aware of and do not care about whether or not we think of them as horses, though they might actively resist our attempt to treat them otherwise.

To extend on Hacking's example, it might follow that if horses were classified as "creatures that fly" and pushed over a cliff with the expectation that they fly like the mythical Pegasus, they would react as indifferent kinds do, which is to say that they would not be aware of or care about the way in which we classify them, though they might resist our treatment of them. We as humans, on the other hand, being interactive kinds, might change our classification of them, such that we might no longer place them in the category of "creatures that fly." Another example Hacking provides of an indifferent kind with which we interact and which is not passive is that of microbes. While microbes react to how we treat them, developing resistant strains, for instance, which may cause us to classify them differently, they are indifferent because they are not self-aware—they do not know what they are doing.

Hacking acknowledges some of the potential limits and slipperiness of his distinction between interactive and indifferent kinds. One might also point to the confusion produced by the fact that while indifferent kinds are said to be "interactive," this is the term reserved to denote the kind with which indifferent kinds are contrasted. From the perspective of embodied in/capacity theory, the language that I am most intent on deconstructing, however, is the use of "indifference" to characterize kinds that do not care about how they are perceived by others because they are not self-aware. To the extent that indifference is the felt incapacity to care about what others feel, it implies the urge to develop this capacity in the form of sympathy, as well as the capacity to emote. Therefore, the kinds whom we ought to think of as indifferent are the kinds who are self-aware rather than those who are not. Furthermore, Hacking's distinction between indifferent and interactive kinds leaves no way of accounting for the difference between horses and rocks. Horses may not be capable of indifference, but they are capable of feeling, while rocks are not.

Inasmuch as I want to be able to discuss the particularities of embodied forms of autonomy, I need to break with Hacking's conceptualization and terminology. To this end I make a practical distinction[1] between embodied and disembodied kinds, with the former pertaining to fleshy things like humans, horses, and microbes, and with the latter pertaining to nonfleshy things like rocks, social systems, and machines. I also make a practical distinction between embodied kinds on the basis of the type of autonomy they are able to practice, whether biological (unindividuated), subjective (self-involved), or moral (other-directed).

Embodied kinds can be distinguished from disembodied kinds on the basis of their fleshy power-driven ability to be transformed by and transform various forces in the achievement of a purpose, in the course of which rules are embodied. Humans, horses, and microbes may all be said to exercise a form of affective, rule-bound transformative awareness, by which I mean the felt and regulated ability to interact with various forces, or stimuli. Embodied autonomy may be distinguished from its disembodied expression on the basis of its affective potential for transformation in the achievement of a purpose. Embodied autonomy is interactive and should not be confused with self-sufficiency.

Since embodied kinds like humans, horses, and microbes cannot all be said to exercise identical forms of awareness, but are distinct in some of the forms of awareness they are able to exercise, it is useful to distinguish between different types of embodied autonomy.

I understand the most basic form of embodied autonomy, which I shall call *biological autonomy*, as the exercise of the embodied capacity to respond to conflict in a manner that promotes homoeostasis, or internal equilibrium. It is a form of fleshy awareness that consists of the rule-bound ability to affectively interact in a noncognitive and nonemotional, or presubjective manner. Biological autonomy is a presubjective form of autonomy, in which the capacity to think and to feel emotional pain and pleasure—the capacity to experience life emotionally through the anticipation of pain and pleasure that constitute fear and desire—does not yet exist. In the biological form of autonomy, awareness is unindividuated.

I place microbes in the category of agents that exercise biological autonomy. The microbe has a power-driven affective potential for transformation in the achievement of a purpose. I suggest that we refer to embodied beings like microbes as *unindividuated* or *biologically embodied kinds*.

I understand a second form of embodied autonomy, which I shall call *subjective autonomy*, as building upon biological autonomy in realizing its affective potential for subjectivity. Subjective autonomy is the exercise of the embodied capacity to respond to conflict in a manner that promotes the overcoming of danger and the implementation of security. It is a form of fleshy awareness that consists of the rule-bound ability to affectively interact in a cognitive and emotional, or subjective, manner and in a premoral manner as well. The ability to experience the world subjectively is the ability to think about and feel emotional pain and pleasure through their individuated anticipation. It is the ability to experience fear—the painful urge that motivates the search for means to overcome danger—and to experience desire—the pleasurable urge that motivates the search for means to implement security. It is the ability to think about and emotionally respond to the affective effects produced by the self's interaction with things in particular as a thing in particular. In the subjective form of autonomy, awareness is individuated.

I place horses in the category of agents that exercise subjective autonomy. While microbes might respond to conflict on the basis of biological awareness in the achievement of a purpose, horses have the additional ability to respond to conflict on the basis of subjective awareness in the achievement of a purpose. Unlike the microbe, the horse has the capacity to interact on the basis of an individuated self that thinks and feels. I suggest that we refer to embodied beings like horses as *self-involved* or *subjectively embodied kinds*.

Subjective autonomy is a premoral form of embodied autonomy, in which the capacity to think and care about the patterns of affective effects that are produced by the self's interaction with other things, or with things in general (including the self as a particular member of things in general), is unrealized affective potential. In the subjective form of autonomy, awareness is self-involved. Where there is no awareness of the self as an other, the objectification of experience that conditions the experience of self-fear, moral pain, self-desire, and moral pleasure remains unrealized potential.

I understand a third form of autonomy, which I shall call *moral autonomy*, as building upon subjective autonomy in realizing its affective potential for morality. Moral autonomy is the exercise of the embodied capacity to respond to conflict in a manner that promotes the overcoming of moral danger and the implementation of moral security. It is a form of fleshy awareness that consists of the rule-bound ability to affectively interact in a moral manner. The ability to experience the world morally is the ability to think about and feel emotional pain and pleasure through their individuated objectified anticipation. It is the ability to experience self-fear—the painful urge that motivates the search for means to overcome moral danger, where moral danger refers to emotional pain patterns for which the self is responsible, and where the means to overcome it imply the transformation of one's agency—and the capacity to experience self-desire—the pleasurable urge that motivates the search for means to implement moral security, where moral security refers to pleasure patterns for which the self is responsible, and where the means to implement it imply the transformation of one's agency. It is the ability to think about and emotionally respond to the affective effects produced by the self's interaction with things in general as a particular member of things in general. In the moral form of autonomy, awareness is individuated and internally divided.

In the self-involved form of autonomy, emotional pain and pleasure are acted upon through subjective consciousness. (For example, when my caregiver leaves the room I am afraid. I anticipate a painful outcome. In desire I find the form of a solution to danger on whose basis I can identify means to implement security. I anticipate a pleasurable outcome. I identify crying as a means to implement security. I am motivated to cry. I cry.)

In the other-directed form of autonomy, emotional pain and pleasure are acted upon as patterned effects for which the self is responsible through moral self-consciousness. (For example, every time my caregiver leaves the room I am afraid of my self's incapacity. I anticipate that I will anticipate a painful outcome. In self-desire I find the form of a solution to moral danger on whose basis I can identify means to implement moral security. I anticipate an anticipated pleasurable outcome. I identify crying as a means to implement moral security. I am motivated to cry. I cry.)

While self-involved embodied kinds have thinking and feeling selves, the capacity to objectify their experience—a capacity that is required for classification awareness—is unrealized. And while unindividuated embodied kinds respond in embodied fashion to other forces, they lack a sense of self about whose place in the world they could think and care. Only other-directed embodied kinds have the capacity to think and feel about their thinking and feeling selves that is required for classification awareness.

I place humans in the category of agents who exercise moral autonomy. Like microbes, humans have the capacity to be affected by adversity. And like horses, they have the capacity to think and feel in responding to conflict. But humans seem to be especially able to exercise the self-control required for the overcoming of moral danger and the implementation of moral security.

To conclude, I suggest that we call the embodied kinds that are morally aware of how they are classified *other-directed* or *morally embodied kinds*. Morally embodied kinds have realized the affective potential to experience their selves as others—an experience that is required for the awareness of classification as a force that can be acted upon in ways that may produce moral pain and moral pleasure. As such, they can be said to exercise three complementary forms of autonomy.

CONCEPTUALIZING EMBODIED AUTONOMY

I propose a number of concepts to ground my conception of embodied autonomy and of its different kinds.

I use the term "force" to designate any cause that is capable of exerting an effect.

I use the term "action" to designate the actualization or movement of a force.

I use the term "agency" to designate embodied purpose-driven actions. In the course of interaction, some forces may be said to exercise agency and others not. I call "actors" those forces that are engaged in actions. I call "agents" those forces that have the capacity to exercise agency.

I use the term "behavioral" to designate the purpose-driven physical actions of agents.

I use the term "cognitive" to designate the purpose-driven mental actions of agents.

I use the term "emotional" to designate the purpose-driven affective actions of agents.

I use the term "sensorial" to designate the purpose-driven sensory actions of agents.

I use the term "biological" to designate the purpose-driven organic actions of agents.

My understanding of interaction corresponds to the view that all matter is involved in relations of co-constitution and that these relations entail action upon action as well as power struggles. I view all forms of interaction as co-constitutive, inasmuch as even the force that exercises power over another that resists it is altered through its contact with this force. All actions are actions upon actions, because all actions cause reactions.[2]

However, not all actions are involved in relations of power.[3] Relations of power are forms of interaction that involve both purpose and affect.

Relations of power—relations of powerlessness and of powerfulness—require an agent whose force either can be directed by another force's greater power or can direct another force's lesser power. They require an embodied agent either who exercises power (is powerful) or over whom power is exercised (is powerless). While one could argue that a rock that crushes another rock has greater power than the other rock that it destroyed, it would not make much sense to speak of one rock's powerfulness and of another rock's powerlessness, since neither rock's purpose is threatened by the other's. Rocks are not agents. Of course it may matter to an agent that one rock crushed the other rock, in which case the rocks are invested with a purpose they do not have in and of themselves. Rocks matter to agents, but not to each other.

Social forces, such as the family structure or the organization of work, but also other forces, such as physical and biographical ones, can only be said to exercise power in their interactions with embodied agents. A prohibition to turn left is a force with particular properties that can interact with the properties of other forces, but it can also be said to exercise power if it blocks my way or causes me injury when its violation happens to result in a costly ticket. Similarly, a rock is a force with particular properties that can interact with the properties of other forces, and it can also be said to exercise power if it blocks my way or causes me injury when it happens to be propelled in my direction. Finally, a personal memory is a force with particular properties that can creatively interact with the properties of other forces, and it can also exercise power if it causes me to feel threatened.

I use the term "potential" to designate the embodied force that can be exercised by all embodied agents.[4]

I use the term "powerlessness" or "incapacity" to designate the insufficient quantity of force exerted by an agent when its actions are directed by another force's actions in a manner that threatens its purpose.

I use the term "powerfulness" or "capacity" to designate the sufficient quantity of force exerted by an agent when its actions direct another force's actions in a manner that overcomes a threat to its purpose.

I use the term "power" to designate the directive force exerted by an embodied or disembodied actor over an embodied agent who has the capacity to exercise biological, subjective, or moral power. "Power" designates the quantity of force exerted by an action. An action can only be deemed to exert greater or lesser power within a relation of power.

I use the term "biological power" to designate the directive force exerted by a biological agent in a driven action that is urged in the overcoming of another action that threatens them by causing them to experience strain.

I use the term "subjective power" to designate the directive force exerted by a subjective agent in a willful action that is urged in the overcoming of an external action that threatens them by causing them to experience pain.

I use the term "moral power" to designate the directive force exerted by a moral agent in a deliberate action that is urged in the overcoming of an internal action that threatens them by causing them to experience moral pain.

Biological, subjective, or moral power is directive action upon threatening directed action. Forces that are not capable of exercising embodied autonomy cannot exercise power outside of their relationship to agents that are capable of doing so. Horses, humans, and microbes can exercise power over rocks, and rocks can exercise power over horses, humans, and microbes, but rocks cannot exercise power over rocks.

I use the term "drive" to designate the purpose-driven, affect-based, strain-avoiding, and release-seeking directive actions of biologically embodied agents.

I use the term "will" to designate the purpose-driven, affect-based, pain-avoiding, and pleasure-seeking directive actions of subjectively embodied agents.

I use the term "intent" to designate the purpose-driven, affect-based, moral pain-avoiding, and moral pleasure-seeking directive actions of morally embodied agents.

I use the term "counterforce" or "reaction" to designate the action that is exercised by actors in the course of interaction. I reserve the term "resistance" for the counterpowering reaction of agents to an exercise of power that causes the agent strain, pain, or moral pain. I use the term "empowerment" for the counterpowering reaction of agents to an exercise of power that causes the agent release, pleasure, or moral pleasure.

I use the term "domination" to designate the power that is exercised by actors in the course of interaction with agents, where agents have little possibility for resistance or for empowerment. I use the term "subordination" to designate the counterforce of agents where the experience is one of persistent strain, pain, or moral pain.

I call "strain" the affect that biologically embodied agents experience when their course of action is directed by another force, embodied or not, that produces the drive to move away from its experience.

I call "release" the affect that biologically embodied agents experience when their course of action is directed by another force, embodied or not, that produces the drive to move toward its experience.

I call "pain" the affect that subjectively embodied agents experience when their course of action is directed by a threatening force, embodied or not, that produces the will to move away from its experience.

I call "pleasure" the affect that subjectively embodied agents experience when their course of action is directed by a friendly force, embodied or not, that produces the will to move toward its experience.

I call "moral pain" the affect that morally embodied agents experience when their course of action is directed by the self as a threatening force that produces the intent to move away from its experience.

I call "moral pleasure" the affect that morally embodied agents experience when their course of action is directed by the self as a friendly force that produces the intent to move toward its experience.

I use the term "biological stress" to designate the drive-based resistance of an agent toward an action that causes them strain.

I use the term "biological resilience" to designate the drive-based empowerment of an agent toward an action that no longer causes them strain.

I use the term "hope" to designate the experience of the potential for the transformation of a lack of capacity into a capacity that motivates the actions of subjectively and morally embodied agents.

I use the terms "fear," "subjective powerlessness," or "subjective incapacity" to designate the will-based resistance of an agent toward an external action that causes them pain. Fear is the painful urge that pushes subjectively embodied agents to move away from anticipated pain in the overcoming of danger. Fear is a form of resistance to external forces that pose a threat to the self. It consists of the hope-based quest for the identification of the form of incapacity to which this threat corresponds, on which is premised the overcoming of danger and the experience of desire.

I use the terms "desire," "subjective powerfulness," or "subjective capacity" to designate the will-based empowerment of an agent toward an external action that causes them pleasure. Desire is the pleasurable urge that pushes subjectively embodied agents to move toward anticipated pleasure in the implementation of security. Desire is a form of empowerment toward external forces that pose a promise to the self. It consists of the hope-based quest for the identification of the means in the exercise of power through which a promise can be realized, on which is premised the exercise of power and the implementation of security.

I use the terms "self-fear," "immoral powerlessness," "immoral incapacity," "immoral powerfulness," and "immoral capacity" to designate the intent-based resistance of an agent toward an internal action that causes them moral pain. Self-fear is the painful urge that pushes morally embodied agents to move away from the moral pain produced by the self in the overcoming of moral danger. Self-fear is a form of resistance to internal forces that pose a threat to the self. It consists of the hope-based quest for the identification of the form of incapacity to which this threat corresponds, on which is premised the overcoming of moral danger and the experience of self-desire.

I use the terms "self-desire," "moral powerlessness," "moral incapacity," "moral powerfulness," and "moral capacity" to designate the intent-based empowerment of an agent toward an internal action that causes them moral pleasure. Self-desire is the pleasurable urge that pushes morally embodied agents to move toward the moral pleasure produced by the self in the implementation of moral security. Self-desire is a form of empowerment toward internal forces that pose a promise to the self. It consists of the hope-based quest for the identification of the means of power through which a promise can be realized, on which is premised the exercise of power and the implementation of moral security.

I use the term "subjective unfreedom" to designate a subjective being's lack of access to the means of exercising subjective power in the implementation of security, while "subjective freedom" designates this access. Subjectively embodied agents are free if they have access to the means of implementing security in the face of an external threat. For example, horses are free if they can bite their caregivers as a means of implementing security, should this be the means through which they feel impelled to exercise power. Horses whose mouths are tied shut do not experience this freedom.

I use the term "moral unfreedom" to designate a moral being's lack of access to the means of exercising moral power in the implementation of moral security, while "moral freedom" designates this access. Morally embodied agents are free if they have access to the means of implementing security in the face of an internal threat. In other words, they are free if they can transform their subjectively embodied urges to exercise power—if they can repress, correct, activate, or form their desire to exercise power in particular ways. For example, humans are free if they can repress or correct their socially transgressive desire to bite their caregivers as a means of implementing moral security, and if they can activate or form their socially competent desire to use words to communicate with their caregivers as a means of implementing moral security. Humans whose capacity to experience (to listen to) their selves is compromised do not experience this freedom. It should be emphasized that the effects of moral self-transformation efforts need not be aligned with dominant social expectations and can be the grounds for significant social change.[5]

SUBJECTIVE, MORAL, AND SOCIAL EMOTIONAL EXPERIENCES AND EMOTIONS

A subjective emotional experience is the feeling based on the perception that one must exercise power over external forces to avoid pain or seek pleasure. Self-involvement, where the self is experienced as equal to itself, leads to the subjective experience of emotions. I experience an emotion like frustration (the fear triggered by the perception that one lacks the ability to confront the forces that stand in the way of one's goals, whose pair is satisfaction) in its subjective form if my incapacity (the pain I anticipate my problem will cause me) is experienced in the moment.

Let us say that I am frustrated that I cannot tie my shoelace, to which problem I apply the subjectively desired, satisfaction-producing solution of the embodied means of power that is ignoring the untied shoelace. Here my experience of both frustration and satisfaction is subjective, inasmuch as I seek to move from one to the other on the basis of an anticipatory subjective awareness. I may of course remain in this subjective emotional pattern, which I do not yet and may never experience as a pattern over which I can act through moral self-control. However, should I develop the embodied awareness of my ability to act upon this emotional experience through its objectification, I may begin to experience frustration/satisfaction in its moral form.

A moral emotional experience is the feeling based on the perception that one must exercise power over internal forces—that one must exercise self-control—to avoid moral pain or seek moral pleasure. Other-directedness, where the self is experienced as another upon which the self can act, leads to the moral experience of emotions. I experience an emotion like frustration in its moral form if my incapacity (the pain I anticipate my problem will cause me) is experienced in objectified form, as something that I have experienced in the past and that I may experience in the future and about which I can and should do something in the present.

Let us say that I am frustrated that I have been frustrated, or that I may again be frustrated, that I cannot tie my shoelace, to which problem I apply the morally desired, satisfaction-producing solution of the embodied means of power that is exercising moral self-control. Thus I might repress or correct my desire to ignore my untied shoelace, or I might activate or form my desire to pay attention to my untied shoelace, as a morally self-interactive solution to the moral problem of frustration/satisfaction, which is a moral problem precisely because I relate to it as part of a pattern upon which I can act, through self-transformation, in the overcoming of moral danger and in the implementation of moral security.

Moral self-interaction begins very early on, such as in learning to deliberately place some objects in one's mouth and not others, or learning to control the time and place of the output of one's urine and feces. As the outcomes of early moral self-transformation efforts are embodied, they can become highly spontaneous. Moral self-control efforts can thereby give way to a process of emotional regulation.[6]

An emotional experience is moral when its object is the unsuccessful resolution of an objectified emotional problem. As such, the moral emotional experience is necessarily one of anxiety/interest or of distress/relief, and it is a condition of the emergence of new emotional-norm pairs through emotional differentiation and blending, which I discussed in chapter 2. The emotional-norm pairs that are formed as a result of moral emotional experience are moral emotions.

All the emotional differentiations and blends that grow out of the three pairs of emotions that serve to strategically orient action—terror/courage, worry/safety, and phobia/escape—are moral emotions, since emotional differentiation is a process that is triggered by the immorally powerful or immorally powerless self's unsuccessful resolution of an objectified emotional problem for which it experiences responsibility. It should be emphasized, however, that the experience of moral emotions does not make for a moral emotional experience, since moral emotions can be experienced subjectively.[7] The moral emotional experience, as I have been arguing, requires that a subject feel compelled to exercise power over internal forces. Should this emotional effort no longer be required, emotional experience should be thought of as subjective.

The way in which I have defined some emotional-norm pairs emphasizes the fact that they are moral emotions that are being morally experienced. For instance, the names I give to the experience of moral emotions involving the self's feeling of disapproval of itself (i.e., self-dislike/self-like, self-disgust/self-purging, and self-hate/self-love) differ from the names I give to the moral experience of these emotions (i.e., shame/pride, personal insecurity/self-esteem). Other examples of emotional-norm pairs that explicitly designate the moral experience of moral emotions in the lexicon I provide include incivility/civility (the felt in/capacity to confront the primitive, animalistic, or bodily impulses that hold one's reason hostage through self-discipline), disempowerment/empowerment (the felt in/capacity to confront the personal shortcomings that compromise one's healthy desire through self-realization), weakness/strength (the felt in/capacity to prevent being controlled by other forces through self-discipline), and vulnerability/invulnerability (the felt in/capacity to prevent being controlled by other forces through self-realization). In short, moral emotions contain the self's unsuccessful resolution of an objectified emotional problem, and morally experienced moral emotions explicitly call for moral self-transformation efforts in the implementation of security.

Any discussion of emotional life would be gravely incomplete without a discussion of its social forms and modalities of experience. I have argued that moral emotional experience requires the experience of the self as another. Social emotional experience is based upon the experience of others as selves. The social emotional experience involves the quality of the relation between a self and another feeling being. It is based on the capacity to experience empathy—the ability to understand what other selves feel. As such, it may require the experience and successful resolution of alexithymia/empathy (the felt in/capacity to confront one's lack of understanding of what other selves feel) should alexithymia be a problem. It should be emphasized that while empathy allows for the exercise of social dis/approval, it does not in itself imply such a judgment. In other words, "understanding" is used here in a value-neutral way.

The capacity to understand what others feel, or the experience of empathy, is the basis of the social emotional experience. The social emotional experience is achieved through a process of situation assimilation[8] where one is able to understand what others feel, as well as the emotional sense of objects. As a means of exercising embodied autonomy, empathy affects the quality of relations between self and other. Agents' capacity to understand what other agents feel affects what they feel and how they act in response to what they feel. For instance, if I understand that another feels anger toward me, I may find ways of resisting through anger/assertiveness, or of conforming through guilt/innocence. Or if I understand that another person experiences terror/courage in the face of a job interview, I may adopt this emotional orientation as well. In turn, others will respond to how I respond.

As such, collective feelings may be said to develop through a process of situation assimilation in which selves adopt others' emotional orientations toward specific objects of fear and desire, namely through the decoding of emotives (Reddy 1999, 1997), as well as the ability to understand those objects once their emotional sense has been acquired. For instance, agents may be prompted by other agents to experience homes without alarm systems as objects of fear and homes with alarm systems as objects of desire through risk/precaution, or to experience smokers as objects of fear and nonsmokers as objects of desire through social disapproval/social approval.

Moreover, affective atmospheres may be thought of as arising from agents' understanding and adoption of other selves' emotional orientations, objects of fear and desire, signs of danger and security, and embodied means of power, as well as through their interactions with human and nonhuman objects of fear and desire that are attuned to specific emotional orientations.[9] For instance, the affective atmosphere of a city street lined with security cameras and bright lights is produced through agents' interactions with an object of desire (a street with security cameras and bright lights) and its implied object of fear (a street without security cameras and bright lights) attuned to the worry/safety emotional orientation, as well as through agents' interactions with each other in this environment. In short, agents' capacity to understand what others feel, as well as their capacity to understand the feelings that become attached to objects, provides them with important information that will affect their capacity to exercise embodied autonomy, the quality of their relations with others, and the quality of relations between selves and others more generally.

The notion of social emotional experience as resulting from empathy-based situation assimilation also helps us understand the institutional and collective basis of some emotional experiences. Agents can be cued by and adopt an institutional or collective emotional orientation, its objects of fear and desire, its signs of danger and security, and its means of implementing security. A member of an institution (e.g., a corporation, a public body, the nuclear family) or of a social group (e.g., based on gender, sexuality, class, ethnicity, disease, age) might therefore experience fear should the institution or group that cues their emotional perceptions be threatened in some way, be moved by the type of promise that fuels the search for the appropriate means of exercising power, and feel compelled to implement security through whatever means of power are deemed appropriate by the institution or group.

We have seen that the social emotional experience is conditioned by the experience of empathy: An understanding of what others feel is a condition of social interaction and affects the quality of this interaction. On the other hand, the social emotion, which I distinguish from the social emotional experience, is an emotion whose structure implies not only the capacity for empathy but also the capacity to care about what others feel. This capacity, which I have called sympathy, belongs to the emotional-norm pair that is indifference/sympathy (the felt in/capacity to confront one's lack of care for what others feel).

I have thought of two ways in which emotional-norm pairs can be structured as social. First, emotions that imply that the self causes hurt to another, such as guilt/innocence (the felt in/capacity to prevent having to hold oneself responsible for causing another hurt), remorse/atonement (the felt in/capacity to avoid having been the cause of hurt to another), and spite/kindness (the felt in/capacity to confront one's treatment of another with illegitimate will), all involve the quality of self–other relations and can therefore be thought of as social. Second, emotions that imply that another causes hurt to the self, such as anger/assertiveness (the felt in/capacity to confront another's hurting of oneself), envy/contentment (the felt in/capacity to confront one's lack of command over the resources required to take pleasure in forces that others are believed to enjoy), and jealousy/possession (the felt in/capacity to prevent another's appropriation of a force the self would like to keep for itself), also involve the quality of self–other relations and can equally be thought of as social.

We have seen that emotions that imply that the self is a cause of moral pain/moral pleasure to itself have a moral structure, such that we can call them moral emotions. Similarly, emotions that imply that the self is a cause of hurt to another self or that another is a cause of hurt to the self have a social structure, such that we can call them social emotions. Social emotions are moral emotions that contain the unsuccessful resolution of an objectified emotional problem pertaining to the quality of relations between selves.

Were we to allow for the further qualification of social emotions as political when they involve the quality of the social distribution of the capacity to exercise power, then the social emotions that imply that one or another unjustly causes hurt to a self—such as outrage/vindication (the felt in/capacity to confront another's illegitimate hurting of oneself), stinginess/generosity (the felt in/capacity to confront the self's illegitimate hoarding of resources), rage/revenge (the felt in/capacity to confront one's victimhood through the causing of retaliatory hurt to one's victimizer), oppression/emancipation (the felt in/capacity to confront forces that illegitimately constrain one's freedom), injustice/justice (the felt in/capacity to prevent being the victim of an illegitimate exercise of power), and heartlessness/compassion (the felt in/ability to confront one's lack of support for those who have been victimized)—should equally or alternatively be understood as political emotions.

While the social relation is an object of danger and security for the social emotion, the social emotion is not necessarily experienced morally. In a subjective experience, the social emotion is a feeling pertaining to the quality of relations between selves. One might be said to experience guilt/innocence or anger/assertiveness subjectively if the object of danger is the self–other relation as an external force. Here selves experience pain/pleasure as a result of feeling that they are/are not capable of preventing having to hold their selves responsible for causing others hurt, or selves experience pain/pleasure as a result of feeling that they are/are not capable of confronting another's hurting of the self.

In the moral experience, the social emotion is a feeling about a feeling pertaining to the quality of relations between selves. One might be said to experience guilt/innocence or anger/assertiveness morally if the object of danger is the self–other relation as an internal force. Here the self experiences moral pain/moral pleasure as a result of feeling the feeling that they are/are not capable of preventing having to hold their self responsible for having caused another hurt, or the self experiences moral pain/moral pleasure as a result of feeling the feeling that they are/are not capable of confronting another's hurting of the self. In the moral experience of the social emotion, the self–other relation has been internalized as a force upon which the self can and ought to act through acting upon itself. It therefore prompts moral self-control and constitutes a means through which individuals relate to themselves and others as the subjects and objects of intervention in the production of moral pain and moral pleasure.

Much like the scope of responsibilization that is present in a social group and the extent to which subjects are able to move with greater or lesser facility from fear to desire or from self-fear to self-desire can serve to distinguish it from other social groups, the extent to which subjects' emotional experiences are based on social emotions can also serve as a basis for comparison in the analysis of emotional economies.

In the comparative analysis of particular emotional economies, beyond the examination of the prevalence of either subjective or moral emotional experiences, of the panic/excitement, anxiety/interest, or distress/relief modalities of fear and desire, of the confrontational, preventative, or avoidant strategic orientations to danger and security, or of the experience of moral problems through immoral capacity or immoral incapacity, we might also wish to consider the specificity of the dynamics of social emotional experiences, as well as the prevalence of the experience of social emotions, and within these, whether self causing other (e.g., guilt/innocence) or other causing self (e.g., anger/assertiveness) emotional experiences prevail. We might also wish to think about whether it is actually the case that highly individuated and individualistic social groups, as is often believed, experience fewer social emotions than highly unindividuated and collectivist social groups (I suspect that this is not at all the case), and whether their experience of the world is based on the highly developed scope of internalized dangers experienced through emotional norms that are characterized by an important range of responsibilities toward the self rather than, or as well as, toward the other (I suspect that a version of this *is* the case).

PART II

Emotional Economies

CHAPTER 4

ANALYZING MORAL DANGER
AND SELF-FEAR

FROM SUBJECTIVE TO MORAL AUTONOMY:
THE PROCESS OF RESPONSIBILIZATION

The relationship between fear and the rise of modern societies is central to some of the arguments made by the late German sociologist Norbert Elias. In his work *The Civilizing Process* (1978, 1982),[1] Elias argued that at the dawn of the modern era sociofunctional forces prompted the need to better regulate social relations. These imperatives are at the heart of what he terms the civilizing process—a process that marks the transition from the seemingly unpredictable, violent, and might-based societies of the Middle Ages to the predictable, pacified, and regulation-based societies of early modern Europe.

For Elias, the newly predictable and pacific nature of early modern conduct is a consequence of the exercise of greater self-control required in the context of the growing division of labor and lengthening chains of social interdependence, and of the development of large states with a monopoly over taxation and the means of legitimate violence. Elias argues that the civility manuals of early modernity contributed to the internalization of fear by making numerous forms of conduct unacceptable. From table manners to elimination and sex, various behaviors were privatized or prohibited, calling upon subjects to watch and sanction their most minute gestures through shame, embarrassment, and disgust.

Elias holds that the intensification of the experience of these emotions is part of the process through which the fear of the self comes to predominate over, without completely supplanting, the fear of others causing one physical harm. He maintains that the more that social structures are differentiated and require minutely regulated conduct, the more that external restraints have been transformed into internal ones, and the more that a person is likely to experience "automatic inner anxieties," whose effects are to produce socially functional self-control or self-discipline in the expression of affects and impulses. According to Elias, the civilizing process is accompanied by an increasing differentiation between the id, the ego, and the superego, between drives and drive controls. With time, self-regulation occurs in a progressively more habitual and spontaneous manner. As violence increasingly gives way to pacification, and as inner fears grow and external fears decline, danger becomes a constitutive part of the self.

Elias also maintains that while medieval subjects benefited from the more spontaneous quenching of their desires, on the other hand they were dominated by their fear of the external world. And while civilized subjects might suffer from the repression of their passions, this self-mastery frees them from being dominated by them. The greater freedom from physical harm comes at a cost, though, since drives and passions can no longer be satisfied directly and spontaneously, such that boredom and restlessness loom large. Moreover, the repression of drives and passions leads to a multitude of painful inner conflicts that prove to be too much in some individuals and lead to chronic pathological unhappiness. Elias holds that most people fit somewhere between the two extremes of high and low levels of gratification and frustration.

Elias seeks to distinguish the dynamics of suffering that characterize the seemingly violent warrior societies of the Middle Ages from the seemingly pacific and civilized societies of modernity. He explains the dynamics of suffering of the latter through the rise of a fear of self brought on by the development of the superego, or moral self. Through a critical reading of Elias's project, I seek to develop a more complex typology of the forms of the fear of self involved in suffering. The greater or lesser importance of one or the other of these forms in a social group might allow us to grasp some of the dynamics of suffering that animate it and could constitute the grounds for comparative analyses.

I begin by considering how the objectification of the self's emotional experience conditions a process of responsibilization toward danger. By "responsibilization," I mean the action of making the self responsible for danger outcomes. While the use of this term is fairly recent in English and seems to be used to denote the neoliberal and politically problematic process through which individuals are made responsible for problems that used to be taken care of by the collectivity (i.e., the welfare state), or over which individuals may have very little control, I use it here in a more general sense, closer to the

French term "responsabilisation," to account for the development of the moral feeling of one's own agency in the management of danger outcomes, on whose basis individuals are prompted—chiefly through their interactions with morally normative social expectations, but also through their interactions with other forces—to act upon themselves in the implementation of moral security. For instance, responsibilization is contained in the modern feelings of evil/righteousness (the felt in/capacity to confront one's lack of rational adherence to moral imperatives) and of its graver equivalent, madness/sanity (the felt in/capacity to prevent one's irrational transgression of moral boundaries), as well as in the late modern feelings of irresponsibility/responsibility (the felt in/capacity to confront one's lack of healthy adherence to moral standards) and of its graver equivalent, mental illness/mental health (the felt in/capacity to prevent one's unhealthy failure to measure up to moral standards).

In the terms of embodied in/capacity theory, let me submit that the process of civilization referred to by Elias involves the increased social and individual treatment of the self's agency as a problem, such that it may be said to constitute an object of fear. The content of this object of fear, or problem, is the dissatisfactory nature of the self's agency, while the content of its associated object of desire, or solution, is the satisfactory nature of this agency. We have seen that this dissatisfaction structures the anxiety/interest modality of emotional experience, which is one of two forms in the moral experience of emotions. I will attempt here to develop more precise and adequate language to discuss some of the potential configurations of the relationship between fear and the self.

On the one hand, Elias can be taken to argue that the cause of fear shifts from the outside to the inside—from the external physical other who poses a physical threat to the self, to the internalized judgment of the social other who poses a moral threat to the self. On the other hand, Elias can be taken to argue that the self becomes a cause of danger for itself, inasmuch as it becomes responsible for transforming its agency in ways that allow it to satisfy the expectations of the internalized social other. On the whole, the process referred to by Elias is one in which the perceived cause of danger shifts from external forces to the self as an internal force that produces danger.

The differing relationships to danger referred to by Elias can be clarified through a distinction between the subjective and the moral experience of danger. The subjective experience of danger is the result of a conflictive interaction between the self and another force, whatever its nature (e.g., social, physical, and the like). This conflict gives rise to the embodiment of an association between this external force and a pain outcome, thereby producing the object of fear. For instance, an agent might fear a parent's reprimand or catching an awful disease. Here the cause of danger (i.e., the cause of anticipated pain) is an external force (i.e., the parent, the disease). By contrast, the moral experience of danger is the result of a conflictive interaction between the self and its self as a force. This internal conflict gives rise to the embodiment of an association between the self as a force and a pain outcome, thereby producing the object of fear. For instance, an agent might fear their self's role in having caused a parent's reprimand or in catching an awful disease. Here the cause of danger (i.e., the cause of anticipated pain) is an internal force (i.e., the self).

Note that subjective experiences of danger do not preclude objects of fear made of socially threatening forces, any more than moral experiences of danger preclude objects of fear made of physically threatening forces. It is simply that in the first case the experience of objects of fear is not mediated by the agent's sense of responsibility for the outcome of threat relations, while in the second case it is. As such, Elias's claim that greater moral self-control efforts lead to a reduced fear of external or physical dangers should be problematized, since it is based on two incorrect premises: first, that external objects of fear are necessarily physical, and second, that self-fear leads to a collective reduction in the exercise of physical coercion and therefore to a collective decline in the fear of physical dangers.[2]

The process of responsibilization can be thought of as a process through which the self becomes internally divided. As a force that can engender pain, the subjective self becomes a cause of danger for the moral self. The subjective self becomes a pain-producing force over which the moral self must act. For instance, subjects who come into conflict with the social force of unemployment when they become unemployed could be said to experience the force of unemployment as an external danger so long as they did not experience it as a danger over which they ought to act through the exercise of self-control. Here, subjects might respond with fear to their condition of being unemployed as caused by an external force and deploy means to implement security that do not involve moral self-transformation. However, were subjects to experience unemployment as a dangerous force that ought to be acted upon by way of moral self-control efforts, unemployment would become a danger for which the self feels responsible.

I have argued that in the subjective experience of danger, danger is felt to be caused by an external force, while in its moral experience it is felt to be caused by the self. All dangers must be embodied to be experienced. But the embodiment of a danger does not necessarily lead to the perception of individual moral responsibility for its occurrence. As such, the embodiment of danger is distinct from the feeling of responsibility for its occurrence, since the latter entails the perception of danger as self-generated and impels moral self-transformation efforts.

The perception of danger that leads to the experience of fear involves the painful capacity to anticipate pain. Fear is the painful urge to move away from the experience of anticipated pain (i.e., of danger) that causes suffering. The perception of danger that leads to the experience of self-fear involves the painful capacity to anticipate anticipated pain. Self-fear is the painful urge to move away from the experience of objectified anticipated pain (i.e., moral danger) that causes moral suffering.

In short, a danger is an anticipated painful outcome caused by an external force (i.e., an object of fear), while a moral danger is an objectified anticipated painful outcome caused by an internal force (i.e., a moral object of fear). Fear is the painful urge to overcome danger, while moral fear, or self-fear, is the painful urge to overcome moral danger. Finally, suffering is the painful experience of fear, while moral suffering is the painful experience of moral fear.

While both modalities in the experience of danger interact with social forces, on the one hand, they are irreducible to these forces (i.e., the individual experience of danger is not simply a reflection of the social forces that help constitute it). On the other hand, it should be emphasized that although the cause of moral danger is perceived by subjects to be the self's morally problematic agency, moral danger emerges relationally and is embodied through subjects' interactions with external forces, and most importantly social forces. In some societies, social norms promote subjects' feelings of responsibility for forces over which they may have very little or no control. As a consequence, subjects are impelled to adapt to these forces through the exercise of moral self-control. I have defined the feeling of adaptation as the felt capacity to prevent self-destruction by conforming to a more powerful force's logic. Dysfunction is the felt form of incapacity with which it is paired.

Contemporary accounts that are critical of the neoliberal and advanced modern self-help rationalities that promote adaptation in the prevention of dysfunction tend to question the extent to which individuals are actually able to exercise power over forces like unemployment, crime victimization, poverty, and disease, or at the very least tend to question the ideological underpinnings of such forms of responsibilization.[3] It is likely that the widespread nature of contemporary forms of moral suffering, whether these correspond to anxiety or distress, have a great deal to do with processes of responsibilization in which agents are prompted to feel accountable for the emotional pain effects of a whole range of forces with which they are or may come to be in conflict. As such, a better understanding of the dynamics of moral pain is required.

Elias's argument should be significantly reformulated into the proposition that in the transition from the medieval premodern to the early modern European societies, subjects' embodied conflicts with physical forces increasingly became experienced as moral dangers, so that it is not the case that physical dangers are replaced by internalized social dangers, but rather that physical dangers become morally threatening. As physical assault becomes an affront to the norms of civility, it is no longer merely a subjectively threatening force producing fear in daily life. It becomes a morally threatening force producing self-fear in a growing number of subjects. In other words, as subjects are expected, under pressure from various social forces that have cultural, political, and economic dimensions, to exercise control over the self's habitual desire to use physical coercion to solve problems in everyday life, the repression of this desire, or its transformation through some other means, becomes a matter of personal responsibility for an increasing number of moral selves. In this particular context, the frequency with which subjects exercise power through physically coercive means can be said to decline through subjects' emotion management of themselves and others.

As I will have the opportunity to discuss later on, whether the habit of using physical coercion to solve problems itself results from self-oriented emotion management efforts deployed during subjects' lifetime is another issue, since it cannot be assumed that physical coercion is a means of power that is habitually engaged in by all subjects in all situations of emotional conflict (i.e., do the warrior subjects that Elias discusses, or the generalized premodern other that these simplistically designate, spontaneously use physical coercion to solve many problems in everyday life, or do they, or some, come to use these means through being emotionally managed by others or themselves?). Before turning to this matter, however, I will explore some of the ways in which experiences of self-fear—the painful urge to overcome moral danger—may be thought of as being on the rise (or not) in any given social context.

EXPLANATIONS FOR THE RISE IN EXPERIENCES OF SELF-FEAR

We have seen that, according to Elias, during the early modern era the moral education of subjects engendered by the increasing circulation and consumption of civility manuals favored the more frequent experience of emotions like shame, embarrassment, and disgust. In turn, these emotions prompted individuals to exercise a repressive form of control over the dangerous impulses that prompted them to violate morally normative social expectations, while also producing new forms of suffering. Modern subjects increasingly came to fear their selves' capacity for moral transgression. The transition from the Middle Ages to modernity is therefore one in which moral self-interaction develops and where the immoral capacity to violate internalized moral norms comes to occupy a dominant position in social relations for Elias.

As it ought to become clear, unlike Elias, I do not view self-fear solely as the result of individuals' conflicts with morally normative social expectations, since moral conflict can come about through agents' conflicts with various forces and is actually a condition, in my view, of social life as we know it (i.e., as based on empathy and sympathy).[4] Self-fear is an urge that develops as a result of subjects' conflictual relations with any force for which the self experiences responsibility. While the importance of morally normative social expectations in the promotion of individual responsibilization is undeniable, other forces, including the social forces with which individuals interact more generally but also physical and biographical forces, for instance, should be thought of as actors with which individuals interact in moral ways. In short, I draw a distinction between individuals' moral experience and the socially produced moral expectations of lawful or adequate selfhood, or moral norms, with which individuals interact and that help constitute this experience.

The self-fearing self experiences moral suffering as a consequence of its self-induced inability to avoid pain through some form of moral self-control. Self-fear motivates the moral self-control efforts through which the moral self transforms the subjective self in its attempt to implement moral security.

I make the case for the existence of two species of self-fear and four means of moral self-control. In this view, the exercise of self-control is not necessarily repressive. It can also be expressive.

The experience of immoral capacity discussed by Elias can be tied to two forms of moral self-control: self-repression and self-correction. To these repressive forms of moral self-control, we can add the two expressive forms that are tied to the experience of immoral incapacity: self-activation and self-formation. The forms taken by self-fear and self-control have implications for how we understand the collective dynamics of moral suffering, and most notably experiences of moral suffering brought about by the inability to repress, correct, activate, or form desires. In particular, the Western tradition of thinking of moral self-control as a matter of self-repression has blinded us to the forms of moral suffering that are tied to moral self-control as a matter of self-expression. I shall later argue that while the former means of moral self-control can be associated with the early modern context, where self-repression is felt to allow reason to emerge, the latter have gained dominance in the advanced modern context, where self-expression is felt to allow health to materialize.

In the terms of embodied in/capacity theory, the dynamics of the subjective experience of danger are as follows. The perception of danger (i.e., a force with which a painful outcome is associated) leads to the experience of fear (i.e., a painful urge to avoid anticipated pain and therefore to overcome danger) that sets in motion the hope-based search for a solution to this problem (i.e., the determination of the form of in/capacity). Once the form of in/capacity has been identified, the perception of security (i.e., a force with which a pleasurable outcome is associated) replaces the perception of danger and leads to the experience of desire (i.e., a pleasurable urge to seek anticipated pleasure and therefore implement security) that sets in motion the hope-based search for a solution to this second problem (i.e., the determination of the means of power).

By contrast, the dynamics of the moral experience of danger are as follows. The perception of moral danger (i.e., of the self as a force with which a painful outcome is associated) leads to the experience of self-fear (i.e., a painful urge to avoid objectified anticipated pain and therefore to overcome moral danger) that sets in motion the hope-based search for a solution to this problem (i.e., the determination of the form of moral in/capacity—whether desire is illegitimate, incorrect, latent, or immature). Once the form of moral in/capacity has been identified, the perception of moral security (i.e., of the self as a force with which a pleasurable outcome is associated) leads to the experience of self-desire (i.e., a pleasurable urge to seek objectified anticipated pleasure and therefore to implement moral security) that sets in motion the hope-based search for a solution to this second problem (i.e., the determination of the means of moral power—the means of repressing, correcting, activating, or forming desire).

I discuss nine ways in which experiences of self-fear may be said to be (or not be) on the rise.

First, one could argue that self-fear experiences are on the rise because agents experience a growing number of conflicts with forces for which they feel responsible. This might be said to occur if the forces for which subjects experience responsibility are very changing, ambiguous, or contradictory. Subjects are more likely to feel threatened by forces in highly complex and demanding environments, in environments with which they are unfamiliar, or in contexts with ill-defined or conflicting demands. However, for any of these conflicting states to contribute to the increase in experiences of self-fear, they must be associated with the practice of moral autonomy, on whose basis they are the subject's responsibility. For instance, if I feel overwhelmed by the unusual and continual appearance of new forms of technology but do not view my ability to make competent use of this technology as a matter of personal responsibility, I cannot be said to experience self-fear as a result of these interactions, though I may be said to experience fear with greater frequency. If, on the other hand, I feel overwhelmed by the unusual and continual appearance of new forms of technology and feel responsible for making competent use of it, I may be said to experience self-fear, or moral conflict, with greater frequency.

Second, it may be that agents relate in a moral manner to conflicts that arise as result of the responsibilization of individuals toward problems that used to be dealt with by a collective body, such as by a clan, a family, a state, or a union, or of the responsibilization of individuals toward conflicts that arise as a result of a collective body's ceasing to exercise responsibility over certain types of social interactions. Here, moral fear experiences are on the rise as a result of a greater number of forces' being subject to individual responsibilization. For instance, the increased scope of responsibilization may be taken to include individuals' responsibility for health or childcare, where these were previously collectively managed, or for chronic experiences of anxiety and distress, where these result from the economic hardship produced by a collective body's failure to ensure an adequate distribution of opportunities.

Third, self-fear experiences could be said to increase as a result of the morally normative social expectation that agents exercise responsibility over a greater number of forces through the cultural promotion of this responsibility. The contemporary self-help ethic is a good example of a cultural form that emphasizes individuals' capacity for personal empowerment in the confrontation, prevention, and avoidance of life problems that includes a growing list of objects of fear. The cultural promotion of responsibilization shares an affinity with the second point.[5] For instance, the contemporary ideal of health as a state of well-being that is increasingly determined by subjects' responsible action in most if not all spheres of everyday life—from finances to relationships, aging, appearance, career path, sexuality, education, and mental and physical activity more generally—should be thought of in its relation to the responsibilization of individuals toward problems that used to be dealt with by a collective body, or in relation to the responsibilization of individuals toward conflicts that arise as a result of a collective body's ceasing to exercise responsibility over certain types of social interactions. These two factors help us make a case for the contemporary extension of the scope of individual responsibility to an increasing number of fields of intervention, such that experiences of self-fear may be said to be currently on the rise.

Fourth, in making the argument that self-fear experiences are on the rise, one might also imply that these experiences are more forceful. Agents might experience moral fear more intensely if difficulties are encountered in aligning themselves with morally normative social expectations (or other forces)[6] through either favorable comparison or compliance, where lack of conformity produces greater moral danger. In other words, agents are likely to fear their incapacities more intensely if their inability to conform to the constraints of a situation causes them to anticipate severe pain. Thus if I fear that I will fail a very important exam for whose outcome I feel responsible, or if I fear that I will behave inappropriately at a very important social function for whose outcome I feel responsible, the intensity of my self-fear will be greater than if I perceive the exam or the social function to be unimportant. This is quite aside from the issue of whether the intensity of fear experiences for which the self is not responsible may be said to have deepened.

Fifth, one might be making the argument that self-fear experiences that have the self as an object that should not experience either suffering or moral suffering are on the rise, such that one morally fears the experience of being a self that experiences one or the other of these, and such that one more and more fears a painful awareness, or the painful experience of being a self. Here, greater than before, self-fear results from the moral understanding of suffering or moral suffering as a morally dangerous force. Thus if I morally fear the suffering caused by a headache, or the moral suffering caused by the loss of a cherished object, the object of my experience of moral suffering is either suffering or moral suffering, and it produces the self-fear-based urge to overcome moral danger.

Sixth, self-fear experiences may also be said to be on the rise in response to various social transformations, whatever their cause. Here self-fear experiences are brought about by subjects' feelings of responsibility for dealing with the relational threats caused by social change. For instance, were subjects to feel responsible for dealing with the role confusion brought about by the destabilization of previously dominant gender roles, they could be said to experience self-fear in response to social transformations.

Seventh, one might also be making the argument that experiences of self-fear are increasingly being morally produced by interested parties through emotion management, as means to achieve their ends. Numerous collective actors (e.g., corporations, organizations, governments, industries) may be said to exercise this type of power in contemporary society, although the deliberate production of self-fear is by no means restricted to the late modern context. For instance, advertising typically seeks to responsibilize agents in the overcoming of the danger caused by a whole range of undesirable situations and promotes specific goods and services as means of implementing security. An array of self-help literatures similarly deploys self-fear as a strategy to prompt moral self-control in line with a whole spectrum of health goals. Of course, fear experiences, rather than self-fear experiences, can also be triggered by these collective actors as means to achieve their aims, in which case the effects of emotion management upon agents are subjective rather than moral.[7]

Eighth, one could be making the argument that self-fear increases because subjects more frequently experience immoral powerlessness, which is the inability to exercise the moral self-control required for the exercise of moral power involving the self's agency's *favorable comparison to an ideal*. The subject who suffers from immoral powerlessness is compelled to overcome the danger he represents for him or herself through the *activation* or the *formation* of a desire that produces moral well-being by causing the self to achieve a moral standard.

This fear of the self treats the self as a source of danger on the basis of its powerlessness, such that the self fears its lack of adequate desire as a force in the production of the problem it represents for itself. The self suffers from being responsible for its powerlessness when, for instance, it feels responsible for its inability to engage in patriotic combat, or for its inability to measure up to standards of beauty, of healthy lifestyle, or of productivity. The self-fear produced by immoral powerlessness implies the self's lack of ability to overcome the danger it represents for itself as a *powerless force of inadequacy*. Once the form of moral incapacity is identified, moving into self-desire should allow the self to free itself through *self-realization*. Here self-transformation requires that the self become what it should be. For example, an individual might feel impelled to activate the desire to exercise, or to form the desire to eat healthy foods, as a means of moving from the feeling of vulnerability to that of invulnerability, or from the feeling of personal insecurity to that of self-esteem.

Ninth, one may be arguing that self-fear is on the rise because subjects more frequently experience immoral powerfulness, which is the inability to exercise the moral self-control required for the exercise of moral power involving the self's agency's compliance with *a command*. The subject who suffers from immoral powerfulness is compelled to overcome the danger represented by the self through the *repression* or the *correction* of a desire that produces moral suffering by causing the self to violate an imperative.

This fear of the self treats the self as a source of danger on the basis of its powerfulness, such that the self fears its excess of transgressive desire as a force in the production of the problem it represents for itself. The self suffers from being responsible for its powerfulness when, for instance, it feels responsible for engaging in acts of illegitimate aggression, for breaching norms of propriety, for hoarding objects that do not belong to it, or for incorrectly wasting precious resources. The self-fear produced by immoral powerfulness implies the self's lack of ability to overcome the danger it represents for itself as a *powerful force of transgression*. Once the form of moral incapacity is identified, moving into self-desire should allow it to free itself through *self-discipline*. Here self-transformation requires that the self cease to be what it should not be. For example, an individual might feel impelled to repress the desire to fall asleep at work, or to correct the desire to leave work early, as a means of moving from the feeling of weakness to the feeling of strength, or from the feeling of shame to the feeling of pride.

Agents' embodied ideals and imperatives necessarily result in part from their embodiment of dominant, morally normative social expectations (i.e., socially determined standards to strive for or commands to be obeyed). However, we should not exclude from consideration the more personal or idiosyncratic ideals and imperatives that develop through individuals' embodied interactions with various forces, as mediated by their unique bodies and biographies, and as mediated also by their social positioning. For instance, a girl brought up in an immigrant working-class family may not relate to the dominant, morally normative social expectations she cannot help but embody in the same way as a girl brought up in a well-established family of professionals.[8]

I have outlined nine ways in which experiences of self-fear could be said to be on the rise. First, through agents' more frequent moral experiences of fear as a result of novelty, ambiguity, or contradiction; second, through the increased scope of moral experiences of fear due to reduced collective responsibility; third, through the increased scope of moral experiences of fear due to the cultural promotion of individual responsibility for problems; fourth, through the increased intensity of moral experiences of fear due to greater anticipated pain outcomes; fifth, through agents' increased moral fear of suffering or moral suffering; sixth, through agents' moral attempts to deal with the effects of social change; seventh, through the increased emotion management of agents by interested parties; eighth, through agents' increased experience of immoral incapacity or powerlessness in the face of moral danger; and ninth, through agents' increased experience of immoral capacity or powerfulness in the face of moral danger.

These explanations for the rise in experiences of self-fear are not mutually exclusive. For instance, an increase in the experience of immoral incapacity can accompany an increase or a decline in the experience of immoral capacity, or an increase or a decline in the experience of emotion management by interested parties or of the cultural promotion of responsibility. The interplay between the different ways in which self-fear may be said to be or not be on the rise may allow one to gain a sense of a particular social group's economy of fear and desire. In other words, the observation of these dynamics can help determine the extent to which the experience and exercise of responsibility in the overcoming of danger and the implementation of security can be said to prevail in any given social context. The more an emotional economy is centered on the exercise of subjective autonomy, the more it might be thought of as a *fear and desire-based* emotional economy, where dangers are perceived to originate outside the self and treated as unavoidable and neutral *amoral problems* with necessary and natural *amoral solutions*. The more an emotional economy is centered on the exercise of moral autonomy, the more it might be thought of as a *self-fear- and self-desire-based* emotional economy, where dangers are perceived to originate inside the self and treated as avoidable and undesirable *moral* problems with identifiable and desirable *moral solutions.*[9]

Whether the moral dangers with which these self-fears are associated are successfully overcome and security implemented, and the degree of difficulty involved in this endeavor, will determine the extent to which a rise in the experience of a given type of self-desire corresponds to the rise in a given type of self-fear. Does the increased frequency, scope, or intensity of experiences of self-fear give way to the increased extent of experiences of self-desire, or do subjects remain permanently caught up in self-fear? Do selves' increased fear of their self's experience of suffering and moral suffering give way to the increased extent of experiences of self-desire, or do subjects remain permanently caught up in these particular self-fears? Do selves' increased experiences of self-fear in the context of social change or of emotion management by other parties give way to the increased frequency, scope, or intensity of experiences of self-desire, or do subjects remain permanently caught up in these experiences of self-fear? Do selves' increased experiences of immoral powerlessness or of immoral powerfulness give way to the increased frequency of experiences of self-desire, or do subjects remain permanently caught up in these experiences of self-fear? Should subjects not remain permanently caught up in self-fear, do they move into self-desire through the modality of anxiety/interest, or through that of distress/relief? Finally, and perhaps most importantly, do the means through which they implement moral security promote heteronomy in their selves or in others? In other words, do experiences of moral well-being and the forms of capacity to which they are tied promote structural forms of powerlessness?

FORMS OF SELF-CONTROL AND FORMS OF SUFFERING

In having outlined some of the various ways in which the self may be thought of as fearing itself, it becomes much less easy to argue, as does Elias, that early modern European subjects or later ones experience greater self-fear than their medieval ancestors. Did the subjects of these warrior societies fear a greater or a lesser number of moral dangers? Did they fear these more or less intensely than subjects of early or late modernity? Did they fear the effects of their moral agency on a greater number of forces? Did they fear suffering and moral suffering more or less than their descendants? Did they undergo experiences of self-fear brought on by social change or by interested parties' emotion management of their emotions more or less frequently, more or less intensely, or pertaining to more forces than we do? And did they experience immoral incapacity or immoral capacity more than we do?

Elias's arguments mostly correspond to the third, sixth, and ninth types of explanation, which have to do with the self's greater moral sense of its own transgressive powerfulness in pain and suffering causation as a result of social transformations and of the cultural promotion of moral responsibility for forces that were not previously moralized. As we've seen, he argues that fear emotions that are aroused by the self in response to the violation of moral imperatives are on the rise and cause the more refined development of the super-ego, or moral self. Shame, embarrassment, and disgust act as internal forms of punishment that ensure compliance with a growing array of social and cultural norms by way of moral ones. In turn, these norms promote the proper functioning of a newly emerging social order and of subjects' morality-driven integration within it.

Perspectives other than Elias's emphasize different explanations to support their view that fear or self-fear experiences are on the rise. In *Risk Society: Towards a New Modernity* (1992), Ulrich Beck argues that in the transition from the "wealth-distributing," scarcity-governed modern world, where a solidarity of need predominates, to the "risk-distributing," overproductive advanced modern world where a solidarity of anxiety predominates, immoral capacity (the ninth explanation) displaces immoral incapacity (the eighth explanation) in the production of self-fear. Human beings increasingly feel responsible for the destructive forces they unleash upon the environment and upon themselves as a consequence of overproduction.[10]

But Beck also views the transition from modernity to advanced modernity as one in which immoral incapacity remains and is exacerbated by immoral capacity. He invokes both explanations in his characterization of postindustrial society, to the extent that the unequal distribution of risks accompanies their universalization, and even exacerbates existing inequalities. In Beck's work the first and fourth explanations I outlined may also be true: Postindustrial society sees the increased frequency of moral fears due to normative conflict and ambiguity in the knowledge forms and expertise through which risks are ascertained. It also sees the increased intensity of moral fears due to the greater anticipation of environmental destruction with catastrophic and apocalyptic dimensions.

Beck contradictorily likens the emotional economy of the Middle Ages to that of advanced modernity in terms of a shared logic of fate. Yet how can we reconcile the logic of fate, which suggests a relationship to danger that is amoral—outside of or beyond moral self-control—with contemporary subjects' feelings of moral responsibility for environmental dangers? Contemporary subjects' relationship to environmental destruction and catastrophe can be explained in the terms of embodied in/capacity theory, by making the argument that some or many subjects resolve immorality/morality (i.e., the felt in/capacity to confront one's failure to adhere to moral imperatives or standards) toward the effects of overproduction by moving into doom/fate (i.e., the felt in/capacity to avoid the self's lack of control over an unfavorable destiny) based on the anxiety/interest modality of emotional experience. As such, it is not simply that (some and perhaps many) subjects feel that they cannot do something about these moral dangers because they are inevitable, it is rather that in many respects they are caught up in anxiety-driven immoral capacity and incapacity, and turn to a logic of fate as an alternative to remaining caught in moral incapacity.

Another perspective that we might usefully contrast with Elias's is that of theorists of the culture of fear.[11] Various collective agents who stand to benefit from subjects' fears (e.g., corporations, experts, politicians, activists) are argued to manufacture fear and self-fear, primarily through the mass media, as a means of furthering their interests, such that those on the receiving end experience immoral incapacity and the urge to implement moral security through whatever means are conveniently being promoted. In this approach, the moral production of self-fear through emotion management is usually politically or economically motivated. Beyond providing the seventh (increase in emotion management of agents by interested parties) and eighth (increase in experiences of immoral powerlessness) types of explanations, culture-of-fear theorists also sometimes invoke the second and third explanations (increased scope of responsibilization) by making the argument that more and more forces are associated with moral danger, as well as the fourth one (increased intensity) by making the argument that subjects experience fear more forcefully than in the past, alongside the argument that these fears are irrational.[12]

Yet another perspective we might contrast with that of Elias's is that of governmentality theorists,[13] of which Nikolas Rose's (1999, 1996b, 1996a, 1989) work is an example. Here the eighth explanation is consistently invoked (immoral incapacity), but so are forms of the second (enlarged scope of responsibilization), third (cultural promotion of new domains of responsibility), and seventh (increased emotion management of agents) explanations. Subjects in the advanced liberal and neoliberal context are urged to exercise freedom and autonomy as a means of countering immoral powerlessness. This self-interactive incapacity is produced through discourses and practices—a "governing at a distance" (Rose, 1996b)—which constitute subjects as responsible for putting themselves and others at risk, thereby prompting them to exercise their autonomy and their freedom as means of resolving immoral incapacity and of realizing moral capacity in the achievement of various state-driven or more widely sanctioned goals such as health, wealth, wisdom, productivity, and success. The concept of risk is also key for governmentality theorists like Mitchell Dean (1997) and Patrick O'Malley (1998), who emphasize the ways in which individuals, families, and communities have become increasingly responsible for insuring themselves against various risks that are no longer under the purview of state protection, from unemployment, to ill health, to crime victimization. This approach to the increased experience of self-fear corresponds to the second explanation (enlarged scope of individual responsibilization due to reduced collective responsibility).

The last perspective I mention here is that of critics of self-help culture. Eva Illouz (2008) invokes a version of the fifth (self-fear of suffering) and third (cultural promotion of responsibility) explanations in writing about how various experiences, such as success and failure in the workplace, intimate relations, and moral suffering, become subject to responsibilization in a culture of self-help. Heidi M. Rimke (2000) and Lisa Blackman (2004) tie the responsibilization of self-help culture to liberal notions of autonomy in which individuals' interdependence is denied, while Micki McGee (2005) and Dana L. Cloud (1998) cite economic hardship and the decline of the welfare state as factors that have prompted the needy to responsibilize themselves through self-help. All four invoke a version of the second explanation (reduced collective responsibility increases scope of individual responsibility) to explain the increased experience of self-fear, as well as the third explanation (cultural promotion of responsibility).

Of course, the various means through which self-fear can be argued to be on the rise do not all count as different species of self-fear. The first four—frequency, scope, cultural promotion, and intensity—have to do with conditions that promote the self's experience of its actions as problematic, and as such they should not be taken to be kinds of self-fear at all. The fifth is an instance of the enlarged scope of moralization, where suffering or moral suffering are subject to moral agency. Here, any number of forces could be substituted for the ones mentioned as objects of self-fear. It is sufficient that a force be perceived as a moral danger for it to become acted upon by way of moral self-transformation, whether it be health, illness, or even the self's fear of itself as an immorally in/capable agent, as the multitude of approaches to contemporary expressions of anxiety and distress testify. As such, these are objects rather than species of self-fear. The sixth and seventh means through which self-fear can be argued to increase—as being triggered by social change or by the emotion management efforts of interested parties—tells us about the trigger for the experience rather than about the nature of the experience, and as such they do not count as species of self-fear either.

Only the last two explanations discussed in our account of the potential forces behind a rise in experiences of self-fear count as actual types of self-fear, because only they can be tied to forms of moral agency in the implementation of moral security.

On the one hand, the self's experience of itself as *immorally incapable* can be acted upon through either *self-activation* or *self-formation*. For example, a subject could deliberately visualize the completion of a marathon in order to activate the latent urge to run as a means of implementing security, or deliberately drink a few cups of strong coffee in order to activate the latent urge to remain awake and study. A subject could also deliberately read a manual on the management of stress in order to form the mature urge to practice meditation as a means of implementing security, or deliberately watch debt-reduction reality television shows in order to form the mature urge to better manage his or her money.

By contrast, the self's experience of itself as *immorally capable* can be acted upon through either *self-repression* or *self-correction*. For example, a subject could deliberately imagine being caught cheating in order to repress the illegitimate urge to cheat as a means of implementing security, or could deliberately put money away in a savings account in order to repress the illegitimate urge to spend it. A subject could also deliberately invoke painful thoughts of a loved one's anger in order to correct the erroneous urge to repeat the same fault as a means to implement security, or could deliberately repeat a spelling exercise until getting it right in order to correct the erroneous urge to make mistakes.

We have seen that self-fear results from the experience of moral danger and is the painful urge to overcome it, while self-desire results from the experience of moral security and is the pleasurable urge to implement it. Once the self becomes an object of fear and desire as a moral agent that causes itself to experience suffering and well-being, it may be said to experience these in their moral form.

Should one be unable to work through a negative feeling for which one feels responsible—should moral self-control efforts be too costly or impossible—something along the lines of defense mechanisms might also be engaged in. For instance, a person who is ignored by others and who feels the need to be noticed, but is unable to act upon himself or herself in such a way as to implement moral security, might seek to reduce the intensity or the constancy of the pain associated with this moral incapacity by denying being ignored, by projecting his or her incapacity onto another person or group, by retreating into the fantasy of being the center of attention, by disassociating the self from the feelings produced by the situation, and so on. I would very much like to pursue elsewhere the ways in which subjects' ability to exercise morally embodied autonomy is facilitated or compromised by their resorting to these kinds of processes, but such is not my purpose here.[14]

On Physical Coercion and Moral Responsibility

I earlier suggested that the shift from a premodern to a modern emotional economy envisioned by Elias could be seen as corresponding to the passage to an emotional economy in which moral autonomy is increasingly exercised—that is, where an increasing number of threatening relations become subject to responsibilization. I shall now argue that while Elias understates the extent to which the premodern subjects of the Middle Ages govern their behavior on the basis of moral self-transformation efforts, it is possible to make the case that the modernization process in the societies he refers to probably brings about an increase in the scope of responsibilization and therefore also effects an increase in the opportunities for the exercise of self-control.

Barbara H. Rosenwein (2002) argues that the assumption that "the history of the West is the history of increasing emotional restraint" informs numerous contemporary approaches to subjectivity from the Middle Ages onward. For instance, it forms the basis of Norbert Elias's civilizing process and of Peter N. Stearns and Carol Z. Stearns's emotionology, as well as the approaches of Max Weber, Sigmund Freud, and Michel Foucault, and of others like Lucien Febvre, Johan Huizinga, and Marc Bloch. According to Rosenwein, the grand narrative of increasing emotional self-control that accompanies the process of modernization is based on a reductionist understanding of the Middle Ages as childlike in its emotional dynamics, as "unadulterated, violent, public, unashamed," in contrast with the "self-discipline, control, and suppression" (5) of the modern period.

This grand narrative, Rosenwein argues, is based on a hydraulic model of emotions as bottled up energy. She notes that the conception of the emotions as universal forces brewing within selves has been replaced by the relational approaches of the 1960s and 1970s. In the 1960s, the cognitive psychology model rejected the notion of emotions as irrational and viewed them as based on the perception and appraisal of anticipated pain or pleasure, harm or goodness. In the 1970s, the social constructionist model also rejected the notion of emotions as irrational. Emotions were seen to be constituted or molded in their expression within specific social contexts, based on rules that govern the expression of feelings and of behavior. In following with these views, Rosenwein maintains that emotions can be thought of neither as being freely expressed nor as being repressed, since they are not natural entities waiting to escape from within. In short, for Rosenwein, emotions are constituted through the social rules that govern their expression. She proceeds to provide examples of emotional regulation in the Middle Ages, while insisting upon the variability of the rules governing emotional expression based on the diversity of medieval emotional communities.

While I fully agree with Rosenwein that there is no such thing as unregulated emotional expression, if only because emotional regulation is operative from the moment that we begin to exercise subjectively embodied autonomy in the course of our interactions with the world, on the other hand I suggest that the extent to which we are called upon to manage our (relationally constituted) desires through moral self-transformation efforts varies from one social context to another. The distinction I draw between emotional regulation and emotion management, which I develop in greater detail in Chapter 5, allows us to account for these differences. This of course does not justify the view that in the Middle Ages subjects were emotionally unregulated.

Embodied in/capacity theory suggests that it is useful to think of subjectively and morally embodied interaction as productive of emotionally structured urges to act. Something like a painful constriction of fearful energy that is relationally produced may therefore be a useful metaphor in explaining the intensity of the emotional pain that characterizes the inability to structure the fear urge in ways that allow one to exercise one's agency effectively in the implementation of security. I have referred to this as the distress/relief modality of emotional experience. Moreover, dissatisfaction with current means of implementing security can be held to promote the channeling of fear energy in ways that correspond to dominant social expectations. I have referred to this as the anxiety/interest modality of emotional experience. It is with Rosenwein's notes of caution in mind that I very briefly explore the possibility that the process of modernization may promote the increase of moral self-transformation efforts, which I refer to as forms of moral self-control,[15] and therefore also an increase in emotional experiences governed by anxiety/interest and distress/ relief. To do so I propose to look at some of Elias's arguments more closely.

Elias argues that in the transition to modern society, the organization of drives shifts as a response to changing social structures and that as a result, internal dangers—dangers, for Elias, that involve a fear of the self's capacity to transgress moral rules—grow in proportion to the decline of external ones—dangers, for Elias, caused by the self's lack of moral self-fear—with a related increase in self-control. Elias also holds that the more that subjects fear the emotional self-punishment brought on by rule transgression, the more they control their violent and unpredictable impulses, the less they pose an external (physical) threat to others. As the self increasingly becomes an object of fear for itself, subjects no longer mainly fear and wish to avoid external or physical dangers, such as the danger of being robbed while walking down the road, but rather those that lie within the self. In short, Elias draws a correlation between an increase in internal danger, a decrease in external danger, and an increase in self-control.

I reformulate this proposition so that the question is whether greater individual responsibilization leads to the decreased exercise of physical assault and to the greater exercise of self-control. For this to be true, one would have to show, first, that the transition to modernity actually involves a greater amount of individual responsibilization; second, that this increased responsibilization necessarily entails a reduction in the exercise of physical assault; third, that the exercise of physical assault is never the outcome of moral self-transformation efforts; and fourth, that the exercise of physical assault is never the outcome of previous emotion management efforts whose outcomes have formed a habit. I hope to show that all premises need qualification and that while the first may be true, the latter three are false.

Before exploring whether greater individual responsibilization necessarily entails a reduction in the exercise of physical assault, I briefly ponder whether the passage to modernity should be thought of as engendering the increased emotion management of self. Do modern subjects engage in more frequent moral self-control efforts than their premodern ancestors? We already know that Elias responds to this question in the affirmative. He argues that individual conduct becomes increasingly subject to social and self-surveillance due to various social changes that include the state's greater monopoly over the legitimate means of violence and the lengthening chains of interdependence. In itself this constitutes insufficient evidence of mounting individual responsibilization for problems—after all, other factors may have promoted the need for moral self-control in premodern societies.

By contrast, it is not improbable that modern and advanced modern life promotes the experience of self-fear and the exercise of moral autonomy in a greater diversity of situations. A growing number of scholars either imply or explicitly note the increased frequency of the emotion management of self and other in modern and advanced modern social contexts.[16] The social forces that promote this emotion management include industrial capitalism's need for a self-disciplined force of workers, and consumer capitalism's need for a self-realizing force of buyers, but also liberal and advanced liberal societies' requirement that individuals govern themselves. The modern and postmodern societies that I characterize based on their respective support for either self-discipline or self-realization certainly involve the promotion of the emotion management of self and other. It remains the case, however, that while these factors explain the dynamics of moral fear in modern and advanced social contexts, they do not demonstrate that other forces did not produce equal or more frequent experiences of moral fear during the Middle Ages, or in other premodern societies. Only a much closer consideration of the dynamics of some of these societies could help us make a case in either direction.

But does increased responsibilization necessarily entail a reduction in the exercise of physical assault? I argue that it does not. Were we to accept that modern societies bring about an increase in experiences of moral fear, we can certainly conceive of modern societies in which morally impelled agents collectively engage in the practice of physical assault to implement moral security. While Elias draws what is probably a legitimate correlation between the rise of large states with a monopoly over the use of violence and the pacification of its citizens' everyday behavior in specific historical cases, one can think of examples that contradict this principle in important respects, such as the morally impelled perpetration of routinized violence against Jews, gypsies, homosexuals, and other "undesirables" by morally impelled perpetrators in Nazi Germany and elsewhere before and during the Second World War.[17]

This same objection leads me to reject the third and fourth premises on which Elias's revised hypothesis would have to rest—that physical assault is never a form of behavior that results from current moral efforts, or from previous moral efforts whose outcomes have formed a habit. While my knowledge of the Middle Ages is limited, it seems impossible to deny that the exercise of at least some, if not many, forms of physical assault was the result not only of moral self-control efforts but also of the morally normative social expectation that physically coercive means be engaged in to implement moral security in a number of situations, such that attacking and being attacked were both potentially morally meaningful actions and susceptible to becoming habitual, subjectively regulated means of responding to conflicts.

While the move from might-based to civility-based societies may have entailed a transformation in the moral meanings of physical assault, such that physical coercion increasingly became an inappropriate way of resolving conflict for the ordinary citizen, it does not follow that greater individual responsibilization for problems, or more frequent experiences of self-fear, bring about the decreased exercise of physical assault as a subjectively compelled or morally impelled means of exercising power.

Does the exercise of physical assault necessarily entail a lack of self-control? Do modern subjects exercise a greater amount of self-control when contrasted with its exercise in medieval warrior societies? I have argued that Elias's view of the reduced incidence of physical assault in everyday life as an expression of increased self-control should be rejected, since the exercise of physical assault can be morally impelled. The culturally produced association between the individual exercise of physical supremacy, various forms of sexual interaction, and moral danger grounds early modern societies in a number of ways. In this view, aggressive and sexual impulses form the basis of individuals' irrational desires, whose repression is required in the name of modern civilization and of the freedom from physical domination it seeks to achieve. It is in the context of this worldview that we should understand Elias's association of the practice of physical assault with the lack of moral self-control.

The best Elias can do is to acknowledge that the premodern societies he discusses were not entirely devoid of moral self-control, inasmuch as warrior subjects engaged in some forms of self-repression. He recognizes, more specifically, that warriors learned to endure severe physical pain with great resolve. However, if we take moral self-control to refer to the self's capacity to exercise power upon itself in the exercise of moral autonomy and make a distinction between the self-control achieved through *self-repression*, that achieved through *self-correction*, that achieved through *self-activation*, and that achieved through *self-formation*, it becomes apparent that the exercise of physical supremacy and of various forms of sexual interaction are in many contexts capacities that evolve from the exercise of complex forms of moral autonomy, and that they cannot be reduced to simplistic forms of spontaneity or impulse, or to amoral agency.

It is true that the exercise of physical aggression may be thought of as spontaneously arising as a habitual embodied response tied to certain forms of relational threat. But it is also true that it can be deliberately activated or formed as an embodied means of morally responding to various kinds of danger, much as it can result from the repression or the correction of the desire not to engage in battle. While the exercise of physical coercion cannot be said to be morally driven in all cases, in some if not many cases it can be shown to be the result of moral self-control.

Elias does not properly demonstrate that, in the earlier societies with which he compares the modern ones, individuals did not commonly relate to their selves through moral self-fear and self-desire. He assumes that this is the case because he reads the exercise of physical aggression and various forms of sexual promiscuity as the expression of an absence of self-control, which he ties to an absence of moral self-fear. He also equates self-control with immoral powerfulness (moral transgression) and therefore fails to account for the various ways in which self-control can also be associated with immoral powerlessness (moral ineptitude) through such means as self-activation and self-formation.

While the exercise of moral autonomy and the modalities through which objects of fear and desire were produced undoubtedly differed in warrior societies in being structured by, perhaps, something like the submission/domination,[18] dishonor/honor, and defeat/victory emotional-norm pairs, subjects can be taken to have had a moral sense of their immoral incapacities and capacities, on whose basis they were impelled to govern their conduct. It may be that the warrior economy of emotions dictated that failure to act through the exercise of aggression, for instance, based on a moral code of honor, made self-fear based on immoral powerlessness of greater prevalence than self-fear based on immoral powerfulness, thereby promoting the exercise of self-control through self-activation and self-formation rather than through self-repression and self-correction.

Self-repression and self-correction may or may not have been the dominant means through which subjects exercised moral autonomy in the premodern or warrior society emotion structure to which Elias compares the modern or civility-based one, but this latter society undoubtedly involved moral forms of agency on whose basis members were prompted to act in concert with morally normative social expectations. And this is to say nothing of the various other emotional styles of members belonging to the diverse communities of this period.

C H A P T E R   5

A NALYZING   S OCIAL   I NTERACTION

E MOTIONAL   R EGULATION , H EDONIC   P OWER , AND   E MOTION   M ANAGEMENT

I wish to begin by making five key points with respect to the role of social norms in the exercise of subjective and moral autonomy.

The first point is that social norms contribute to the perception of certain forces as dangerous, and of others as securing. For example, subjects may learn to perceive germs, mental illness, self-defeating thoughts, and unprotected sex as dangers, and they may learn to perceive aseptic environments, mental health, productive thoughts, and protected sex as securing. I have called these problems and their solutions objects of fear and desire, while I have called the signs that trigger their experience signs of danger and security.

Social norms promote the discrimination between bad and good forces through cultural means—through producing the meaning of these forces in representations—as well as through positive and negative emotional outcomes. Thus agents will be more likely to fear germs if these are associated with a force already determined to be bad like dirt or illness, or with a painful outcome like the feeling of dirtiness or of illness, and they will be more likely to desire aseptic environments if they are associated with a force already determined to be good like sanitation or health, or with a pleasurable outcome like the feeling of cleanliness or of health. Similarly, agents will be more likely to fear mental illness if it is associated with a bad force like violence or ugliness, or with a painful outcome like the feeling of shame or of stigma, and they will be more likely to desire mental health if it is associated with a good force like youth or freedom, or with a pleasurable outcome like the feeling of self-esteem or of belonging.

The second point is that social norms contribute to the determination of the means of power through which security is implemented, when these are acquired by subjects in the course of their social interactions with others, whether through mass mediatized means (e.g., in a chat group, on a sitcom, in a government pamphlet) or through more proximate contact with others (e.g., in a doctor's office, chatting with a neighbor, through notes from their child's teacher). Social norms may prompt subjects to move away from the painful consequences associated with germs, mental illness, self-defeating thoughts, and unprotected sex by washing their hands, taking an antidepressant medication, reading self-improvement literature, and using protection during intercourse, much as they may prompt subjects to move toward the pleasurable consequences associated with aseptic environments, mental health, productive thoughts, and protected sex through the same means.

So far we have established that through interacting with social norms, subjects may learn to associate some forces with already existing bad forces and painful outcomes, and others with already existing good forces and pleasurable outcomes, and to develop socially normative means of moving away from the painful outcomes associated with these objects of fear (problems) and of moving toward the pleasurable outcomes associated with these objects of desire (solved problems).

My third point is that social norms contribute to the determination of the experiential structure of threats and promises in the form of felt in/capacities. We have seen that relational threats are structured as problems and that relational promises are structured as solution orientations to these problems that themselves pose the problem of the determination of the means of power required in the implementation of security. While they are not the only forces involved in this process, social norms are fundamental to the production of the structured experience of relational threats and promises that I have called emotional norms.

To know how to respond to a threat in a manner that moves one away from pain, one must determine the form of one's in/capacity. For instance, social norms might suggest that the form of one's fear of germs is disgust (where disgust/purging is the felt in/capacity to avoid further contact with disruptive forces), or that the form of one's desire for sex is precaution (where risk/precaution is the felt in/capacity to prevent a harmful outcome based on a calculation of its probabilities, whatever the form taken by this estimation). And to know how to actualize a promise in a manner that moves one toward pleasure, one must determine the means of power through which to implement security. We have seen that social norms are influential in the determination of these means. For instance, social norms might suggest that cleaning is the means of power through which to implement security in the presence of disgusting germs, or that protecting oneself is the means of power through which to implement security in the presence of risky sex.

My fourth point is that the specific means through which power is exercised in the implementation of security may already be associated with a desire form, or become newly associated with it. For instance, if social norms have helped determine that the form of one's fear of germs is disgust, the desire form that is its pair, purging, may be associated through habit with the action of removing germs from one's environment. Social norms may also attach new or more specific means to this desire form, such as cleaning with a particular product, getting rid of household pets, and so on. Or if social norms have determined that the form of one's desire for sex is precaution, the desire form, whose pair is risk, may be associated with the habitual action of protecting oneself. Social norms may also attach new or more specific means to this desire form, such as monogamy or the use of a condom. Knowing how to implement security is therefore conditioned by the fear/desire form (i.e., the form of in/capacity) through which one perceives objects of fear and desire, to which a particular means of exercising power is or becomes associated.

My fifth and last point is that social norms often contribute to the production of the signs of danger and security that trigger emotional experience. For instance, in the contemporary North American context, a consistent lack of energy is a socially produced sign of danger that may trigger the experience of clinical depression/being oneself (the felt in/capacity to prevent one's empirically determined moral deviance through observable depressive symptoms), while the smell of one's favorite fast food is a sign of security that may trigger the experience of craving/indulgence (the felt in/capacity to prevent one's unhealthy hunger for a pleasurable stimulant).

In the second chapter, we discussed how, through the processes of affective, agential, and symbolic attunement, objects of fear and desire, emotional orientations, means of power, and signs of danger and security could interactively merge to produce individual and collective forms of emotional experience. Now we have seen that social norms act on the determination of objects of fear and desire, on the production of emotional orientations to these objects, on the means of moving from danger to security, and on the signs of danger and security that trigger emotional experience. The concepts of emotional regulation, hedonic power,[1] and emotion management are useful in the further clarification of these processes.

Emotions are aroused through the perceived in/capacity to move away from pain or toward pleasure. Inasmuch as they consist of the structured urge to find the means to move away from forces associated with pain and the structured urge to move toward those associated with pleasure, they have a regulatory effect on agency. By *emotional regulation*, I mean the power effect of emotional experience on agential means (on cognitive, emotional, biological, sensorial, moral, and behavioral processes). Emotional regulation designates the problem-based, will-driven urge to seek the avoidance of pain and the pursuit of pleasure that grounds the exercise of subjective autonomy.

Actions can be willfully (subjectively) or intentionally (morally) prompted through the threat of a painful emotional outcome, or the promise of a pleasurable one, whether the object of this threat or promise is already in existence or is newly created. *Hedonic power* designates the felt directive force that pushes subjectively or morally embodied beings away from pain and toward pleasure. Hedonic power is the directive force that subjectively and morally embodied beings experience that pushes them to overcome danger and implement security. Hedonic power lies at the heart of both emotional regulation and emotion management.

Emotion management refers to any intention-driven exercise of power over agential means (over cognitive, emotional, biological, sensorial, moral, or behavioral processes), whether others' or one's own, through the problem-structured mobilization of hedonic power. In other words, emotion management is the triggering of emotional experiences on whose basis subjects are compelled to act, with the intention of directing subjects' actions. As such, emotion management is the moral expression of emotional regulation. It can result in the moral control of other selves or in moral self-control.

In emotional regulation, the felt perceptions that trigger emotional experience and the agential course they promote are embodied normative effects. For instance, an individual may have embodied the knowledge that sharp objects cause pain (are dangerous) and require proper handling (security measures). The desire to implement the normatively appropriate solution to the problem of the anticipated pain of interacting with sharp objects, perhaps on the basis of the worry/safety emotional-norm pair, causes this individual to implement security through the safety solution orientation and through the specific means of prevention that is proper handling.

In this example, the agential process through which security is achieved is produced through emotional regulation, but security outcomes may be and are quite often the result of earlier emotion management efforts. For instance, it may be that a parent has instilled in their child the fear of sharp objects as well as the need to exercise moral self-control in the prevention of the hurt that might result from their inappropriate handling. Thus a parent might have taught a child to repress its desire to run around with a knife or to form its desire to properly handle knives. It might also be that a child learned through morally objectified personal injury to exercise moral self-control in the presence of knives. In any event, whether through the promotional efforts of another or of the self, emotion management was engaged in at some point. Inborn fears and desires, and the means of implementing security with which they are attached, if such inborn phenomena are held to exist,[2] may also have been acquired through earlier emotion management efforts.

This does not mean that all emotionally regulatory effects stem from earlier emotion management efforts. Indeed, subjectively embodied beings who are not able to exercise moral autonomy cannot be said to engage in emotion management efforts. The emotional regulation effects with which they interact did not grow out of the earlier exercise of moral self-control. Some emotional responses are therefore embodied through the exercise of subjective consciousness—through selves' subjective interactions with other forces—rather than through the exercise of moral self-consciousness, even though they may result from emotion management efforts on the part of others who are capable of moral action (i.e., of actions that result from the objectification of emotional experience).

For instance, a domesticated horse may learn to move from the feeling of hunger to that of satiety through access to his stall, which he comes to desire. While it is true that his owner may have deliberately ingrained this association in the horse in an emotion management effort, the horse can probably not be said to exercise a great deal of moral self-control in the emotional transformation of his own behavior, such that his actions should be thought of as predominantly resulting from a subjective rather than a moral exercise of autonomy, and are therefore an expression of emotional regulation rather than of emotion management.

In emotion management, emotional experiences and the agential course with which they are already associated, or with which they become deliberately associated, are purposefully triggered so as to become embodied normative effects. Whether they aim at the self or another, emotion management efforts are efforts at emotional socialization.

Emotion management efforts often involve two morally embodied parties and take on the form of a campaign. For instance, the collective embodiment of the moral knowledge that coughing into one's hands promotes the spread of harmful germs, and that this problem should be resolved through the application of the crook of one's arm to the opening of the mouth, is the result of a governmental campaign whose aim is to manage the population's health. It is likely that this campaign operated by way of something like the guilt/innocence emotional-norm pair, such that failing to apply the appropriate agential means to this particular problem should make selves feel guilty, while succeeding in doing so should make them feel innocent.

I have argued that three basic inborn affective forms structure the agential strategies through which the urge to move away from pain and toward desire is expressed. A force that is experienced through terror will trigger confrontation in the courage-bound implementation of security; a force that is experienced through phobia will trigger avoidance in the escape-bound implementation of security; and a force that is experienced through worry will trigger prevention in the safety-bound implementation of security.

I have also argued that all other emotions are blended and differentiated expressions of these basic emotional-norm pairs. For instance, frustration/satisfaction is structured by terror/courage and involves confrontation, alarm/reassurance is structured by phobia/escape and involves avoidance, and surprise/predictability is structured by worry/safety and involves prevention. Knowledge of the agential orientations to which particular emotional forms are tied can be used in the emotional management of subjects. For example, I might imply that a particular outcome is frustrating in order to trigger confrontational actions, that a particular group of people are alarming in order to trigger avoidant actions, or that a particular behavior is surprising in order to trigger prevention actions.

In the course of an emotion management effort, I may wish to create a new object of fear or desire, or transform the valence of an existing object of fear or desire.[3] Let us say that I am a parent who wishes to get my children to eat healthy foods. I might seek to create unhealthy foods as an object of fear by associating them with a painful outcome (e.g., by emphasizing that they promote cavities, by explaining that a role model would never eat them, and so forth), or I might also or alternatively seek to transform healthy foods into an object of desire by associating them with a pleasurable outcome (e.g., by presenting them through play, by cooking them in tasty ways, and so forth). Finally, through these same means I might seek to transform an existing felt perception of healthy foods from an object of fear into an object of desire, or an existing felt perception of unhealthy foods from an object of desire into an object of fear.

I will also need to propose specific means of dealing with objects of fear and desire. Should I favor a fear-based approach, I might prompt a child to repress the urge to eat unhealthy foods through impulsivity/self-restraint (in this case the child is required to engage in moral self-control in the presence of unhealthy foods), to experience unhealthy foods through disgust/purging (in this case the child is not required to engage in moral self-control but is taught to experience disgust toward unhealthy foods), or to protect themselves from unhealthy foods through risk/precaution. Should I favor a desire-based approach, I might prompt a child to eat healthy foods through dislike/like by making sure they are prepared in ways that appeal to the child, to experience healthy foods through alarm/reassurance by creating rituals around their consumption, or to experience the consumption of healthy foods as a form of belonging to a select club of healthy food eaters through rejection/belonging.

In these examples, where the child is successfully emotionally managed through emotional regulation effects, no further efforts will be required, since the objects of fear and desire and the emotional forms through which their effects are regulated are embodied. For instance, if the child is taught to avoid certain foods through the feeling of disgust, their emotional experience will simply compel them to avoid these foods. However, where the child is required to perform some moral action upon himself or herself in order to conform to the parent's expectations, the parent's emotional management efforts can only be said to be successful once the child develops the desire to emotionally manage himself or herself. For instance, the child who is prompted to repress the urge to eat unhealthy foods through impulsivity/self-restraint must develop the desire to engage in this effort. And should the child's desires become permanently transformed in such a way as to ensure that the desire to eat unhealthy foods no longer needs to be repressed, emotion management efforts would no longer be required in the production of conformity to social expectations.

Emotion management effects become transformed into emotional regulation effects when an embodied action, whether an emotional, a cognitive, a sensorial, a biological, or a behavioral process, no longer requires the exercise of moral self-control to become realized. How then does it come to pass that emotion management effects no longer require the exercise of moral self-control to become realized? It is not sufficient that the exercise of moral self-control become habitual, because I might habitually engage in the repression of my desire to eat too much such that it remains a moral self-control effort. For emotion management effects to become emotional regulation effects, the desire that forms the object of emotion management efforts must cease to exist and come to be replaced with a desire that produces the effects the emotion management intended. For example, if, after a time, my desire to eat unhealthy food is replaced by my desire to eat healthy food such that I no longer have to seek to transform myself in the achievement of this latter desire, emotion management gives way to emotional regulation.

Let me illustrate this through the distinct means of discipline-based and realization-based emotion management efforts, where a child's efforts are enlisted in the parent's emotion management effort. In wanting to act upon a child's hitting behavior, one could attempt to get the child to repress the desire that motivates the behavior by exclaiming: "Stop hitting, it is wrong to do so," thereby triggering a shame response and the desire to implement pride-driven security through the repression of the illegitimate desire to hit. Alternatively, one could attempt to get the child to correct the desire that underlies the behavior by exclaiming: "Your brother does not deserve to be hit, it is wrong to do so," thereby triggering a shame response and the desire to implement pride-driven security through the correction of the erroneous desire to hit. Should means of self-realization be favored rather than means of self-discipline, one could attempt to get the child to activate the desire that underlies an alternative behavior by exclaiming: "Big sisters should look over their little brothers, why don't you try teaching him how to share?," thereby triggering a personal insecurity response and the desire to implement self-esteem-driven security through the activation of the latent desire to protect. One could also attempt to get the child to form the desire that underlies an alternative behavior by exclaiming: "Let me give you some tips on how to negotiate with your brother," thereby triggering a personal insecurity response and the desire to implement self-esteem-driven security through the formation of the mature desire to negotiate. Over time, the displeasure of a conflict with one's brother might come to be remedied without further recourse to emotion management efforts if a new desire (other than that to hit) becomes associated with the resolution of conflicts over the sharing of objects.

However, it is likely that the security that is implemented through the self-repression of an illegitimate desire will continue to require a form of self-repression and therefore of moral self-control to be achieved, unless the repressed desire is replaced by a corrected, activated, or newly formed desire that more or less permanently takes its place. As such, repressed desires are less prone to be transformed into a form of emotional regulation than are corrected, activated, or newly formed desires, if their repression "works" for subjects, or if no alternative exists.

In emotional regulation, the objects of fear and desire are already tied to a form of emotional experience, with which an agential orientation (confrontation, avoidance, or prevention) or particular actions are also associated. For example, I encounter a snake, I experience phobia, I run away. In emotion management, the objects of fear and desire are intentionally[4] tied to a form of emotional experience, with which particular actions become associated. For example, I encounter a snake, I experience phobia, I run away, my parents tell me I am wrong to fear snakes because they are harmless, I experience self-dislike as a result of their disapproval, I decide to agree with them and take ownership over my fear/desire, I experience shame, I correct my desire to run away every time I see a snake and eventually develop the desire to stay and watch, or perhaps even play with the snake, and my future encounters with snakes constitute experiences of security rather than experiences of danger. Once I no longer need to manage my phobia and have moved into a new embodied perception of snakes, which might include the experience of courage since I confronted my fear/desire, my relationship to snakes is no longer one that involves an object of fear, but rather one that involves an object of desire. Moreover, my relationship to snakes is now one that I experience subjectively rather than morally, since I am no longer required to manage this emotional experience, and it therefore becomes an instance of emotional regulation.

For the sake of nuance, let me provide another example. I am a child, I encounter a baby, I experience love, I move to cover it with my body. Here my experience of love is triggered by an object of desire with which an action is already associated: the desire to cover the loved object with my body. In other words, my experience of love is governed by the process of emotional regulation. Should I come to experience dissatisfaction with any element of this process, my experience of it will shift from panic/excitement to anxiety/interest. Let us say that I encounter a baby, I experience love, I move to cover it with my body, my parents shout "No, don't lie over the baby, you'll harm him!," I experience self-dislike as a result of their disapproval, I decide to agree with them and take ownership over my fear/desire, I experience a guilty form of shame[5] for having almost hurt the baby, I repress my desire to cover the baby with my body, I experience anger as well as a guilty form of shame because I still unconsciously desire to cover the baby with my body. In my attempt to move from a guilty form of shame to an innocent form of pride through self-repression, I am getting stuck in self-repressive anger and am compelled to continue my emotion management efforts. I may feel anger and a guilty form of shame in the presence of babies. I may even come to blame babies for these feelings if the relational threat constituted by my parents' disapproval becomes symbolized by babies, such that they act as signs of danger that trigger these felt incapacities.[6]

Both examples show that moral self-transformation efforts result from subjects' interactions with forces that produce relational threat because existing means of implementing security are felt to be wanting. The second example also shows that self-repression may lead to recurring, potentially self-destructive feelings of incapacity, since one is required to repress illegitimate desire each time this desire is triggered. On the other hand, it should be emphasized that the self-transformative effects of the other three means of moral self-control do not necessarily produce effects that are caring of selves and others. For instance, one might form one's desire to achieve moral and social security through contempt for one's self or others. Treating oneself or others as being of little or lesser worth than oneself is hardly caring.[7]

In an alternative scenario, my parents, recognizing my love and enthusiasm for the baby, show me how to touch and handle the baby with care, I experience self-dislike as a result of their implied disapproval, I decide to agree with them and take ownership over my fear/desire, I experience personal insecurity as well as ignorance for not having known how to touch and handle the baby with care, I form my desire to touch and handle the baby with care, I experience knowledge and competence in the presence of babies. Since I am no longer required to manage this emotional experience, it becomes an instance of emotional regulation.

Self-repression, self-correction, self-activation, and self-formation refer to the moral self's action upon a desire that is experienced as illegitimate, erroneous, latent, or immature. These self-transformation efforts are forms of emotion management, since they produce a particular, normatively structured, morally driven emotional experience. But do all emotion management efforts require or produce the exercise of moral self-control? What is the relationship between the emotion management of the self, the emotion management of the other, and the exercise of moral self-control?

The emotion management of self or other involves a deliberate effort on the part of a subject to mobilize the hedonic power of emotional norms. Whether the work of emotion management requires the exercise of moral self-control on the part of the self depends on whether the self is required to exercise power over itself in the achievement of the structured hedonic effects it seeks to achieve.

If the object of the emotion management effort is the self, the exercise of moral self-control is necessarily involved, since the production of an emotional experience other than that which is currently being experienced will require the self's repression, correction, activation, or formation of its desire. Here moral self-control is a condition of emotion management, whether I want to repress my desire to go to sleep in the afternoon, correct my desire to fall asleep in front of the television, activate my desire to sleep at ten o'clock, or form my desire to sleep eight hours every night.

If the object of the emotion management effort is another self, the exercise of moral self-control over the self is only required if the self's emotional transformation is a condition of the emotion management of another self. For instance, if I have to repress my desire to move from anger to assertiveness through shouting in order to make another person feel respected, then in this case as well moral self-control is a condition of emotion management.

On the other hand, there are circumstances in which I need not exercise moral self-control as a precursor to the emotion management of another self. For instance, I might be able to make another person feel respected if my desire to act in a way that will have this effect is already in place. Thus I may not have to repress, correct, activate, or form my desire in order to manage another's emotions.

Finally, the other self that the self seeks to emotionally manage may or may not have to engage in moral self-control efforts in response to the emotion management effort deployed upon it. In other words, the other self may or may not have to repress, correct, activate, or form their own desire in response to the emotional experience produced by the self engaged in emotion management efforts. This will depend on whether the danger that is produced is experienced as moral or not. For instance, if I induce another self to feel guilty for failing to recycle, their ability to implement security is likely to involve moral self-control efforts, since they will be required to transform their existing desire in such a manner as to have it give way to the action of recycling. But if I induce another self to feel saddened by showing them a film about loss and they are able to spontaneously move into happiness once the film ends at the thought of not having to prevent such loss, their ability to implement security does not involve moral self-control efforts. Whether the emotion management effort induces the exercise of moral self-control on the part of the other self on whom emotion management efforts are being deployed will depend on whether this self becomes impelled to exercise moral power over itself in response to the structured hedonic effects that have been exercised over it. In other words, an emotion management effort can simply have emotional regulation effects and need not compel the exercise of moral self-control.

Because emotion management is based on the appropriation of the hedonic forces involved in emotional regulation, like emotional regulation, it is deeply anchored in human corporeality. Agents are not necessarily conscious of engaging in emotion management through moral self-control efforts, and they are even less likely to be conscious of their having acquired the propensity to feel and otherwise act in particular ways through their own moral efforts, once their fears and desires become the effect of emotional regulation. Emotional regulation and emotion management speak to the processes through which social norms help constitute the practices of subjective and moral autonomy, but they also speak to the processes through which they help constitute the norms with which they interact. As such, emotional regulation, hedonic power, and emotion management engender an understanding of social norms as the interactive produce of embodiment.

Emotional regulation and emotion management, as the outcome and means of emotional socialization, are key means through which subjects are compelled and impelled to conform to social expectations. In considering the relationship between social and emotional life, many analysts hold the perspective that positively valenced emotions promote socially expected behavior, whereas negatively valenced emotions tend to favor the avoidance of behaviors that violate normative expectations. For instance, in their feedback theory of emotions, Baumeister et al. (2007) maintain that the negative and positive valence of emotions impacts behavior in alignment with social norms. Barbalet (2002b) argues that emotional pleasure is more likely when we engage in forms of behavior that conform to social norms, while emotional pain is more likely to be the fruit of behaviors that fail to do so. Prinz (2004) maintains that emotions act to positively reinforce behaviors through reward or nonpunishment and to negatively reinforce them through punishment or nonreward.

In considering the self's conception of what it ought to be in its relation to others' confirmation or disconfirmation of the image they have of themselves (i.e., of the kind of force they are)—in other words, in considering what I discuss later on as the moral experiences of pride/shame and personal insecurity/self-esteem—Stets and

Turner (2007b) argue that subjects experience positive emotions in the course of identity verification if their identities are confirmed, and negative emotions if their identities are challenged. Should their identity be threatened, subjects are prompted to modify their behavior or to pay selective attention to the feedback of others. Stets and Turner also argue that an individual's moral identity (their transsituational self-conception) acts as a master identity that governs their selection of other, more situational identities, such as those operating in smaller groups or through the taking on of roles. The moral identity is the self's conception of what it ought to be as a moral agent, which ranges from the most abstract sense of being a good person (i.e., of being a person who acts desirably in general) to the most specific sense of being a good person (i.e., of being a person who acts desirably in specific situations). Defensive processes are further accounted for by Turner (2007) elsewhere.

Whether an emotional experience is pleasurable or painful is thus at the heart of the matter of its relationship to behavior, if we work with the assumption that individuals are generally inclined to avoid pain and to seek pleasure, which I do.[8] In short, through positive and negative valence, emotions are an important form of agency that impact behavior and other forms of agency.

In line with these views, Claire Armon-Jones (1988b) maintains that interactions that produce painful emotions are more likely to be avoided, whereas interactions that produce pleasurable emotions are more likely to be sought. As a consequence, social order can be achieved by teaching subjects to experience painful emotions in response to interactions that ought to be avoided, and by teaching subjects to experience pleasurable emotions in response to interactions that ought to be sought. For example, if one learns to feel happy after having taken pictures of loved ones, one is more likely to repeat this behavior, and if one learns to feel alarm when one fails to brush one's teeth, one is less likely to repeat this behavior. In this perspective, social conformity is accomplished through the rewarding of certain actions and the punishing of others.

This latter point requires further clarification, however. A negative emotional experience that is produced through social interaction—deliberately or not—can induce social conformity in general, or conformity with more locally produced social expectations, through its being already associated or through its becoming associated with a particular action that is itself socially desired. For example, I may seek to trigger the feeling of alarm in a potential consumer because I desire them to achieve reassurance through the purchasing of an extended warranty. Or the sadness that is experienced when one loses a friend whom one treated with spite might cause one to choose to treat other friends with kindness. Moreover, some painful experiences are sought as means of implementing pleasurable security. For instance, intentionally attending school implies that one deliberately seeks the painful experience of ignorance as a condition of the pleasurable experience of knowledge.

Social conformity is achieved through subjects' existing or more recently acquired emotionally governed actions in response to particular interactions, sometimes painful and sometimes pleasurable, and in both cases through subjects' desire and attempt to fit in—to belong—whether through subjective means or through moral ones. By actions of social conformity, I mean the self's attempts to conform to another's expectation of how they ought to act or be. Actions of social conformity can be local (e.g., a subject might attempt to conform to another subject's expectation that they speak to them quietly), much as they can be global (e.g., a subject might attempt to conform to a social group's expectation that they eat healthy foods). It is to a further consideration of some of the emotional dimensions of actions of social conformity that I now turn.

SOCIAL DIS/APPROVAL: SHAME/PRIDE AND PERSONAL INSECURITY/ SELF-ESTEEM AS MORAL EXPERIENCES OF SOCIAL DANGER AND SOCIAL SECURITY

I call the feelings of responsibility for social approval that trigger repressive or discipline-based self-control efforts shame/pride, whereas I call the feelings of responsibility for social approval that trigger expressive or realization-based self-control efforts personal insecurity/self-esteem.[9] Shame/pride is an expression of the self-fear I also refer to as immoral capacity (or immoral powerfulness), which is the danger the individual represents for their self as a powerful force of transgression. Personal insecurity/self-esteem is an expression of the self-fear I also refer to as immoral incapacity (or immoral powerlessness), which is the danger the individual represents for their self as a powerless force of ineptitude. In order to shed light on the central role played by these emotions in agents' desire to conform to local and global social expectations, I consider the work of Mary Douglas (1966) on secular defilement, of Claire Armon-Jones (1988a, 1988b) on the sociocultural dimensions of emotions, and of William I. Miller (1997), Jack Barbalet (2001), and Elspeth Probyn (2005) on shame.

Douglas (1966) argues that "danger rituals" produce the solidarity, social order, and cultural innovation that ensure a group's survival. These rituals can involve the exclusion or the expulsion of threatening behaviors, people, places, or objects, such as those that are ambiguous or in excess of that which is known or normal, but also their inclusion through innovation or the creation of new ways of seeing. For instance, the Nuer view babies born with anomalies as baby hippopotamuses and return them to their proper place in the river, while some West African tribes wring the necks of cocks that crow at night so that they do not contradict their understanding of cocks as birds who crow at dawn (40). Douglas argues that there are countless instances of such practices in all cultures, from contemporary Western hygienic practices to Haviks' treatment of cooked and uncooked foods.

Douglas understands danger rituals in terms of their ordering function. Forces are impure, or disgusting, because they are categorically abnormal—because they do not conform to a culturally established order of things.[10] Danger rituals have the social function of reestablishing this order. Dirt, she writes, is "matter out of place": "Shoes are not dirty in themselves, but it is dirty to place them on the dining-table; food is not dirty in itself, but it is dirty to leave cooking utensils in the bedroom, or food bespattered on clothing… In short, our pollution behavior is the reaction which condemns any object or idea likely to confuse or contradict cherished classifications" (Douglas 1966, 36–37)

To build on Douglas's insights, I suggest that dislike/like, disgust/purging, and hate/love are the felt forms of in/capacity that pertain to socially disruptive forces. I have argued that there are three basic strategic orientations to danger and security: present-directed confrontation, past-directed avoidance, and future-directed prevention. Dislike/like corresponds to confrontation, disgust/purging to avoidance, and hate/love to prevention.

The desire form to which dislike is related, like, suggests means of power in the implementation of security having to do with the *inclusion* of forces that cause disruption in the present (e.g., I dislike it, you, or your actions. I require it, you, or your actions to change. I like it, you, or your actions). The desire form to which disgust is related, purging, suggests means of power in the implementation of security having to do with the *expulsion* of forces that have caused disruption in the past (e.g., I am disgusted by it, you, or your actions. I require it, you, or your actions to exit. I feel purged of it, you, or your actions). Finally, the desire form to which hate is related, love, suggests means of power in the implementation of security having to do with the *exclusion* of forces that are anticipated to cause disruption in the future (e.g., I hate it, you, or your actions. I do not allow it, you, or your actions near me. I love the absence of it, you, or your actions).

These same observations apply to these emotional forms when they are directed toward the self, with the experience of self-dislike/self-like leading to means of power that involve *self-inclusion*, the experience of self-disgust/self-purging leading to means of power that involve *self-expulsion*, and the experience of self-hate/self-love leading to means of power that involve *self-exclusion*.

Miller (1997, 4) points out that Douglas's theory does not properly account for the fact that disgust relates not only to matter that is out of place but to matter that is out of place in relation to a personal shortcoming. He argues that if soup on a man's beard elicits disgust, it is not only because the soup belongs in the man's mouth and not on this beard but because the man should have been able to place the soup in his mouth. As such, Miller (1997, 34) emphasizes the connection between self-disgust and shame, which he understands as a feeling of inadequacy. Barbalet (2001, 103–125) identifies shame as an emotion that is central to social conformity, since it involves a subject's feeling of being judged by another.

Building on these further insights, I tie shame to experiences of moral transgression, and personal insecurity to experiences of moral inadequacy. Shame and personal insecurity can take the form of self-dislike, self-disgust, or self-hate. Shame-based moral self-transformation efforts in the form of self-dislike, self-disgust, or self-hate will consist of self-disciplinary means of obedience involving self-inclusion, self-expulsion, or self-exclusion, while personal insecurity-based moral self-transformation efforts in the form of self-dislike, self-disgust, or self-hate will consist of self-realization means of competence involving self-inclusion, self-expulsion, or self-exclusion.

In short, it is not only a self's incompetence that elicits feelings of social disapproval such as dislike, disgust, and hate but also a self's disobedience. If disobedient and incompetent selves are grounds for others' dislike, disgust, and hate, we must therefore include the self and the objects it contaminates among the forces that are potentially dislikable, disgusting, or hateful. It is because the self is disruptive, through its disobedience or incompetence, that it elicits dislike, disgust, or hate. And it is because they become associated with this categorical abnormality—the category of disobedient or incompetent things that fail to conform to a command or to a standard—that certain forces (ideas, people, places, smells, foodstuffs, forms of entertainment, behaviors, and so on) elicit dislike, disgust, or hate.

Disruptive selves are forces that violate social commands. They are also forces that fall short of social standards. I have called shame the emotion that names the experience of oneself as disruptive when it results from a violation of social commands for which one experiences responsibility, and personal insecurity the emotion that names the experience of oneself as disruptive when it results from a falling short of social standards for which one experiences responsibility. Thus when we feel ashamed, we feel that we do not belong to a particular order of things whose principles we have intentionally[11] violated: We feel unruly because our self, for whom we are responsible, is unruly. And when we feel personally insecure, we feel that we do not belong to a particular order of things whose standards we intentionally do not meet: we feel inadequate because our self, for whom we are responsible, is inadequate.[12] Similarly, when we seek to shame someone or to make them feel insecure, we seek to make them responsible for their lack of social conformity.

While there may be different implications to differentiated forms of shaming or of rendering insecure—for instance, contempt[13] can be thought of as a differentiated form of shaming or of rendering personally insecure that implies the degradation of the other's worth as a means of elevating oneself—whether we treat others or ourselves with dislike, disgust, or hate, the effect is a call to order that feeds off the desire to belong. As Probyn (2005) observes, shame is an experience of being out of place related to the other's gaze, and it is born of our desire for connection.

In Chapter 3 we saw that the experience of alexithymia/empathy conditions the self's ability to be affected by the emotional orientations of others through the capacity to understand them, and that the experience of indifference/sympathy conditions the moral self's ability to care about what others feel. The self's felt perception of whether the other views it as disruptive is of prime importance to actions of social conformity. Experiences of self-dislike, self-disgust, or self-hate, and their moral experience in experiences of shame/pride and personal insecurity/self-esteem, involve caring about how others view us because this affects the quality of our place in the world, and therefore our ability to exercise power in the implementation of security. Most basically, these experiences affect our capacity to survive.

When others treat an individual like a disruptive force, they may seek to include it, expulse it, or exclude it. We have seen that the purpose of the danger ritual is to reinstate an order that has been disturbed. But what is the effect of these rituals on the selves who are treated as disruptive? A number of emotional-norm pairs tell us about what it feels like to be treated as disruptive and have in common the importance of fitting in, of belonging, of appealing to others. These include separation worry/attachment, sadness/happiness, ugliness/beautifulness, exclusion/inclusion, stigmatization/attractiveness, embarrassment/politeness, humiliation/dignity, anger/assertiveness, and guilt/innocence. Some of these emotional-norm pairs, such as ugliness/beautifulness and exclusion/inclusion, have to do with the fact that one experiences marginalization, such that one's desire to belong is denied. Others tell us about how the self's vitality and integrity are threatened by marginalization, such as separation worry/attachment, sadness/happiness, and anger/assertiveness. Yet others tell us about the strategies people use to get us to conform to their expectations, such as anger/assertiveness, which may produce guilt/innocence, and inferiority/contempt, which may produce humiliation/dignity, or reproduce inferiority/contempt.

The effects on selves of the rituals that treat selves as disruptive will also depend on whether the experience is a subjective or a moral one. If the danger remains external, the self will simply respond to it through embodied means that are already at its disposal. For instance, a person who is ignored by others might simply seek to gain their attention if they have a need for it. In other words, the subject will respond to the effects of the force in question through the experience of emotional regulation—through the experience of a panic/excitement-driven form of self-dis/approval, with which an embodied action through which to implement security is likely associated.

If on the other hand the self develops a moral relationship to danger, it will seek to engage in moral self-control efforts. A person who is ignored by others and who feels the need to be noticed might seek to repress, correct, activate, or form the illegitimate, erroneous, latent, or immature desire they perceive as responsible for their disruptive self. In other words, the agent will respond to this object of fear through emotion management—and in this particular case through the experience of anxiety/interest-driven or distress/relief-driven shame/pride or personal insecurity/self-esteem.

In Chapter 3 I argued that the subjective experience of moral emotions should be distinguished from their moral experience.[14] How can we explain agents' subjective desire to conform to social expectations, as well as their moral desire to transform aspects of their selves that do not allow them to conform? We have seen that self-dislike/self-like, self-disgust/self-purging, and self-hate/self-love are experiences of social dis/approval that are directed toward the self by the self. As social emotional-norm pairs, they are conditioned by subjects' ability to experience two even more basic social emotional-norm pairs: alexithymia/empathy (the felt in/ability to confront one's lack of understanding of what others feel) and indifference/sympathy (the felt in/ability to confront one's lack of care for what others feel). Self-dislike/self-like, self-disgust/self-purging, and self-hate/self-love orient subjects' actions through the desire to belong. They are triggered by others' evaluations of the disruptive nature of the self or of its actions.

For instance, telling a child that it is wrong to waste food or that the child should strive to share toys is likely to trigger the subjective experience of one of these forms of self-disapproval. Here the subjective self may seek to implement security by conforming to a request in the spontaneous or habitual attempt to please and be pleasing, should it be able to do so, but will need constant reminding of this request, since the danger remains external and is not the self's responsibility. When, on the other hand, this emotional-norm pair is experienced morally—when a subject develops a feeling of responsibility for the transgressive or inadequate nature of his or her actions as determined by another's social expectation—it will likely give rise to moral self-control efforts. Here the moral self will seek to implement security by conforming to a request, should it be able to do so, and will no longer need constant reminding of this request by another, whether through vertical authority relations (e.g., by a parent, by an employer) or through horizontal peer relations (e.g., by an advertisement, by a chat group member), since the danger is now internal and has become the self's responsibility.[15] The righteous child might come to repress the desire to take too much food in order to avoid wasting any, while the responsible child might come to activate her desire to share her toys by thinking of how happy it will make her parent. In short, the difference between the subjective experience and the moral experience of the emotional forms of self-disapproval is the difference between feeling compelled (from without) and feeling impelled (from within).

We have seen that self-dislike/self-like, self-disgust/self-purging, and self-hate/self-love move into shame/pride or personal insecurity/self-esteem if the self comes to feel responsible for the implementation of social security (i.e., if the self becomes responsible, as the dangerous cause of danger to itself, for being disruptive, for not fitting in, and feels impelled to engage in moral self-transformation efforts). If the self develops a relationship to itself as a dangerous force that must be repressed or corrected, the emotional-norm pair that designates its experience is shame/pride, and if the self develops a relationship to itself as a dangerous force that must be activated or formed, the emotional-norm pair that designates its experience is insecurity/self-esteem. It is to a more detailed consideration of these anxiety/interest and distress/relief-driven moral actions of social conformity that I now turn.

MORAL ACTIONS OF SOCIAL CONFORMITY

Danger rituals—the inclusion, the exclusion, and the expulsion of socially disruptive forces—are conditioned by and promote social order. When they target morally embodied beings, danger rituals are demands for social conformity that achieve their emotion management effects by prompting moral agents' moral self-control efforts. I call *moral actions of social conformity* the morally embodied actions through which agents seek to resolve the shame/pride or the personal insecurity/self-esteem that these rituals produce.

Moral actions of social conformity always require a moral effort (i.e., the repression, correction, activation, or formation of desire), as when one represses the desire to shout at one's children as a means of moving from the shame associated with being a bad parent to the pride of being a good one. Moral actions of social conformity are morally embodied means of overcoming social danger and of implementing social security—of moving from the feeling of unruliness or of inadequacy to the feeling of ruliness or of adequacy. They are the strivings for goodness of subjects who feel responsible for dealing with the objectified painful effects of social demands for conformity. Moral actions of social conformity may eventually become subjective actions of social conformity—that is, actions that ensure that one experiences social approval but that do not require self-transformation efforts.

Moral actions of social conformity might involve behavioral (e.g., saving money as a means of moving from the personal insecurity associated with being unable to own a home to the self-esteem associated with being able to do so), cognitive (e.g., thinking about how to improve one's appearance as a means of moving from the personal insecurity associated with being ugly to the self-esteem produced by being beautiful), and sensory processes (e.g., wine tasting as a means of moving from the personal insecurity associated with being unable to appreciate wine to the self-esteem of having acquired the taste of doing so). They might also involve the emotional processes I have called emotional blending and emotional differentiation.

The emotional-norm pairs that subjects tend to turn to, and the differentiated forms that emerge in a given social group and its stratifications, can tell us a great deal about its economy of fear and desire.

For instance, the contemporary emotional-norm pair of emotional stress/resilience may be a means of moving from the personal insecurity associated with suboptimal productivity at work to the self-esteem associated with optimal productivity, in a social order in which work environments are characterized by unpredictability, novelty, rivalry, and oppression.[16] Emotional stress/resilience (the felt in/ability to confront the demands of everyday life in ways that promote health) may itself be thought of as a blend of surprise/predictability (the felt in/ability to prevent unexpected occurrences), unfamiliarity/ familiarity (the felt in/ability to confront forces with which one is unacquainted), rivalry/advantage (the felt in/ability to confront one's failure to measure up to standards in the context of a competition), and oppression/emancipation (the felt in/ability to confront forces that illegitimately constrain one's freedom). In what follows I will focus my interest on the processes of emotional blending and emotional differentiation involved in moral actions of social conformity.

Claire Armon-Jones (1988a, 1988b) argues that emotions are triggered by interactions for which an appropriate emotional response has been acquired. She explains that the social constructionist perspective[17] on emotions is based on the notion that the ability to experience specific emotions is conditioned by one's cognitive knowledge of the beliefs, values, and other norms of one's culture. Emotions are socially prescribed responses to various situations that serve to reproduce a given social order through agents' responsibility for acting appropriately. Aspects of this understanding of emotions[18] correspond to what I suggest is the moral experience of emotions—an emotional experience that involves intentionality and self-transformation, and that is consistent with the anxiety/interest-driven and the distress/relief-driven modalities of fear and desire.

I have suggested that the subjective experience of emotions, which corresponds to the panic/excitement-driven modality of fear and desire, is one in which emotions, the objects of fear and desire tied to signs of danger and security that trigger them, and the means of power with which they are associated, are already embodied. I call this process emotional regulation. I have also suggested that the moral experience of emotions, which corresponds to the anxiety/interest-driven and the distress/relief-driven modalities of fear and desire, is one in which emotions, the objects of fear and desire tied to signs of danger and security that trigger them, and the means of power with which they are associated, become embodied. I call this process emotion management. Emotion management efforts have the effect of transforming a basic emotional landscape through processes that include emotional blending and differentiation. Group specificity is expressed and maintained through morally produced emotional blends and differentiations, among other means of emotion management.

The examination of a social group's emotional orientations, of the objects of fear and desire to which these correspond, of the signs of danger and security that trigger these, and of the particular actions through which security is implemented, should allow us to gain insight into the specificity of a social group's emotional means of prompting social conformity, and of the larger social conditions within which this prompting takes place. For example, one might come to feel at risk (emotional orientation) for a particular disease (object of fear), where this experience is triggered by the idea of certain social groups (sign of danger) that one excludes from one's life (means of power) in order to implement security. Or one might come to feel satisfied (emotional orientation) by one's ability to arrive on time at work (object of desire), where this experience is triggered by the sound of one's alarm clock (sign of security) one carefully sets before falling asleep (means of power) in order to implement security.

William I. Miller (1997) and Elspeth Probyn (2005) highlight the relationship between disgust or shame and positive emotions such as love, interest, and dignity. Embodied in/capacity theory seeks to formally and meaningfully explain this relationship as one in which painful emotional experiences structure pleasurable ones. Thus painful emotions are felt incapacities that serve to orient emotional action toward the development of capacity, and pleasurable emotions are the felt capacities that serve to orient emotional and other forms of action as embodied means of power in the actualization of capacity. In this sense, disgust is a way of helping agents find means of avoiding further contact with disruptive, categorically abnormal forces by structuring the desire to purge, while self-disgust is a way of avoiding the self's disruptive nature or actions by structuring the desire to self-purge.

As the feelings that cause us to painfully notice when we do not fit in, self-dislike, self-disgust, self-hate, and their moral experience in shame and personal insecurity, structure our desire to do so. They lead us into the experience of the desire to belong and prompt the determination and actualization of the means of doing so. As such, the various emotional-norm pairs that have the feeling of being disruptive at their core can all be said to be structured by this basic danger. Examples include embarrassment/politeness, exclusion/inclusion, being ignored/being noticed, isolation/connection, humiliation/dignity, rejection/belonging, difference/integration, ugliness/beautifulness, and stigmatization/attractiveness.

It should be recalled that emotional differentiation is a process in which a new emotional perspective on a problem is produced in the face of its nonresolvability, such that a new agential content emerges. I have argued that emotional differentiation is driven by the distress/relief modality of fear and desire. The emergence of new emotional orientations to the problem of belonging tells us something about how individuals in this group are prompted to conform. For example, abnormality/normality—the felt lack of ability to prevent one's empirically determined moral deviance—is an emotional-norm pair that is peculiar to social groups that have undergone a scientizing process. The experience of this emotional-norm pair constitutes a form of embodied knowledge that channels agents' actions (biological, sensory, cognitive, emotional, and moral) in particular directions.

An emotional-norm pair that is a differentiated form of abnormality/normality in contemporary Western social groups is clinical depression/being oneself,[19] where subjects' inability to conform to social expectations is experienced through empirically observable depressive symptoms (depressed mood, anhedonia, lack of energy) that determine the nature of one's problem as one that involves disruptive moral agency, and to which specific actions are associated (e.g., psychopharmaceuticals, regular exercise and sleep, healthy diet, self-help, and psychotherapy) as means of regaining the feelings of normalcy and of being oneself.[20]

The political implications of processes of emotional differentiation ought to be considered. For instance, in *The Antidepressant Era*, David Healy (1997) examines the powerful role of the psychopharmaceutical industry in producing and disseminating knowledge about disease categories and their chemical basis. In *Creating Mental Illness* and in *The Loss of Sadness*, Allan V. Horwitz (2002) and Horwitz and Jerome Wakefield (2007) maintain that the overestimation of actual cases of depression[21] is of value to numerous social actors, including the psychiatrists who enjoy a more important clientele, the advocacy groups that see the banalizing of depression as a factor that reduces stigma, the pharmaceutical companies that profit from increased sales, and the patients whose emotional distress acquires legitimacy through medical diagnosis. Finally, in *Making Us Crazy* (1997), Stuart A. Kirk and Herb Kutchins (1997) argue that the *Diagnostic and Statistical Manual of Mental Disorders* is an authoritative document with highly political effects. Among these are the validation of mental health professionals' expertise, a foundation for governmental and private support, a framework for thinking about social troubles that pathologizes everyday behavior and has profound consequences on institutions such as the judicial system, prisons, and schools, and above all a means to legitimate and maintain the current political order at the expense of those who are least able to exercise power.

Two less recent[22] differentiated emotional-norms pairs that are structured by the self's disapproval of itself or of another are worth mentioning here: guilt/innocence and anger/assertiveness. The first designates the self's unruliness or inadequacy in its hurting of others, while the second designates the other's unruliness or inadequacy in being the cause of one's hurt. Guilt/innocence and anger/assertiveness may therefore be thought of as two sides of a same coin involving a self who is problematic for being on the giving or the receiving end of a selfhood that offends social order by causing another hurt.

The feeling that one is unruly or inadequate when one hurts another is at the heart of the emotional orientation I call guilt/innocence. Similarly, the feeling that the other is unruly or inadequate when they hurt one's self is at the heart of the emotional orientation I call anger/assertiveness. Because they involve the quality of relations between selves, and are means through which embodied selves can orient their actions in order to influence their own and others' agency in the determination of this quality, these emotional-norm pairs ought to be thought of as key social emotions in social contexts in which individuals are encouraged to have a distinct sense of self-bound, freely governed agency. They may also be thought of as forming the basis of the morally driven political emotions, which more properly designate the quality of relations between selves that results from differences in the social distribution of the capacity to exercise power.

One is positioned to respond with guilt/innocence when faced with another's anger/assertiveness if that anger is directed toward oneself, since the assertion of anger involves a charge of wrongdoing, much as one is positioned to resist this charge through anger/assertiveness should one feel wrongly charged of wrongdoing or hurt in some other way. One might therefore use anger/assertiveness as a means of triggering an experience of guilt/innocence or of anger/assertiveness in another. Moreover, the means through which an agent expresses their anger—the means through which they assert themselves—can also trigger an experience of anger/assertiveness in another, since the means through which anger is expressed can be the object of social norms that condemn them. This is an important dimension of contemporary anger management.[23] In short, guilt/innocence and anger/assertiveness are powerful means of social conformity, whether they are experienced subjectively or morally.

When guilt/innocence is experienced subjectively, it promotes actions that are already associated with the implementation of security. For instance, one might spontaneously or habitually recoil on realizing that one has hurt another. When, on the other hand, guilt/innocence is experienced morally, it promotes moral self-transformation efforts that require that one act upon one's existing desire to act in particular ways. For instance, one might seek to correct the desire to recoil on realizing that one has hurt another and seek to repair the hurt caused instead. Similarly, when anger/assertiveness is experienced subjectively, it promotes actions that are already associated with the implementation of security. For instance, one might spontaneously or habitually seek to strike another who has caused one hurt. When, on the other hand, anger/assertiveness is experienced morally, it promotes moral self-transformation efforts that require that one act upon one's existing desire to act in particular ways. For instance, a subject might seek to activate the desire to obtain reparation from another who has caused them hurt instead of asserting their self through physically or verbally hostile means.

In the Western context, guilt/innocence and anger/assertiveness are emotional orientations that are frequently triggered in social interactions and that serve to produce conformity with social expectations. But these emotional experiences are by no means the only differentiated emotional-norm pairs through which agents are able to achieve social conformity. All the emotions that contain the feeling of being disruptive or disapproved of by oneself or by others may be said to promote conformity, even though in some cases, as we shall soon see, this conformity is achieved through agents' promotion of social changes that will allow them to conform. Thus on the one hand, one may be said to achieve social conformity through conventional means by moving from the felt incapacity that is embarrassment to the felt capacity that is politeness based on the practice of personal hygiene, by moving from the feeling of notoriety to that of prestige by becoming a well-regarded professional, by moving from the feeling of abnormality to that of normality based on the advice of self-improvement manuals, or by moving from the feeling of ugliness to that of beautifulness by undergoing cosmetic surgery. But on the other hand, one might also seek to achieve social conformity by transforming the order to which one fails to conform.

The social changes brought about through political struggle ought necessarily to be explored in making manifest the political implications of processes of emotional differentiation and blending, since forms of in/capacity structure social movements and political protest. Embodied in/capacity theory helps shed light on the ways in which felt forms of incapacity such as shame, personal insecurity, outrage, rage, resentment, and oppression structure the political forms of agency through which pride, self-esteem, vindication, revenge, fairness, and emancipation are sought. Moreover, inasmuch as the emotion management of self is often thought to be the result of a pressure that is placed over individuals to adapt, or in other words to conform to a more powerful force's logic in order to survive, exploring instances in which emotional self-control is engaged in as a means of effecting social change underscores agents' ability to exercise power in more subversive ways, and more specifically in ways that subvert the socially rewarding actions, or the actions of social conformity, which produce heteronomy.

In their discussion of emotions in politics and protest,[24] Goodwin and Jasper (2007) highlight the importance, for activists, of the emotions they bring to a social movement. They argue that emotions like shame, resignation, and depression hinder effective political action, whereas emotions like anger, outrage, and pride promote it. As I illustrate in the example I discuss below, I suggest that felt forms of incapacity like shame, anger, and outrage orient effective political action by promoting pride-based, or more specifically assertiveness-based and vindication-based, implementations of security. As a felt form of capacity that is oriented to avoidance, resignation is obviously not an effective means of political action. By contrast, as a form of fear produced by the perception that one lacks the ability to confront burdensome forces, misery, whose pair is joy, might constitute an effective basis for action.

Gould's (2001) analysis of the struggle for social inclusion of lesbians and gay men provides a way of concretely illustrating how members of social groups who have been made to feel shame or personal insecurity can exercise power over themselves and others in ways that promote or thwart their capacity to exercise embodied autonomy based on the emotional orientation through which they interact with danger. As we shall see, in their struggle to move from social and self-disapproval to social and self-approval, lesbians and gay men made themselves responsible[25] through a confrontational activism that ensured greater social inclusion on the basis of a pride-based identity. However, the fear of losing this newfound status was given voice in a form of avoidant activism that did little to counter renewed social disapproval and seemed to promote its exacerbation instead. Finally, the radicalization of threats to lesbians' and gay men's vitality and integrity helped reinvigorate their struggle for social inclusion.

Gould argues that while the Gay Pride movement's militant activism achieved significant change on behalf of lesbians and gay men from the late 1960s onward, in the 1980s, renewed and intensified shame in the wake of the AIDS epidemic gave way to emotional orientations that favored the maintenance and even the aggravation of this shame rather than its subversion. Lesbians and gay men urged each other to repress their anger in the name of pride, such that pride came to designate avoidance rather than confrontation. In other words, a confrontation-based emotional energy gave way to a loss of confidence and an avoidance-based emotional energy in the attempt to achieve conformity. Lesbians and gay men moved to implement pride-based emotional security through "volunteerism, remembrance of the dead, relative quietude despite the government's glaring failures, and stoic nobility in the face of a deadly epidemic, rather than confrontational or oppositional politics" (385). Gould argues that 1986 marked the renewal of confrontational militancy in response to the increased awareness of threats to lesbians and gay men, spurred on, among other things, by a repressive U. S. Supreme Court ruling (the *Hardwick* ruling) that sought to deny the right to gay sex by comparing it to "adultery, incest, and other sexual crimes" (387).

While the confrontational activism discussed by Gould was achieved through actions that allowed shamed agents to implement pride-based security by producing a social order to which they felt they could belong, renewed shaming and experiences of shame were dealt with through moving into emotional orientations that caused them to implement pride-based security through avoidance rather than through confrontation. Shame/pride became blended with avoidant and compensatory emotions—emotions that promoted self-repressive and self-corrective emotion management efforts in the struggle to avoid "rocking the boat"—instead of being blended with confrontational and revolutionary emotions—emotions that promoted self-activating and self-forming emotion management efforts in the struggle for inclusion by disapproving others.

In other words, when the existing means of implementing pride-based security were experienced as inadequate (i.e., when confrontational activism was publicly disparaged by lesbians and gay men), avoidant emotions like torment/resignation (the felt in/capacity to avoid extreme hardship) and victimhood/surrender (the felt in/capacity to avoid being the systematic object of an illegitimate exercise of power) were moved into as means of achieving pride. As such, the original struggle for inclusion by way of outrage/vindication (the felt in/capacity to confront another's illegitimate hurting of oneself) and oppression/emancipation (the felt in/capacity to confront forces that illegitimately constrain one's freedom) gave way to an emotional dynamic involving the disciplining of disruptive selves. But when outright exclusion became a threat in 1986, the response shifted again to confrontation.

The shifts in emotional orientation in the evolution of the Gay Pride movement discussed by Gould show that emotional blending is, together with emotional differentiation, a means through which subjects may seek to conform. It should be recalled that emotional blending is a process in which a felt form of in/capacity is resolved through recourse to another emotional-norm pair. Emotional blending is driven by the anxiety/interest modality of fear and desire, where an existing solution to a problem is experienced as inadequate. Should this process become habitual, a blended emotional-norm pair that incorporates the agential content of the secondary emotional-norm pair may develop. In the example we were discussing, blended outcomes might include an emotional-norm pair that involves the achievement of pride through torment/resignation and victimhood/surrender, or alternatively through anger/assertiveness and outrage/vindication.

Where the moral experience of being a disruptive self is involved, various emotions could be moved into as means of identifying and of implementing a satisfactory solution to the experience of social disapproval, most of which should not be thought of as effecting significant social change through activist, outward-directed moral means. For instance, one might implement pride-based security by moving into poverty/wealth and engaging in a lucrative business venture, one might implement self-esteem-based security by moving into ignorance/knowledge and obtaining a college or university education, one might implement self-esteem-based security by moving into risk/precaution and taking a multivitamin daily, or one might implement pride-based security by moving into sadness/happiness[26] and making regular payments on one's mortgage toward the possession of one's house.

The emotional-norm pairs that might be moved into as a means of progressing from shame to pride or from personal insecurity to self-esteem are in fact endless. The appeal of some rather than others will depend on the social context. One might therefore wish to consider the group specificity of the forces that promote some emotional blends over others. To the extent that a confrontational orientation to problems entails a feeling of confidence in one's ability to wield an amount of power that is sufficient to overturn an adversarial force, and that avoidant and preventative orientations to problems entail little or no confidence in one's ability to do so, a dimension that is worth exploring is the extent to which social groups that commonly experience emotional blends that involve avoidant or preventative emotional orientations as means of achieving social conformity are groups that are positioned within socially structured forms of incapacity (e.g., the poor, the exploited, the marginalized).

In calling our attention to the culturally relative nature of morals and manners, classical sociologist Émile Durkheim (1982, 1963) sought to argue that their legitimacy lay in their social ordering function. Thus notions of goodness and of badness, and the behaviors with which they are associated that we observe in groups other than our own, may seem immoral from our perspective, but are nonetheless moral for that group, inasmuch as they allow that group to function according to its particular historical social needs. It is easy to slip into the problematic argument that (dominant) social expectations ought to function as a foundational measure of that that is desirable (or moral) for the group, as does Durkheim, because moral norms are collective products that serve an ordering function (or have an ordering effect). However, there is a difference between acknowledging that moral norms are relative to one's social group and that they produce that group's order, and saying that this order is desirable. In particular, this socially determinist approach downplays the role of political forms of agency—of power struggles—in the determination of dominant social expectations of conformity (i.e., of moral norms).

All social orders are desired to some extent by some (collective) agents, since social orders are the outcome, in some measure, of collective agents' exercise of embodied autonomy. But that a social order is desired by some who manage to impose it as the norm—that the desire of some produces social order—certainly does not make it desirable in and of itself. Karl Marx's lifelong collaborator, Friedrich Engels (1987), also points to the group relativity of morals. Unlike Durkheim, however, he emphasizes the collective power dynamics that underlie this relativity, such that the morality of the ruling classes, in serving their interests, is necessarily different from that of those who are ruled, even though the latter may be (temporarily) deluded into taking on the morality of their oppressors. Engels ends up arguing that the proletarian morality is the universal morality, inasmuch as it signifies the end of class struggle and represents the interests of all as equals.

The difficulties associated with the determination of a universal principle on which to rest moral norms are many, and I do not propose to account for them here. I simply mean to emphasize that while the self may feel ruly or adequate when it conforms to social expectations, and unruly or inadequate when it does not, the self may also feel conflicted about this call for conformity. As such, it is crucial that we attend to instances in which it is morally painful to conform to moral norms via expectations of social conformity, or in which it does not feel morally painful to deviate from these. These embodied forms of resistance to morally normative social expectations may not only tell us something about problems in the social distribution of the embodied capacity to exercise power and implement security; they may also help us distinguish between emotion management efforts that promote the embodied exercise of autonomy and those that promote heteronomy. In short, it does not follow that moral norms are desirable, or that they are beyond critique, because they are relative to one's social group, are desired by some of its (collective) members, and produce social order. As such, the collective forms of biologically, subjectively, and morally embodied resistance to moral norms can be thought of as a motor of change that is potentially respectful of all embodied selves, and as an embodied basis for critique.[27]

C H A P T E R   6

ANALYZING EMOTION MANAGEMENT

INTERACTING WITH THE MANAGED HEART

To further develop an approach to the self grounded in the notion of embodied autonomy, and to help increase the coherence and relevance of the concept of emotion management as it pertains to the differential access to the means of exercising power, it is worth discussing the pioneering work of Arlie R. Hochschild on emotion management. A student of Irving Goffman's, Hochschild takes an interactive and dramaturgical approach to the analysis of emotions. In her first book, *The Managed Heart: Commercialization of Human Feeling* (1983), she discusses the culturally specific "feeling rules" that guide the learning of appropriate emotion displays, such that emotions are subject to individual management. Hochschild argues that the work we perform on emotions is part of what these emotions are. As a result, emotions are highly subject to techniques that reshape them. She makes a distinction between surface acting, which involves changing one's outward appearance in order to deceive others through the dissimulation of real feelings, and deep acting, which involves deliberately changing one's feelings, so that subjects not only deceive others about the nature of their feelings but also may deceive themselves. In other words, in deep acting, subjects may end up altering themselves through a form of deep pretending.

Hochschild pays particular attention to the commercialization of emotional work in jobs such as flight attendance and bill collecting. In the case of flight attendance, she argues that the job involves the attempt to feel and display certain emotions (e.g., calm, sincerity, compassion) while avoiding the feeling and display of others (e.g., alarm, anger, ridicule). Flight attendants are therefore prompted to manage their own emotions with a view to managing passengers' emotions (e.g., fear, anger). "Emotional labor" is the work of bringing about or stifling a feeling in order to produce a facial representation of emotion that affects others' subjective state in a desired fashion in exchange for a wage. For Hochschild emotional labor is a form of self-estrangement. "Emotion management" (or emotion work) is the same work but done in private for its use value rather than exchange value. It is therefore not a form of self-estrangement.

While I respect the spirit within which Hochschild delivers her critique of the capitalist commercialization and commoditization of human feeling, I propose to broaden the scope of the concepts of emotion management and emotional labor so that they include emotional self-transformation efforts that do not involve the physical display of emotion, as well as emotional self-transformation efforts whose goal is not the emotion management of another. I will also show how the concept of emotional regulation that I developed in Chapter 5 can help solve some of the shortcomings of Hochschild's framework—in particular the problematic distinction she draws between a private and authentic self and a public and artificial self—and provide hypotheses as to why workers might experience their selves as artificial. Finally, I suggest that it is more useful to make sense of self-destructive forms of agency on the basis of the notion of embodied heteronomy than on the basis of the notion of self-estrangement.

While it is an important reason for the increase in emotion management and emotional labor efforts, the growth of frontline service work is by no means the only factor that serves to explain this augmentation. In Chapter 4, we considered some of the many ways in which we might make sense of the contemporary increase in selves' emotion management efforts, such as the increased frequency of moral fear experiences due to novelty, ambiguity, or contradiction, the increased scope of responsibilization, the greater intensity of pain produced by problems, the increased frequency of emotion management efforts deployed by interested parties, and the increased frequency of experiences of transgression or of failing to meet standards. For instance, Micki McGee (2005) points to the contemporary belabored self—a self who is constantly made to work on itself as a means of countering socioeconomic vulnerability; Eva Illouz (2008, 133) points to the objectification of emotions that is central to contemporary therapeutic action upon the self; and Cas Wouters (1989b, 115) maintains that in complex societies individuals necessarily develop a more instrumental relationship to feeling due to the "increase and intensification" of "social constraints toward self-constraints." As such, Hochschild's conceptualization of emotion management and emotional labor is too narrow.

Hochschild's definition of both emotion management and emotional labor is tied to the making visible of an internal state: "I use the term *emotional labor* to mean the management of feeling to create a publicly observable facial and bodily display; emotional labor is sold for a wage and therefore has exchange value. I use the synonymous terms *emotion work* or *emotion management* to refer to these same acts done in a private context where they have *use value*" (Hochschild, 1983, 7) She also writes,

> The work done by the boy in the wallpaper factory called for a coordination of mind and arm, mind and finger, and mind and shoulder. We refer to it simply as physical labor. The flight attendant does physical labor when she pushes heavy meal carts through the aisles, and she does mental work when she prepares for and actually organizes emergency landings and evacuations. But in the course of doing this physical and mental labor, she is also doing something more, something I define as *emotional labor*. This labor requires one to induce or suppress feeling in order to sustain the outward countenance that produces the proper state of mind in others—in this case, the sense of being cared for in a friendly and safe place. This kind of labor calls for a coordination of mind and feeling, and it sometimes draws on a source of self that we honor as deep and integral to our individuality. (Hochschild, 1983, 6–7)

This means that Hochschild cannot account for the emotion work potentially performed in the course of manual labor, nor can she account for the fact that the emotion management of others is not necessarily achieved through the emotion management of self or through visible displays of emotion. For instance, one can act on others' emotions through one's words or lack thereof through sensory means such as touch, smell, and taste; through providing entertainment; and so on.

There is a need to broaden what counts as emotion management and emotional labor to better account for the various ways and contexts in which individuals seek to transform their selves and others through deliberate action upon their own and others' emotions—through what I have called emotional socialization. Emotion management is not only a means of transforming oneself through moral self-control (i.e., through self-repression, self-correction, self-activation, and self-formation). It is also a means of transforming others' selves through emotional regulation effects, or through prompting them to engage in moral self-control efforts, and may therefore be a means through which one's self is transformed by others' efforts to emotionally manage one's self. Emotion management is a means of transforming selves through the exercise of moral power over felt in/capacity. One might therefore simply manage oneself, but one might also manage oneself in order to act upon another, much as one might simply manage another, or manage another in order to prompt them to emotionally manage themselves. Finally, emotion management may involve a self-transformation effort whose purpose is to effect observable signs, but it is not limited to this effect.

Similarly, emotional labor, as a species of emotion management engaged in by an agent for compensation, may involve a self-transformation effort whose purpose is to effect observable signs, but it is not limited to this effect. Thus Hochschild's example of the boy laboring in the factory, which she contrasts with the flight attendant dealing with passengers, does not point to the absence of emotional labor in the first and its presence in the second, since the boy can be said to engage in emotion management of his self in the course of doing his job (one can imagine the self-transformation efforts required for a young boy to sit hour upon hour performing the same task over and over again, especially before habit develops). The exploitation of the boy's labor is therefore also an exploitation of his capacity to instrumentalize his feelings in exchange for compensation. In short, the laboring boy in Hochschild's example, or any physical laborer for that matter, may have to deploy moral self-control efforts in order to do their job—from showing up on time, to taking breaks at the preordained time, to performing the physical and mental tasks that are required throughout the laboring period. This means that they too engage in emotional labor.

It remains necessary to account for the specific features and effects on embodied selves of service industry jobs that involve direct customer contact (i.e., frontline service jobs).[1] A key difference between the laboring boy and the frontline service worker is that in order to manage clients' emotions, the frontline service worker must ensure the proper display of emotions, such as the friendly or reassuring smile, whereas the laboring boy, presumably, is not responsible for producing such displays. Frontline service jobs involve not only the emotion management of self but also the emotion management of others through display work (and presumably other forms of work, such as making sure that passengers' requests are promptly attended to, and so forth). While the emotion management of others does not necessarily require display work, in order to account for the specific type of emotional labor performed by the frontline service worker, I suggest that we use the term *emotional display labor*.

I can only provide hypotheses as to the potential implications of emotional display labor on embodied selves. Beyond the fact that both the boy's and the frontline service worker's capacity to exercise embodied autonomy may be compromised by their lack of control over their conditions of labor (i.e., by way of oppression/emancipation), this capacity may be threatened in particular ways for the service sector worker. In becoming responsible for the emotions of others, the frontline service worker may cease to listen to his or her own embodied desires through confusing them with or ranking them beneath those of others.[2] As such, I am suggesting that the frontline service worker must be able to practice some form of detachment from others if the worker is to exist as a discrete entity whose unique embodied needs are honored. Moreover, the frontline service worker may be exposed to a greater number of relational threats as a result of their interaction with the public, which not only requires that they exercise some control over what this public feels but also may involve the frequent experience of the four emotional-norm pairs that I have argued constitute emotional stress/resilience (surprise/predictability, unfamiliarity/familiarity, rivalry/advantage, and oppression/emancipation).[3] These hypotheses ought to be considered in relation to the findings of Amy Wharton's study (1993), which shows that it is not the requirement to perform emotional labor per se that has a negative impact on workers, but rather the degree of job autonomy and involvement as well as the ability to self-monitor.

I now turn to a discussion of the usefulness of the concept of emotional regulation as a counterpoint to Hochschild's distinction between a natural and an artificial self. As Cas Wouters (1989b) argues,[4] Hochschild invokes a problematic split between the private and public spheres, where the former is the realm of authenticity, freedom, welfare, and pleasure, and where the latter is the realm of artifice, control, harm, and suffering. Given that human beings acquire the bulk of their mechanisms of self-regulation through social learning, whose constraining effects become unconscious and therefore come to feel natural, Hochschild also draws a problematic opposition between natural self-regulation and artificial emotion management.

Wouters (1989a, 1989b) and I are not in agreement on all aspects of the conditions and effects of emotion management and emotional regulation. For instance, like Norbert Elias, he fails to properly account for the expressive dimensions of emotion management and is overly focused on the repressive containment of violent and sexual impulses. Moreover, like Hochschild, he tends to slip from a more comprehensive understanding of emotion management as a practice that can be performed upon the self as well as upon the other, to a practice that is uniquely performed upon the self with the aim of acting upon others' emotions through display work. However, we are in agreement on the fact that Hochschild's reliance on a natural, asocial self to produce her critique of the commercialization of feeling is inadequate.

The emotional experiences produced through the emotional labor form of emotion management (i.e., for the purpose of their exchange value) may be of interest or of concern for a variety of reasons, including their tie to workplace exploitation, but they are no more or no less artificial than those that are the outcome of any other emotion management effort. In all instances, they are the product of a process whereby an emotion is deliberately acted upon in the goal of achieving a particular end. Emotional experiences produced through the moral self-control efforts of emotion management can feel unnatural for a variety of reasons, whether or not they are the result of emotional labor.

While we may wish to reject the understanding of emotional experience as either real or artificial, given the problematic nature of the private/public distinction on which it rests, we might still wish to account for the feeling of artificiality if such a feeling is indeed operative in the experience of frontline service workers. One might begin by asking how emotion management efforts could transform emotional experience in the workplace into something that is felt to be artificial. It may be the case that certain kinds of work, or the context in which work takes place, make emotion management efforts more explicit, more frequent, or more intense, thereby increasing the possibility that they become experienced as constituting a break with the natural or habitual course of things. Training periods, jobs that require greater self-transformation, jobs that require more frequent self-transformation, or jobs in which self-transformation efforts go against one's existing beliefs, may make emotion management efforts more explicit or more frequent. Moreover, the increased painful consequences of the failure to properly engage in the emotion management of the self or others may be greater in some jobs than in others, thereby making the experience more intense.

It is interesting that Hochschild's analysis is based on interviews with flight attendants in training, since training usually involves a great amount of self-transformation and can make the self that is the object of emotion management efforts feel that it is being denaturalized. Moreover, flight attendance is the sort of work in which the failure to engage in the required management of self and other can lead to serious, life-threatening consequences. The resulting increased pressure to follow rules and to perform well is likely to make emotion management efforts more explicit.

Two of the defining features of the general context of work relations in capitalism that may be said to favor experiences of artificiality are the greater place occupied by frontline service work (Wharton 1993) and the greater role of psychological principles and practices in the management of work relations (Rose 1989; Illouz 2008). Late liberal cultures frequently promote emotion management as a means to transform agency in the achievement of various ends in multiple spheres of life, including greater or better productivity and health, and the workplace is certainly no exception.[5] Moreover, the prevalence of frontline service work in the contemporary capitalist economy means that beyond the emotion management of the self that is required to a greater or lesser extent at some point in all forms of labor, the emotion management of others by way of work on one's self in the course of doing one's paid work makes the emotional transformation of selves and others more frequent, more explicit, and therefore more susceptible to provoke the experience of denaturalization that underlies the feeling of artificiality.

One might also consider the psychological trends that contrast authentic emotional experience and getting to know and to express one's true self with the oppressive consequences of discipline, together with the consumerist mass mediatization of this particular ethic, as contributing to the production of a conflict between the disciplinary logic that lies behind a number of workplace-based emotion management expectations and the logic of self-realization that increasingly governs social relations more generally, such that the emotion work performed in the context of the former is more likely to be experienced as unnatural in the face of the emotion work performed in the context of the latter.

While these are all reasons that might explain subjects' sense of their emotional experiences as objects that are artificial and separate from them—an experience that might also lead to the feeling of self-estrangement or of alienation—they are not sufficient grounds for making the argument that emotional labor leads to a destructive relationship to self.

Emotion management efforts performed in the context of capitalist forms of work are, like many other emotion management efforts, attempts to ensure that embodied subjective actions (emotional, cognitive, sensorial, and the like), and more often than not behavior, conform to morally normative social expectations. One might argue, in following with a Marxist perspective, that in the context of capitalist

relations of production, emotional labor is a form of emotion management in which the surplus value produced by emotional laboring
over oneself and others does not belong to the self in a strict economic
sense and that in this sense it produces self-estrangement or alienation, which I have defined as the felt in/capacity to confront one's
separation from a valuable part of oneself, whose pair is wholeness.
One might also draw a distinction between the instrumentalization of
feeling that is achieved through all emotion management efforts, and
the instrumentalization of feeling that is achieved through exploitative emotion management efforts. Finally, one might also adopt a
Marxist understanding of human beings as defined by their laboring capacity—a capacity from which they may then become alienated
through its instrumentalization by capital—as well as an understanding of human beings as defined by their feeling capacity—a capacity
from which they may also become alienated through its instrumentalization by capital.

Alternatively or additionally, as the case may be, a compelling
case can be made for the self-destructive nature of capitalism's special brand of instrumentalized feeling if we argue that it is not the
compensation-bound instrumentalization or making use of emotion
per se that is a problem, but rather the worker's heteronomous relationship to this instrumentalization. In other words, if the ability to
emotionally manage oneself and others requires a making use of feeling that allows agents to exercise embodied autonomy, it is not the
act of managing emotion per se that is potentially destructive, but
rather embodied agents' lack of control over this management as a
means of overcoming danger and of implementing security, whether
this lack of control is understood more locally, in the context of
specific workplace demands, or more globally, in the context of the
overall dynamics of labor relations. And to be fair, as Simon Williams
(2001, 24) notes, this is the spirit in which Hochschild produces her
critique of the capitalist managed heart. How then might we account
for self-destructive forms of emotion management, if not through
the notion of alienation?

We have seen that Hochschild draws a distinction between emotions that are tied to the self and emotions that are estranged from the
self on the basis of their instrumentalization in the context of work
demands. She also articulates this difference on the basis of a distinction between surface acting as a form of pretending or of dissimulation
where original feelings are left intact, and deep acting as a form of
pretending or of dissimulation where original feelings are transformed,
such that one is no longer whom one truly is. While Hochschild's

interactionist approach is built on the implicit notion that the self is continuously transformed and called upon to transform itself emotionally in the course of everyday interactions, it also rests on the notion of an original self who undergoes these transformations, and from which one can become estranged.

Given the problems associated with this distinction between a natural and an artificial self, I propose that we understand those forces that pose serious challenges to the exercise of embodied autonomy through the notion of heteronomy, as self-destructive self-regulation. The notion of self-estrangement implies a natural and authentic self that stands outside the operations of social and other forces—a pure self who is at a remove from the theater of everyday life—whereas the notion of heteronomy implies that the vitality and integrity of the self that emerges through its co-constitutive exchanges with social forces is compromised.[6]

LYING, ACTING, AND EMOTION MANAGEMENT

Hochschild uses the metaphor of acting in order to demonstrate that emotions that are the result of emotion management are artificial. This makes the emotions that result from acting in the private sphere just as artificial as those that result from acting in the workplace, but only those produced through emotional labor are artificial in a problematic sense for Hochschild.

Hochschild's understanding of the emotional experience that results from acting as artificial stems from the fact that she confounds the manner in which emotions are triggered with the emotional experience that ensues. Unlike Hochschild, I view these processes as distinct. As a result, I hold that the quality of emotional experience is not affected by the nature of its trigger, whether it is spontaneous or contrived. As I have already argued, emotional experience is governed by the anticipation of an outcome, not by the probability of its actualization.[7]

Whether I feel an emotion as a result of a manufactured trigger produced in the attempt to make myself sad (e.g., by imagining losing someone I love), as a result of a manufactured trigger in somebody else's attempt to make me feel sad (e.g., by being shown images of someone who loses a loved one), or as a result of a spontaneous trigger produced in my interaction with a force that makes me feel sad (e.g., by experiencing sadness for my neighbor's loss of a loved one), in all instances I should be thought of as truly feeling sad.

Hochschild attempts to redeem what she views as the artificial emotions produced through acting for fun or in professional acting by making the argument that it is their context that makes them problematic or not. She provides the example of the professional theater actor in order to draw a distinction between rewarding forms of acting and its self-estranging forms. She argues that unlike flight attendants who are "forced" to act in the course of doing their jobs, professional actors "choose" to act in the course of theirs, and moreover the effects of their actions are socially rewarding. Notwithstanding the fact that professional acting can involve a highly exploitative work context and that the effects of flight attendants' acting can be socially rewarding—a fact that falsifies the opposition between good and bad artificial emotions as it pertains to these particular examples—the attempt to distinguish between forms of acting on the basis of whether the intention behind them is freely willed, or socially rewarding, fails to generate the grounds for a distinction in kind between emotion management efforts that produce heteronomy (i.e., which threaten the self's vitality and integrity) and those that do not, since both freedom-based implementations of security and socially rewarding actions can produce heteronomy.[8]

Part of Hochschild's uneasiness seems to lie with the emotional experiences that result from emotion management efforts as expressions of moral self-control, inasmuch as she tends to view these as artificial and alienating forms of feeling. In contrast, she views the emotional experiences that result from what I have called emotional regulation as more authentic forms of emotional experience. However, the emotions that are produced through emotion management efforts cannot be said to be any less true or authentic, per se, than those that result from emotional regulation, even where these are not deemed to be freely willed or socially rewarding. While the emotions that result from emotional regulation may be experienced as natural and as belonging to a core self in contrast with the fabricated emotions that result from emotion management, as differentiated and blended structured experiences of felt in/capacity,[9] they too came into being through emotion management efforts.

To further clarify, it is useful to think through the relationship between actions like acting and lying and emotion management.

In social interaction, subjects may be more or less frequently expected to act differently than they do. As a consequence, they may be more or less frequently prompted to dissimulate or represent their actions in a manner that corresponds to social expectations, such that a form of "lying" or of "acting" may be of use in the avoidance of the pain caused by social punishment and in the pursuit of the pleasure caused by social reward, owing to the absence or presence of conformity with social norms.

Lying consists of the intentional,[10] morally self-transformative dissimulation of an embodied action such as a cognitive, emotional, behavioral, sensorial, or biological process. Lying can be achieved through different means. Thus one might hide what one truly thinks of mystery novels, behave as though one likes a relative one actually dislikes, speak untruths about one's visualized personal appearance, deny the fact that one has consumed alcohol, or conceal one's wrinkles with filler. Lying often depends on the practice of acting.

Acting consists of the intentional, morally self-transformative performance of a behavior as a means of representing an action, such as a cognitive, emotional, behavioral, sensorial, or biological process. Unlike biological or subjective forms of agency, acting, like lying, requires embodied action upon one's own agency—a self-transformation I have referred to as moral self-control. Thus one might behave as though one were thinking about a loved one, as though one were feeling angry, as though one saw bright sunshine, as though one were riding a bike, or as though one were physically tired. Acting is not necessarily a form of lying, since it does not necessarily involve dissimulation (e.g., I might deliberately behave as though I am feeling hot and actually be feeling hot), and lying is not necessarily a form of acting, since it does not necessarily involve a behavioral performance (e.g., if I hide what I truly think of mystery novels by refraining from speaking I am not engaging in a behavioral performance).

How do lying and acting relate to the emotion management of self and other?

Lying (the intention-driven dissimulation of undesirable actions) and acting (the intention-driven behavioral representation of desirable actions) may be involved in the emotion management of other selves, but they are not necessarily involved. Emotion management requires the intentional production of an emotional experience in the self or in another self as a means of exercising power over the actions of a self or other self. Lying and acting might be convenient means of inducing this effect in other selves, but they certainly are not the only means of intentionally triggering emotional experiences in others. For instance, one might serve a friend a few cups of strong coffee to help them feel energized, tell a loved one sincere words of affection to help trigger in them a feeling of love, or send someone a joke to cheer them up, none of which is an instance of lying or of acting, even though all involve intention and emotion management.

Further, the emotion management of the self is not necessarily involved in lying and acting. For instance, I do not have to induce a specific emotional experience in myself in order to lie about the wrinkles under my eyes that I am concealing by having injections of filler, and I may be able to convince another self that I dislike apple pie without having to actually make myself feel one way or another about either the pie or the social interaction. Here the verbal performance of my dislike of apple pie through the motivating effects of emotional regulation might suffice if my emotional motivation is simply that I subjectively will the other person to feel accepted. By contrast, the emotion management of the self often is involved in lying and acting, since it is effective to intentionally induce a particular emotional motivation in the self as a means of acting upon others' agency. For instance, it may be useful to trigger in myself the emotional experience of relaxation if I wish to effectively dissimulate my nervousness to another self, or to trigger in myself the emotional experience of anger if I wish to effectively convey to another self that I am angry.

Finally, the emotion management of other selves is most likely involved in lying and acting, since presumably lying and acting have intention-driven emotional effects on the selves to whom one lies or for whom one acts. Thus if I lie to someone about my financial situation by making it appear better than it is, it is likely with the intention of inducing some sort of emotional response in them. Or if I behave as though I were hungry when presented a meal made of plastic vegetables by a small child, it is also likely with the intention of inducing some sort of emotional response in them. Of course, my emotion management efforts, whether through lying, through acting, or through some other means, can be said to fail if the emotion I intended to induce in another self is not the one they end up experiencing, or at the very least if the action that my emotion management efforts meant to induce is not effected.

EMOTIVES, MODALITIES OF FEAR AND DESIRE, AND MORAL SELF-CONTROL

William M. Reddy (1997, 1999) developed the concept of "emotives" in an effort to move beyond social constructionism and the extreme relativism of Foucault's and Bourdieu's hypermalleable subjects, while avoiding the pitfalls of essentialism, which do not provide any grounds on which to anchor emancipatory politics. Rather than view emotional statements as "constative," where what is said about an emotion describes or represents that emotion (e.g., saying "I am angry" represents the internal state of being angry)—a stance that corresponds to the dominant Western view; and rather than view emotional statements as "performative," where the performance of the emotion is the emotion (i.e., saying "I am angry" is being angry)—a stance that can be associated with social constructionist ethnographic approaches—Reddy maintains that emotional statements do not simply represent an internal state or create it. He urges us to view emotional statements as "emotives," where the statement's referent simultaneously precedes it and is altered by it.

As Reddy writes, "Emotives are themselves instruments for directly changing, building, hiding, intensifying emotions. There is an 'inner' dimension to emotion, but it is never merely 'represented' by statements or actions. It is the necessary (relative) failure of all efforts to represent feeling that makes for (and sets limits on) our plasticity" (1999, 331). It is because it fails in representing the emoting subject's internal state that the emotive transforms this state. In other words, the feeling is transformed by the attempt to express it (i.e., saying that one feels a certain way can induce that emotion, intensify the feeling, or cause it to dissipate).

Reddy argues that conventional emotives serve to shape (rather than to create) subjects' emotional experience by producing expected forms of emotional expression. Conventional emotives are particularly powerful in situations where subjects experience a conflict between the desire to conform to social expectations and the desire to deviate, such as in the desire to conform to the expectation that one marry and the desire not to marry, since they act in favor of social conformity by providing a conventional emotive through which to resolve it—an emotive that is ultimately tied to pleasurable social rewards. Emotional deviance, then, can be understood as the consequence of the self's resistance to the resolution of ambivalence in favor of conventional emotives. As such, argues Reddy, when a social system is destabilized, competing norms can be turned to as alternatives by those who experience greater frustration or exclusion. Indeed, Reddy wonders whether some types of social systems promote greater emotional deviance than others. Hence for him, "Emotional control is the real site of the exercise of power: politics is just a process of determining who must repress as illegitimate, who must foreground as valuable, the feelings and desires that come up for them in given contexts and relationships" (1999, 335). In short, for Reddy the expression of conventional emotives is a form of emotion management that functions by repressing inappropriate feelings and by emphasizing appropriate ones.

If I were to put this in the terms of embodied in/capacity theory, emotives are among the embodied means of power through which subjects seek to implement security, and are therefore means of moving from incapacity to capacity. As such, emotives always entail a form of lack, on whose basis blended and differentiated fear and desire forms may come into being. It is useful to distinguish between moral emotives and subjective emotives, where the former are statements or displays of emotion that require self-control efforts and where the latter do not. For example, the habitual statement "I am angry" could be a means of exercising power if it causes me to experience a particular form of felt incapacity that allows me to implement security through assertiveness. This same statement could also be a moral means of exercising power if I deliberately utter it as a means of exercising self-control or of emotionally managing another.

Deliberately producing anger in oneself might involve self-repression (i.e., I might repress the feelings of rejection/belonging as means of moving into anger/assertiveness), self-correction (i.e., I might correct the feelings of rejection/belonging as means of moving into anger/assertiveness), self-activation (i.e., I might activate the feelings of anger/assertiveness as means of replacing the feelings of rejection/belonging), or self-formation (i.e., I might form the feelings of anger/assertiveness as means of replacing the feelings of rejection/belonging).

The statement "I am angry" could also bring about a particular form of felt incapacity in another, such as guilt. In this case it would be a means of triggering a specific fear and desire form in another. For instance, one might express anger at another self's failure to fulfill an obligation, thereby triggering the feelings of guilt and, perhaps also, the innocence-motivated implementation of security by way of a commitment to do so in the future. The uttering of this statement may or may not require a self-control effort on the part of the subject who makes it, and it may or may not require a self-control effort on the part of the subject who receives it. In this way, emotives can be seen to constitute means of exercising subjective and moral power over oneself and others in the production of social conformity.

As a means of further defining the dynamics of emotion management, I would now like to explore its relationship to three modalities of emotional experience (panic/excitement, anxiety/interest, distress/relief) together with the means of moral self-control (self-repression, self-correction, self-activation, self-transformation) as they pertain to "lying" and "acting," both of which involve emotives.

The reader should be reminded here that the panic/excitement modality of fear and desire corresponds to the perception of a threat/promise for which satisfactory means of threat/promise resolution are already in place. As a result, the actions through which security is implemented are spontaneous or habitual. The anxiety/interest modality of fear and desire is one in which existing means of power are perceived to be inadequate, such that alternative means are sought. Here actions are suspended but not frozen. Finally, the distress/relief modality of fear and desire designates emotional experiences in which actions are frozen due to the absence of an orientation to danger, or the absence of the knowledge of or access to means of exercising power in the implementation of security.

If a flight attendant or anybody else learns that they should feel a certain way in order to meet the conditions of their employment, what they are probably learning is that they are required to feel a certain way in order to behave in a certain way. In the service industry, for instance, if the panic/excitement-based manner in which one responds to a particular relational threat, such as a client's anger, is to match this anger with one's own and to spontaneously grimace or shout, then one will typically be compelled by one's employer and service culture more generally to change one's means of responding to an angry client's anger, whether or not one continues to experience anger. In other words, it is not so much the angry feeling that conflicts with service culture, but rather some of the common behavioral means of dealing with it, which is to say its emotive outcomes, since these fail to effect in the client the desired emotional response. The panic/excitement-driven response becomes a problem and prompts the service industry worker to move into anxiety/interest.

To be rid of the anxiety/interest-driven burden or relational threat an expectation represents in the event that one's present feelings and behavior fail to conform to it, whether by comparing to it favorably or by complying with it, a number of things could take place. First, one might attempt to dissimulate inappropriate emotions, made manifest through emotive outcomes, by engaging in the acts of anxiety/interest-driven moral self-transformation that are self-repression or self-correction—in this case the intentional dissimulation of the undesirable actions that are one's anger and one's behavioral expressions of it through "lying." Transforming the socially recognizable form of anger in facial gestures or shouting through the repression or correction of the urge to implement these means as assertiveness solution orientations to anger are two potential means of implementing moral security in this situation.

Hence I might urge myself not to grimace or shout (e.g., by deliberately thinking about the ensuing job loss), thereby repressing my urge to do so and transforming it into the self-repressive urge not to do so, much as I might urge myself to smile or to lower my voice (e.g., by deliberately thinking of my superior's evaluation of my performance), thereby correcting my urge to do so and transforming it into the self-correcting urge to smile or lower my voice.

While it is true that the repression or correction of one's urge to implement a particular solution to a threat can be thought of as a kind of self-estrangement or as an instance of going against one's self, self-repression and self-correction are nonetheless expressions of desires that equally belong to the self, albeit to the moral self rather than to the subjective one. The fact that these desires emerge in the context of subjects' interactions with the normative expectations of a particular workplace do not make them desires that do not belong to them, since all desires can be said to develop in the course of interaction.

Setting aside for now the issue of the autonomous or heteronomous nature of one's intentions, one can argue that the more one feels one's desires result from an exercise in moral self-control in the avoidance of moral pain and in the pursuit of moral pleasure, the more one is likely to experience them as objectified others. As I have already argued, this is more prone to happen in the course of learning to resolve novel relational threats and promises, such as in the course of job training, and it is less likely to be the case once moral self-control efforts have become more habitual or have given way to emotional regulation effects through the transformation of old desires that required repression or correction efforts, into new ones that require no such efforts. So how might we explain the process through which new desires emerge and replace older ones rather than counter them?

Notwithstanding the emotional energy that must continuously be expended in the processes of self-repression and of self-correction and the likelihood of their lesser efficiency overall in ensuring that emotions and behaviors correspond to normative imperatives,[11] in contemporary culture these are likely to be experienced as threatening, to the extent that in a culture of "emotional authenticity" one will be inclined to feel that one's real self is buried while an artificial self takes its place, and that one is misleading others about the true nature of one's self. Moreover, the contemporary preference for self-activation and self-formation as means of moral self-control is apt to increase the perception of emotional self-transformation efforts achieved through self-repression and self-correction as problematic.

In consequence, should self-repression and self-correction not be satisfactory solutions to the dual problem of one's anger and of its emotive outcome, the expectation that one refrain from further offending angry clients through one's verbal or facial output signifying anger might be said to further prompt the anxiety/interest-driven search for more satisfactory means of moving away from it. Thus we shift from what Hochschild refers to as "surface acting," which I rather think of as the self-repressive and self-corrective efforts that might involve "lying" and "acting," to what she refers to as "deep acting," which I rather think of as the self-activating and self-forming efforts that might involve "acting."

Thus one might attempt to display appropriate emotions, made manifest through emotive behaviors, by engaging in the acts of anxiety/interest-driven moral self-transformations that are self-activation or self-formation (in this case the intentional behavioral representation of the desirable actions that are one's alternative to anger and one's behavioral expression of this alternative through "acting"). Transforming the socially recognizable form of anger in facial gestures or shouting, through the activation or formation of alternatives to the urge to implement these means as assertiveness solution orientations to anger, is another potential means of implementing moral security in this situation.

Hence I might urge myself to achieve relaxation (e.g., through deep breathing), thereby activating my urge to move from anger/ assertiveness to tension/relaxation (the felt in/capacity to confront strain by releasing it) and transforming anger/assertiveness into the alternative tension/relaxation, much as I might urge myself to achieve patience (e.g., through looking at the situation differently), thereby forming my urge to move from anger/assertiveness to impatience/ patience (the felt in/capacity to confront the forces that cause the self to suffer without complaint) and transforming anger/assertiveness into the alternative impatience/patience. In these examples I behave as though I were relaxed or patient through a process of moral self-transformation that allows me to become relaxed or patient.

Here one is able to move away from one's anxiety/interest-driven anger through recourse to another emotional-norm pair—a process I earlier referred to as emotional blending. An emotionally blended means of dealing with anger allows one to implement security through means of power newly made available by another emotional-norm pair, where none was satisfactory before.

Any of these anxiety/interest-driven responses to a client's anger—through self-repression, self-correction, self-activation, or self-formation—might come to more or less permanently supplant the initial, panic/excitement-driven one as the habitual means of dealing with one's anger. But even if they become habitual, anxiety/interest-driven means of exercising moral self-control remain self-management efforts. Thus I might habitually come to transform my original angry feelings and behavioral solutions to them by not grimacing or shouting, by smiling or lowering my voice, by achieving relaxation, or by achieving patience. However, should any of these moral anxiety/interest-driven responses to anger come to no longer require moral self-control efforts, they might then be said to replace the initial, panic/excitement-driven ones as the new panic/excitement-driven means of implementing security in response to the danger posed by one's anger. The emotion management of the self would give way to a process of emotional regulation, such that moral self-control efforts would cease to be required in achieving conformity with the norms of one's work.

To be clear, the previously acquired urges that promote specific behavioral means of implementing security (e.g., dealing with one's anger through grimacing or shouting) are not any truer or more natural than the newly acquired ones that promote the repression or correction of existing desires (dealing with one's anger through the repression or correction of the urge to grimace or shout), or the activation or formation of new ones (dealing with one's anger through the activation or formation of an alternative urge to achieve relaxation or patience). Existing means of overcoming danger and of implementing security may feel truer or more natural by virtue of their habitual nature, if they are mediated by moral self-control efforts, or by virtue of their subjective nature, if they no longer or never required the moral self-control efforts of emotion self-management, but they are no less the product of interaction and of learning than are newer means of doing so.

In short, one should not confound the repression or correction of an existing means of resolving conflict, or the activation or formation of another means of doing so, with emotional artificiality, even though these may involve "lying" or "acting." It is more useful to think of the anxiety/interest-driven transformation of an existing means of responding to a particular form of conflict as an instance of emotion management, which is to say, as a deliberate means of acting upon one's self and others through the mobilization of hedonic power, and as a consequence of which the transformation of both self and other may take place.

Now let us say that a flight attendant is incapable of fruitful self-repression, self-correction, self-activation, or self-formation in the production of a normatively appropriate response to clients' anger. Let us say, in other words, that anxiety/interest-driven attempts to find more satisfactory means of overcoming the danger produced by the urge to grimace or shout at clients remain unsuccessful, but that the desire to practice flight attendance be maintained or remain possible. In the absence of the identification of more satisfactory means to deal with relational threat/promise, distress/relief-driven attempts to do so might evolve and result in the production of new means through the creation of a new emotional-norm pair.

For instance, in the face of an angry client, a flight attendant might develop the ability to experience something along the lines of the emotional-norm pair of unprofessional involvement/professional detachment, where unprofessional involvement is the emotion triggered by the perception that one lacks the ability to avoid experiencing undesired emotions as a result of their unwanted emotive outcomes in the context of the requirements of one's service-oriented work, and where professional detachment is its pair. Any number of means to implement professional detachment-driven security might here be identified, such as the deliberate view of clients as an unindividuated mass. In any event, should this new norm pair develop and be triggered, and should it prompt emotive behavior that conforms to normative expectations, anger might be dealt with by way of a newly created emotional-norm pair in a process I earlier named emotional differentiation, with self and other being transformed in the process.

The manner in which Hochschild sets up her discussion of emotion management in terms of surface acting (behavior modification) and deep acting (feeling modification) results in the common analytical tendency of failing to account for the specific dynamics of the felt nature of this management, which can for this very reason be easily confounded with behavior management or feeling artificiality. Thus the repression of the urge to shout when one is angry is not simply a form of behavior modification. Rather it is an action performed upon a structured emotional experience. And the activation of the feeling of relaxation that results from the transformation of the feeling of anger through deep breathing is not simply an artificial outcome. It also is an action performed upon a structured emotional experience.

The felt nature and structure of emotions is central to their impact. Emotion management does not merely produce emotional and behavioral outcomes. It must also be taken to entail the deliberate exercise of hedonic power over other agential forces, such as moral, cognitive, sensorial, and biological ones. The painful and pleasurable nature of emotions as well as their normative form means that their experience can influence individual and collective agency and be generated to manage it.

ANALYZING EMOTIONAL CAMPAIGNS

MASTER EMOTIONAL-NORM PAIRS: FROM SELF-DISCIPLINE TO SELF-REALIZATION

How do the subjects who make up Western social groups control or exercise directive action upon their selves, other selves, and the world more generally? Do they more frequently do so through the feelings of shame/pride or through those of personal insecurity/self-esteem? Do they privilege confrontational, avoidant, or preventative strategic orientations to dangers and securities? Do the emotional modalities of panic/excitement, anxiety/interest, or distress/relief predominate? Are emotional differentiation and emotional blending common? To what objects of fear and desire, signs of danger and security, and means of power are emotional orientations attached? Is displacement common? Are subjects primarily directed by themselves or by others? And when they are being directed by others, are they or are they not prompted to act upon themselves? Is the scope of the moral forces that threaten subjects extending the reach of responsibilization? Which emotional experiences are typical of or unique to Western societies' attempts to overcome danger and implement security? Which ones are most common? What are their varying intensities? How are these experiences aligned with the various forces (social, physical, spatial, climactic, and the like) with which they interact? How are they aligned with stratifications in the incapacities and capacities that structure social relations of power and of domination?

In previous chapters, I proposed that we think about these questions as they pertain to distinct emotional economies. Emotional economies can be conceived of as large sociohistorical formations, but they can also be thought of as smaller complexes within these larger configurations, whether these are based on small groups or communities, or on social positions such as gender, race, class, sexual orientation, age group, health status, and so on. For instance, the emotional experiences of a twenty-first-century white middle-class heterosexual North American female in her thirties with a history of chronic pain and living in a small rural community have distinct features. In what follows, I develop a rudimentary sketch of some of the general features of modern and advanced modern emotional economies based on the concept of the master emotional-norm pair, which I use to designate the organizing felt in/capacity or emotional principle of an emotional economy. To breathe life into this concept, I initially produce a brief reading of Norbert Elias's analysis of early civility manuals. I further attempt to illustrate its potential by exploring how emotional differentiations and blends are structured by a master emotional-norm pair in the popular late eighteenth century gothic novels of Ann Radcliffe, and in a contemporary bestselling self-improvement guide written by Susan Jeffers.

The master emotional-norm pair organizes and actively generates differentiated and blended emotional norms. It emerges in times of large-scale social change and may be thought of as being spawned by this change but also as contributing to it in significant ways. The perspective it embodies is actively promoted by members of society for whom it produces new forms of capacity. This dominant pair more or less progressively replaces another dominant pair whose desire form it transforms into an incapacity. In other words, the new master emotional-norm pair is the solved content of a problem (an object of desire) made up of a dominant felt form of capacity, which it contests. As such, it acts to subvert the incidence of the dominant pair and the incidence of the pairs that are its differentiated and blended forms, as well as the means in the exercise of power through which security is implemented in the context of these emotional experiences. More specifically, inasmuch as existing emotional means of moving from incapacity to capacity feel inadequate or begin to fail them, it promotes agents' moral self-control efforts in the transformation of existing, morally problematic desires, whether these are experienced as illegitimate and in need of repression, erroneous and in need of correction, latent and in need of activation, or immature and in need of formation.

The idea of sociohistorical emotional organizations rests on the principle that these more or less stable structures are subject to transformation in the wake of social change. It follows that an emotion that is experienced as a pleasurable capacity in one context can come to be experienced as a painful incapacity in another, in which case it will constitute an object of fear for agents who may seek to repress, correct, activate, or form the problematic desire with which it is associated.

I emphasize that the brief comparison that follows between a master emotional-norm pair that I attribute to the Middle Ages and a master emotional-norm pair that I attribute to the modern period is entirely based on a reading of Norbert Elias's arguments and evidence in his study of the rise of civility. While I venture it here for illustrative purposes, I nonetheless hope that it is of some historical relevance. I later speculate about a master-norm pair for the advanced modern context and feel more confident in my knowledge of this emotional formation.

It can be hypothetically inferred from Elias's (1978, 1982) work that a master feeling we might call domination (the felt capacity to confront one's failure to conquer one's adversary through self-realization), whose matching fear form is submission, constituted a pleasurable desire form in the context of the warrior societies of the Middle Ages, but became a painful incapacity prompting self-discipline in the context of the later civility-based, pacified[1] societies of the modern era. The master-norm pair we might attribute to the early modern era, incivility/civility (the felt in/capacity to confront the primitive, animalistic, or bodily impulses that hold one's reason hostage through self-discipline), can be thought of as a means of rejecting and of replacing the main form of felt capacity in the might-based society that precedes it—a felt capacity becoming felt incapacity.

The emotional differentiations and blends that stem from and therefore contain incivility/civility are emotional-norm pairs on whose basis agents can learn to repudiate the forms of desire through which they implement security in a society no longer governed by the importance of activating and of forming physical supremacy, strength, and skill, but by the importance of restraining the use of physical coercion in everyday life through self-discipline. Thus we see that the new master emotional-norm pair not only subverts the master pair that precedes it but also produces a new means of governing conduct. The capacity that is the realization of masterful desire gives way to the capacity that is the disciplining of irrational desire.

While Elias views the increased promotion and inferred experience of emotional experiences of shame, embarrassment, and disgust as a feature that distinguishes early modern subjects from their warfaring ancestors, I do not believe these particular emotional experiences to have been unique to early modernity. If shame, embarrassment, and disgust become so important during this period of transition, it is perhaps not so much because the members of warrior societies did not experience these emotions, but because these emotions are more intense and more prevalent in contexts of large-scale social transformations, where they act as means of prompting agents' moral actions of social conformity—promoting the moral self-transformation efforts required for the development of new forms of capacity in the context of changing morally normative social expectations.

As was discussed in Chapter 5, danger rituals in which deviant subjects are rendered dislikable, disgusting, and hateful favor the social and self-inclusion, exclusion, and expulsion of those who fail to conform, thereby also promoting the experiences of shame/pride and of personal insecurity/self-esteem, on whose basis moral agents can develop the means of achieving conformity. Moreover, the objects of fear and desire, signs of danger and security, and means of power associated with these emotions would have differed from those with which Elias was familiar, making it difficult, perhaps, for him to recognize them in another emotional economy.

In short, experiences of shame, embarrassment, and disgust were in all likelihood not absent from the emotional landscape of the Middle Ages, and cannot therefore be said to have been newly experienced during the early modern period. Yet there were undoubtedly emotional blends and differentiations that developed and grew out of the master-norm pair of this emerging civility-based emotional formation—new emotions having to do with the need for new forms of sociability and sexual propriety, for instance. If I am correct in my (highly speculative) hypothesis that means of moral self-realization were generally favored in the Middle Ages, and that means of moral self-discipline were generally favored in the modern period that follows, it is also possible that feelings of personal insecurity/self-esteem were a more frequent emotional basis for the production of moral conformity in the warfaring societies of the Middle Ages, while feelings of shame/pride were a more frequent emotional basis for the production of moral conformity in the newly pacified societies of the modern era.

I venture another comparison here between the modern incivility/civility master emotional-norm pair and the advanced modern master pair I have chosen to call disempowerment/empowerment. One might argue that the pleasurable master feeling of civility, whose matching fear form is incivility, which constituted a pleasurable desire form in the context of the modern societies of the Western world, has become a painful incapacity prompting self-realization in the context of the later empowerment-based, consumerist societies of the advanced modern period. The master-norm pair I have attributed to the advanced modern era, disempowerment/empowerment (the felt in/capacity to confront the personal shortcomings that compromise one's healthy desire through self-realization), can be thought of as a means of rejecting and of replacing the main form of felt capacity in the civility-based society that precedes it—a felt capacity becoming felt incapacity.

The emotional differentiations and blends that stem from and therefore contain disempowerment/empowerment are emotional-norm pairs on whose basis agents can learn to repudiate the forms of desire through which they implement security in a society that is no longer governed by the importance of restraining the use of physical control in everyday life through rational self-discipline, but governed by the importance of promoting the use of psychological control in everyday life through healthy self-realization. Thus we see that the new master emotional-norm pair not only subverts the master pair that precedes it but also produces a new means of governing conduct. The capacity that is the disciplining of irrational desire gives way to the capacity that is the realization of healthy desire.

The different logics of these master emotional-norm pairs, as well as the manner in which they resist and seek to replace the logic of their rivals, can be illustrated with a brief comparison between two bodies of bestselling works of literature, the one modern, the other advanced modern. Both can be understood as moral attempts to form the subjectivity of readers in the context of large-scale social change, and are in this respect comparable to the civility manuals of the early modern era analyzed by Elias. As such, they should also be thought of as other-directed emotion management efforts on the part of agents for whom a new logic in felt in/capacity solves problems and who therefore stand to benefit from its spread.

In Ann Radcliffe's bestselling gothic novels *The Mysteries of Udolpho* (1784) and *The Italian* (1787), written with the explicit intent of elevating readers' souls (Radcliffe 1826), the in/ability to discipline irrational desire structures the various emotional experiences that produce the narrative. Notable examples include the heroines' frequent experiences of prejudice/enlightenment (the felt in/capacity to confront one's preconceived irrational beliefs), corruption/virtue (the felt in/capacity to prevent immoral temptation through self-discipline), arbitrariness/impartiality (the felt incapacity to confront another's irrational exercise of power), gullibility/skepticism (the felt in/capacity to prevent being misled by one's irrational beliefs), impulsivity/self-restraint (the felt in/capacity to confront one's irrational failure to delay gratification), evil/righteousness (the felt in/capacity to confront one's lack of rational adherence to moral imperatives), and madness/sanity (the felt in/capacity to prevent one's irrational transgression of moral boundaries). In both novels, security is ultimately achieved when the heroine emancipates herself from the fear-producing oppressive forces of her irrational desire through self-discipline.

Radcliffe's novels were written during the French revolutionary period, and rest upon a moral and emotional contrast between the culture of the Enlightenment and that of the so-called Dark Ages that precedes it. The medieval setting of the heroines' ordeals forms the basis of their eventual emancipation from oppressive circumstances through courage, enlightenment, virtue, impartiality, skepticism, and self-restraint. Heroines eventually acquire the empirical knowledge required to subvert the threat of victimization, superstitious prejudice, and gullibility, and develop the self-restraint they need to counter arbitrary and corrupt influences on their lives, thereby warding off both evil and madness. In short, terror is confronted and courage is implemented through the disciplining of irrational desire, which forms the basis of moral, civil conduct, and of its pleasurable effects in Radcliffe's gothic universe.

In Susan Jeffers's bestselling personal improvement guide *Feel the Fear and Do it Anyway* (1987), the in/ability to realize healthy desire structures the various emotional experiences that produce the narrative. Notable examples include the author's frequent mention of experiences of passivity/proactivity (the felt in/ability to confront one's unhealthy failure to take command of one's life), negativity/positivity (the felt in/ability to confront one's unhealthy negative thinking in the improvement of one's life), self-doubt/self-confidence (the felt in/ability to implement security [i.e., health] effectively), emotional stress/resilience (the felt in/ability to confront the demands of everyday life in ways that promote health), self-stagnation/self-growth (the felt in/ability to confront one's unhealthy inability to take risks), dependence/independence (the felt in/ability to confront one's unhealthy reliance on another force to be happy), irresponsibility/responsibility (the felt in/ability to confront one's lack of healthy adherence to moral standards), and mental illness/mental health (the felt in/ability to prevent one's unhealthy failure to measure up to moral standards). Security is ultimately achieved when readers learn to emancipate themselves from the fear-producing oppressive forces that stunt the emergence of healthy desire through self-realization.

Jeffers's self-improvement guide was written during a period of sustained economic crises in the 1980s, and rests upon a moral and emotional contrast between the culture of neoliberalism and that of the interventionist regime (i.e., the welfare state) that precedes it.

While the former is associated with healthy risk taking, self-confidence, proactivity, independence, and resilience, the latter is conceived of as an oppressive disciplinary institution that promotes negative thinking, depression, paralysis, and insecurity. Enthusiastic risk taking is presented as the solution to readers' painful circumstances, and individuals are urged to take responsibility for achieving their own health, wealth, and well-being, as well as for the negative outcomes of their inaction, such as disease, stagnation, and joblessness. Jeffers's book promises a profound self-transformation. Irrespective of age, gender, and social status, fear is said to be a human trait that prevents people from fully experiencing life and from expressing their true potential. Unlearning our fearful relationship to the world is thus a condition of becoming emancipated from the insecurities that imprison our true selves. In short, terror is confronted and courage is implemented through the realization of healthy desire, which forms the basis of moral, empowered conduct, and of its pleasurable effects in Jeffers' self-help universe.

We can infer from these examples that in the modern discipline-based emotional economy, civility is grounded in the ability to negate, chiefly through self-discipline, the aspects of the self that curb one's potential for reason. In contrast, in the advanced modern realization-based emotional economy, empowerment is grounded in the ability to express, chiefly through self-realization, the aspects of the self that curb one's potential for health.[2] Both reason and health should be thought of, in these respective social contexts, as the bases for moral conduct.

The social philosopher Michel Foucault (1979, 1990) argued that power was more productive than repressive in disciplinary societies, because he wanted to emphasize that subjects were being increasingly governed through the knowledge being produced about them. I do not dispute the importance of the practices of subjectivity formation identified by Foucault in the various disciplinary contexts he discusses. However, I am making the alternative argument that while societies we might qualify as disciplinary do indeed have as an explicit goal the shaping of subjectivity as a means of "conducting conduct"—as a means of getting individuals to govern themselves— the modern disciplinary logic is one that aims to repress and correct, or to have subjects repress and correct, the internal irrational forces that cause agents to violate moral commands. In contrast, the advanced modern realization logic is one that aims to activate and form, or to have subjects activate and form, the internal healthy forces that cause agents to achieve moral standards. As such, in disciplinary societies individual desire is conceived of as transgressive—as illegitimate or as incorrect—whereas in realization societies, individual desire is conceived of as inadequate—as latent or as immature. In the one, subjects are conceived of as immorally capable, and in the other, as immorally incapable.

To illustrate, in the modern disciplinary logic, a child's hitting behavior will be thought of as the expression of an irrational desire that must be repressed or corrected so as to enable the emergence of the rational and moral capacity not to hit. In the advanced modern logic of realization, a child's hitting behavior will be thought of as the lack of expression of a healthy desire that must be activated or formed so as to enable the emergence of the healthy and moral capacity to be gentle. In the first instance, moral self-control involves the repression or correction of an inborn or learned response to relational threat and promise, while in the second it involves the activation or formation of an inborn or learned response to these. For the one, irrational fears and desires constitute the object of fear, while for the other, the lack of healthy fears and desires are the problem.

Karl Marx, Max Weber, Émile Durkheim, Sigmund Freud, Norbert Elias, Michel Foucault, and many other thinkers interested in the relationship between the individual and society have sought to account for the forces that promoted the development of modern disciplinary societies. For instance, we have seen that for Elias, the early modern states' growing monopoly over the legitimate means of violence, as well as the greater need for collaboration and predictability owing to the lengthening chains of interdependence between individuals, causes existing forms of agency to fall into disfavor. Many of us are also familiar with Foucault's argument: Prompting subjects to self-discipline is a more efficient means in the exercise of state and capitalist power than is their repression through physical force. Thus in the dominant emotional and moral logic of developing liberal regimes, the exercise of physical mastery as a means of social control becomes an irrational capacity whose effects are unpredictable and inhumane.

On the other hand, Anthony Giddens, Ulrich Beck, Nikolas Rose, Stuart Ewen, Marcel Gauchet, Zygmunt Bauman, and others have sought to explain the forces that favor individual self-realization in advanced modern societies. For instance, one might make the argument that consumer capitalism is stunted by the self-denying and standardized logic favored by its earlier production-oriented forms,[3] such that civility falls into disfavor. One might also make the argument that prompting subjects to self-realize through concern for their personal security and well-being is a more efficient means in the exercise of state and capitalist power than is their disciplinary repression and correction.[4] Thus in the dominant emotional and moral logic of late liberal capitalist societies, the exercise of civility as a means of social control becomes an unhealthy capacity whose effects are to stunt human freedom and potential.

While I do not propose to account for these forces in any more detail here, I do wish to develop a framework within which we can attempt to identify some of the particularities of the self-discipline and self-realization approaches to the moral control of subjectivity. To this end, I initially turn to the task of comparing and contrasting two rhetorical approaches to the management of emotional selves in the emotional campaign.

CAMPAIGNS OF FEAR, CAMPAIGNS OF DESIRE

Embodied in/capacity theory emphasizes the felt and structured dimensions of perceptions as conditions for action. In what follows, I consider two main rhetorical strategies through which objects of fear and desire (i.e., problems and their solved forms) and means of exercising power are deliberately produced. I refer to these efforts as emotional campaigns. Emotional campaigns are rhetorical attempts to emotionally manage subjects—to direct agency through emotional regulation effects, or through prompting subjects' emotion management efforts. Emotional campaigns affect social practices by transforming individual and collective forms of embodied perception. For example, Nancy Tomes (2002) shows that the mass-mediated manufacture of concern by public health officials, scientific researchers, and health activists and reformers over tuberculosis in the early twentieth century served to popularize the new germ theory, to produce the new authority of the laboratory, and to legitimate reforms dealing with problems of urbanization and industrialization.

Fear campaigns are commonly understood as morally or ideologically suspect operations that make deliberate use of fear in order to achieve a particular end. They are negatively associated with an illegitimate, manipulative use of power as well as with repressive and irrational effects. But given that all forms of emotion management entail the more or less implicit use of fear in order to achieve their ends, the unilateral nature of this view must be called into question. Nor can emotion management per se be thought of as inherently problematic. It is true that the emotion management of others can involve an abusive instrumentalization of these others. It is also true that the emotion management of self can be prompted by the self's abusive instrumentalization by others. On the other hand, emotion management is fundamental to humans' deliberate interactions with other sentient beings.

As morally embodied social beings, we are emotionally managed by others, much as we emotionally manage others and emotionally manage ourselves. The moral exercise of power through emotion management is certainly not always a bad thing; and since we cannot avoid either emotional regulation or emotion management—nor should we wish to—what we ought to question is the manner in which we formulate and solve problems in terms of their effects on the increase or reduction of some agents' capacity to exercise embodied autonomy, or to care for their selves.

I propose a brief critical reading of Brian P. Bloomfield's and Theo Vurdubakis's work on emotion management (1995) as a means of furthering a distinction between two modes in the management of emotions: self-discipline and self-realization. I argue that these modes correspond to distinct rhetorical approaches: campaigns of fear and campaigns of desire. As we shall see, in both types of campaign, fear and desire are produced through the modality of anxiety/interest. However, the underlying structure of this production differs in the one and in the other.

In a short article inspired by the previous work of Michael Mulkay, Bloomfield and Vurdubakis examine how individuals' feelings of either anxiety or expectation toward new reproductive technologies are rhetorically produced. They argue that the rhetoric of fear uses a language of boundary transgression, violation, and disintegration to inhibit the use and development of these technologies, whereas the rhetoric of hope uses a language of therapeutic restoration, enablement, lesser evil, and promise to legitimate and promote them. The rhetorical strategies are also said to feed off one another, with the rhetoric of hope seeking to mitigate the worries produced by the rhetoric of fear, and the rhetoric of fear pointing to powerful popular images of well-intentioned science gone wrong, such as Frankenstein's monster.

In my conceptualization of the dynamics of emotional experience, I maintain that the hope response is constituted both by the painful quest for the identification of a form of in/capacity as a means of moving away from the anticipated pain that constitutes the threat relation and by the pleasurable quest for the identification of a means of power as a means of moving toward the anticipated pleasure that constitutes the promise relation. Thus rather than understanding emotion management campaigns on the basis of fear-based and hope-based rhetorical strategies, I suggest that both are governed by hope. We are better served by speaking of a rhetoric of fear based on the disciplining of desire, and a rhetoric of desire based on its realization.

What one might call the *rhetoric of fear* either invokes a previously constructed association between a force and a painful outcome or produces a new one with the aim of disciplining this outcome. Its purpose is the repression or correction of the desire to produce this painful outcome such that moral self-transformation leads to the repression or correction of an illegitimate or erroneous, danger-producing desire. As such it emphasizes the painful, destructive, and norm-transgressing consequences of the desire it challenges.

What one might call the *rhetoric of desire* either invokes a previously constructed association between a force and a pleasurable outcome or produces a new one with the aim of realizing this outcome. Its purpose is the activation or formation of the desire to produce this pleasurable outcome such that moral self-transformation leads to the activation or formation of a latent or immature, security-producing desire. As such it emphasizes the pleasurable, constructive, and norm-enhancing aspects of the desire it seeks to actualize.

Both types of campaign rely on the production of danger and of the urge to overcome it and implement security. However, the mechanics of the fear campaign revolve around the disciplining of a desire (the desire rhetoric's), constructed as immoral, whereas those of the desire campaign revolve around the overcoming of a danger (the fear rhetoric's) that stands in the way of the realization of a desire constructed as moral. In the first, immoral desire is at stake, whereas in the second, moral desire is at issue. In short, the fear campaign is a response to the desire campaign, and the desire campaign is a response to the fear campaign.

The late eighteenth century, highly popular gothic novels of Ann Radcliffe constitute a good historical example of a fear campaign whose battleground is fiction. Interestingly her novels were themselves the object of both fear and desire campaigns in which Radcliffe herself took position. The interaction between fear and desire campaigns is clearly brought to view in the interplay between Radcliffean gothic texts, the author's view on her own literary production, and critics' view of this production and of the author's view of it.

Radcliffe's novels can be situated in a context in which discipline is an increasingly culturally valued social form in the exercise of power over the self and others, and in which normatively disruptive forms of desire and of pleasure become the object of a growing variety of disciplinary measures. In particular, the so-represented immoral desires and pleasures of women, workers, and children become the increasing focus of fear campaigns in the light of these populations' growing ability to exercise power. Incidentally, gothic novels were avidly consumed by female readers.

Inspired by the writings of philosopher Edmund Burke, Radcliffe (1826) endorsed her own writings in a desire campaign in which she argued that the calculated production of sublime terror, which produces mental pain through sensory deprivation and through the suggestion of physical pain, produced delight once all threats had been lifted, and elevated the soul in the process. In concrete terms, for Radcliffe's heroines, soul elevation or sublimation is the painfully achieved pleasurable result of the repression or correction of immediate, ego-driven desires in favor of the achievement of future, superego-driven ones, causing these narratives that systematically promote self-discipline to belong to the rhetorical genre of the fear campaign.

In short, Radcliffe views the reading of her novels as desirable inasmuch as they activate or form in their readers the desire to self-discipline. Thus while her views on her writings constitute a campaign of desire that encourage the action of novel consumption as a means of self-realization, the novels themselves constitute a campaign of fear, inasmuch as they prompt readers to discipline their existing desire to transgress normative expectations.

In voicing their opposition to Radcliffe's views and to those who praised the genre, many critics waged fear campaigns in which they charged that this literature was responsible for promoting rather than containing immoral desires and urged the public to discipline their irrational urge to consume it.

The children's picture books discussed by Jackie Stallcup (2002) can also be seen to constitute instances of the distinct approaches to emotion management I have been discussing. Stallcup argues that the current cultural disapproval of what she describes as the direct use of fear in the education of children has led to the trend of fear-alleviating books.[5] She explains the difference between earlier and more contemporary children's literature on the basis of the formers' direct production of fear through graphic depictions of the painful consequences of rule violation, which she contrasts with contemporary children's literatures' indirect production of fear through fear-alleviating scenarios. Stallcup highlights that, paradoxically, even the contemporary fear-alleviating books must produce fear before they alleviate it.

The difference between the older and the more recent books discussed by Stallcup can be coherently explained as a difference between two emotion management styles: that of the rhetoric of fear, which corresponds to the older books' approach, and that of the rhetoric of desire, which corresponds to the more recent books' approach. The older books depict the frightening consequences of transgressive action in order to prompt the repression or correction of illegitimate or erroneous desire, as well as the negation of the conduct with which it is associated. Their message is that you must not behave in this way, because it will cause you to experience pain. In contrast, the contemporary books depict the reassuring consequences of ideal action in order to prompt the activation of formation of latent or immature desire, and promote the conduct with which it is associated. Fear results from unrealized desire rather than from the need for discipline. Their message is: You must behave in this way, because it will cause you to experience pleasure. These books make use of the rhetoric of desire.

Both rhetorical strategies produce fear in order to achieve their emotion management goals, and to be effective, neither can entirely free its subjects from the fear experience that prompts either emotion self-management or emotional regulation. The first is tied to an emotional economy of self-discipline, and the second to one of self-realization. As we have seen, the rhetoric of fear and the self-disciplining form of emotion management ground the discipline-based emotional norm structure, whereas the rhetoric of desire and the self-realizing form of emotion management ground the realization-based emotional norm structure.

Both the discipline-based and the realization-based forms in the moral government of conduct through emotion management involve the deliberate production of danger and security. It is simply that in the disciplinary form, the means to overcome the former and achieve the latter involve the repression or correction of immoral (illegitimate or erroneous) desires, whereas in the realization form, the means to overcome the former and achieve the latter entail the activation or formation of moral (latent or immature) desires.

Ultimately, whatever their rhetoric, all the books promote the overcoming of danger and the implementation of security. Whether the suggested means of moving from felt incapacity to felt capacity also promote the exercise of embodied autonomy is another issue. Stallcup argues that the fear-alleviating books do not necessarily promote children's autonomy. For instance, in *Go Away, Big Green Monster!* (1992), while the promotion of play may be subversive of adult authority and of the value of self-control, it is not empowering for the child, who is encouraged to remain in a world of fantasy. Or in *Ghost's Hour,*

Spook's Hour (1987), Stallcup notes that scary images and text are used to prompt children to turn to adults for reassurance. She charges that the book produces a fear of child autonomy that reinforces adult authority and presumably causes the child to repress his or her own desire for autonomy. When the ghost that the child sees ends up being the child's own reflection in the mirror, the child in this story learns that it is ultimately himself or herself that should be feared. On the other hand, Stallcup praises the book *The Boy and the Cloth of Dreams* (1994) for its promotion of child empowerment. In this story, a boy is gently encouraged by his grandmother to confront his fears as he learns to move away from adult security in a quest for maturity. In short, we see that that the books that use a fear-alleviating rhetoric of desire do not necessarily promote children's autonomy, since they can activate and form dependence-producing desires instead.

We cannot assume that those who engage in a campaign of fear promote forms of agency that thwart autonomy, any more than we can assume that those who engage in a campaign of desire promote forms of agency that favor autonomy. These are rhetorical devices that do not in themselves determine whether an action supports embodied autonomy or undermines it. For instance, in her discussion of cosmetic surgery, Sue Tait (2007) points to the discourse of feminists for whom the surgical turn is dangerous, pathologizing, and racist, as well as to the discourse of postfeminists for whom the surgical turn is empowering, self-loving, and a matter of individual choice. Both these discourses produce truths about the conditions and effects of cosmetic surgery, but we need to go beyond discourse[6] to get a sense of how these truths and the very real practices they criticize or endorse affect embodied subjects. Thus, as Tait further argues, while the surgeries may be understood to relieve acute suffering through individual empowerment, they do little to subvert the cultural ideals of femininity and of youthful and Caucasian appearance that produce this suffering in the first place. Moreover, cosmetic surgery needlessly endangers lives, and its representation as a valuable solution to culturally deviant bodies both normalizes this solution and makes its results seem attainable and a matter of individual responsibility.

Lisa Blackman's (2007) analysis of the Hearing Voices Network concretely illustrates a shift from a disciplinary to a realization model in the emotion management of self. It can also help us think further about some of the conditions that favor or hinder the exercise of embodied autonomy. Blackman argues that our fears and anxieties toward those who hear voices arise out of a risk discourse through which disordered subjects' refusal to comply with biomedical treatments is constructed as dangerous or pitiful. Pharmaceutical treatment is required to transform this subject position into a victorious and nonthreatening one. Fear is thus initially produced in the perception of voice-hearers as a problem requiring biomedical attention, and hope is generated through the adoption of a biomedical solution independently of its efficacy. In psychiatry, those who hear voices are expected to resist and deny their voices. In contrast, the Hearing Voices Network is a support group that helps guide and counsel voice-hearers so that they may reconfigure the voices and connect them to their self. As such, they may be said to resist and subvert what Blackman refers to as psychiatry's technology of hope.

Translated into the approach I have been developing, we might argue that in a disciplinary model, voice hearing, and presumably the behavior with which it is associated, is initially constructed and experienced both as an immoral desire or capacity—as an immoral powerfulness—that should be repressed or corrected through psychopharmacological treatment and as a means of moving from the inability to discipline irrational desire to the ability to do so. The Hearing Voices Network subverts this model in favor of a realization one. Rather than construct the problem as one in which voice-hearers should develop the capacity to not hear voices and therefore not behave as if they did, the network reformulates voice hearing and the behavior with which it is associated as one that has to do with an immoral lack of desire or incapacity—as an immoral powerlessness—that should be replaced with an activated or formed desire through self-help therapy, and as means of moving from the inability to realize healthy desire to the ability to do so. Voice hearing is reconfigured so as to constitute a form of unhealthy incapacity to self-realize, instead of a form of irrational incapacity to self-discipline.

In this particular example, the shift from self-discipline to self-realization also involves a shift from vertical to horizontal power relations. In other words, in the older emotion management model, voice-hearers are prompted to manage their irrational desires by way of solutions produced by psychiatric authority, whereas in the newer model, they are prompted to manage their unhealthy desires by way of solutions produced by their peers. This need not be the case, however, as we saw in an earlier discussion of a book for children, in which self-realization was achieved by way of a vertical power structure.

We should also be careful in generalizing from this example the principle that self-realization-based forms of emotion management favor the exercise of embodied autonomy, while self-discipline-based ones hinder it. Both self-discipline and self-realization can help individuals exercise subversive power over the forces that hinder their autonomy. By contrast, particularly when emotional regulation effects or expectations of moral self-transformation are produced with little or no regard for the embodied autonomy of those on the receiving end of this power, the capacity for individual autonomy can be seriously undermined. This is perhaps the most important difference between the moral efforts deployed by the Hearing Voices Network and institutional psychiatry: In the former, those who hear the voices are invited to listen to their embodied selves as a condition of moral self-control, whereas in the latter these embodied selves are ignored and rendered incapable.

Painful feelings are felt incapacities that, together with the felt capacities toward which they tend, found our capacity to exercise subjective and moral forms of embodied autonomy. As such, the goal is certainly not to be rid of fear.[7] Ultimately, fear emotions and their expression in moral suffering are the very basis of our capacity to transform ourselves and the world in ways that promote collective care. As such, it is important that we pay increased attention to and produce nuanced, effective understandings of the subjective and moral forces that undermine care-based (as opposed to destruction-based) processes of social change. While we may trouble the objects to which our fears and desires become attached, and the means through which we implement security, including emotional orientations themselves—for instance, we might trouble the use of inferiority/contempt as means of obtaining social approval, and its expression in racist, homophobic, classist, and sexist emotional orientations—this critical orientation would be impossible without the experiences of moral fear through which we become interested in confronting these associations.

I now propose an analysis of two contemporary emotion management campaigns that are respectively tailored to discipline-based and realization-based approaches.

Contemporary Emotion Management Efforts

I have argued that threat and promise resolution are processes that are moved forward by both pain and pleasure, inasmuch as the painful urge to move away from anticipated pain prompts subjects to search for the means of overcoming danger (i.e., the form of in/capacity), and the pleasurable urge to move toward anticipated pleasure prompts subjects to search for means of implementing security (i.e., the form of power).

I have designated as "discipline based" the emotional economy in which danger is overcome and security implemented based on the principle that irrational desire must be painfully repressed or corrected in the production of moral capacity. I have designated as "realization based" the emotional economy in which danger is overcome and security implemented based on the principle that healthy desire must be pleasurably activated or formed in the production of moral capacity.

Emotional self-discipline is both an expression of conflict (of the conflict between an existing undisciplined desire and the desire to discipline it) and a means of conflict resolution (of the conflict between an undisciplined desire and the normative imperative that it offends). Similarly, emotional self-realization is both an expression of conflict (of the conflict between an absent unrealized desire and the desire to realize it)and a means of conflict resolution (of the conflict between an unrealized desire and the normative ideal of which it falls short).

I shall now produce two contemporary examples of emotional campaigns that respectively make use of discipline-based and realization-based rhetorical strategies. My first example is that of Health Canada's antismoking campaign, while my second is that of a Colgate Total prohygiene campaign.

A series of images that depict the painful consequences of tobacco use, accompanied by captions that deepen the impact[8] of these images, are printed on all cigarette packages legally sold in Canada today.[9] The form of felt in/capacity and the means of power through which to implement security are suggested by the images and outlined in the captions. For instance, an image of yellow teeth and blackened and receding gums, along with a large caption that reads "Cigarettes Cause Mouth Diseases," can be said to trigger[10] moral disgust/purging (the felt in/capacity to avoid further contact with disruptive forces) toward smokers. Should one assimilate this situation[11] from the stance of the responsibilized smoker, one might also experience shame/pride (the felt in/capacity to confront one's self as a disruptive force through self-discipline). Another image is that of a premature infant wearing an oxygen mask, along with the caption "Tobacco Smoke Hurts Babies." In this instance, moral outrage/ vindication (the felt in/capacity to confront another's illegitimate hurting of oneself) might be aroused toward those who smoke, should one assimilate the situation from the responsibilized baby's or the baby's parent's stance, as well as moral guilt/innocence (the felt in/capacity to prevent having to hold oneself responsible for causing another hurt), should one assimilate this situation from the stance of the responsibilized smoker. Finally, the master emotional-norm pair that structures these advertisements may generally be said to be incivility/civility (the felt in/capacity to confront the primitive, animalistic, or bodily impulses that hold one's reason hostage through self-discipline). As such, they may also produce moral experiences of disobedience/obedience (the felt in/capacity to prevent one's failure to comply with imperatives through self-discipline).

In my second example, a Colgate advertisement for Total whitening toothpaste,[12] a young man is seen walking out of a store with a new pack of cigarettes. He proceeds to awkwardly light and begin smoking a cigarette—presumably one of his first. Along with two other slightly older men, including one who is also smoking, he is impressed by an older attractive blonde woman who suggestively walks by them with a cigarette between her fingers. The woman blows a kiss to the young man and he smiles timidly with the force of inexperience. However, when she smiles back, her unattractive blackened teeth produce a shocking contrast with her otherwise desirable appearance. As he sheds his naiveté, the horrified young man promptly puts out his cigarette and a caption states "Image is nothing. Hygiene is everything," followed by an image of Colgate's Total toothpaste and another caption that reads "The true whitening paste." All this occurs to the sound of Bananorama's song "Venus," whose lyrics include "I'm your Venus, I'm your fire, At your desire."

The Colgate Total advertisement represents a personally insecure young man's attraction to an older woman, who eventually and shockingly puts her unsightly smile on display. Should one assimilate this situation from the youth's position, the shocking appearance of the woman's unsightly smile might be said to trigger the moral experience of horror/order (the felt in/capacity to prevent the shocking appearance of disruptive forces), as well as the ensuing feeling of personal insecurity/self-esteem (the felt in/ability to confront one's self as a disruptive force through self-realization). This campaign also plays on the feelings of stigmatization/attractiveness (the felt in/capacity to prevent being marginalized by others as a result of being visibly disturbing), should one assimilate the situation from the woman's position.

Finally, the master emotional-norm pair that structures this advertisement may generally be said to be disempowerment/empowerment (the felt in/capacity to confront the personal shortcomings that compromise one's healthy desire through self-realization). As such, they may also produce the moral experience of incompetence/competence (the felt in/ability to prevent one's failure to measure up to standards through self-realization).

We have seen that the structured emotional arousal produced through the emotional campaign determines the form of the in/capacity as well as the objects of fear and desire to which it is tied. In the moral experience produced by the emotional campaign, the object of fear is made up of both the initial object of fear and the secondary moral object of fear. The problem content is not only that smoking causes mouth disease, that it harms babies, and that it ruins your smile; it is also that smoking makes you feel disgusting and ashamed, that it makes you feel outraged and guilty, and that it makes you feel horrified, personally insecure, and stigmatized. In other words, the moral relationship to problems produced by the emotional campaign involves an initial object of fear as well as the emotionally painful and unsatisfactory, anxious relationship to this object of fear. Similarly, the object of desire or solved form of the object of fear contains the security not only that not smoking prevents mouth disease, that it prevents harming babies, and that not smoking/practicing oral hygiene prevents ruining your smile; it also contains the secure feelings of purging and pride, of vindication and innocence, and of order, self-esteem, and attractiveness.

Both fear and desire campaigns are based on the expectation that the responsibilized or moral anticipation of emotional pain can cause a subject to seek to transform a morally threatening, pain-producing desire, whether this desire is illegitimate, erroneous, latent, or immature, into a morally promising, pleasure-producing desire—that is, a legitimate, a correct, an activated, or a mature desire. The campaigns structure subjects' moral responses. In the fear campaign, self-discipline will constitute the moral means through which morally problematic desire can be acted upon in the implementation of security, while in the desire campaign, self-realization will constitute these means.

In the Health Canada antismoking campaign, the emphasis is placed on the painful, destructive, and norm-breaking consequences of the desire to smoke. Smoking is constituted as a dangerous force—as an irrational desire that ought to be disciplined in the pleasurable implementation of security. In the Colgate prohygiene campaign, the emphasis is placed on the pleasurable, constructive, and norm-enhancing aspects of the desire not to smoke. Not smoking is constituted as a securing force—as a healthy desire that ought to be realized in the pleasurable implementation of security.

Historically, smoking has been structured in various ways by fear and desire campaigns. It has been represented as a solution to any number of problems—as a means of power—much as it has been represented as the cause of various problems—as a cause of incapacity. To get individuals to adopt smoking behaviors, tobacco companies have waged various desire campaigns in which they aimed to produce an association between smoking and security-producing capacities such as emancipation,[13] coolness, proximity with nature, and relaxation. These campaigns focused on the realization of the desire to smoke as a means to experience moral pleasure.

To counteract the desire to smoke engendered by tobacco companies and other forces, the Health Canada antismoking fear campaign aims to produce an association between smoking and danger-producing capacities that are centered on punishment, such as disease production and emotional pain. Its focus is on the repression or correction of the irrational desire to smoke as a means to achieve moral pleasure. In contrast, the Colgate Total prohygiene desire campaign aims to produce an association between not smoking and the practice of personal hygiene and security-producing capacities that are centered on gratification, such as health production and emotional pleasure. It focuses on the activation or the formation of the desire not to smoke/ to practice personal hygiene as a means to achieve moral pleasure.

In short, tobacco companies have constructed smoking as a desirable solution to a number of problems. As such, their representations of smoking constitute desire campaigns that seek to activate or form the desire to smoke as a form of capacity. The Health Canada campaign, on the other hand, constructs smoking as the undesirable cause of a number of problems. As such, its representations of smoking constitute a fear campaign that seeks to repress or correct the desire to smoke as a form of incapacity. Finally, the Colgate Total prohygiene campaign constructs not smoking in its association with the practice of hygiene as a desirable solution to a number of problems. As such, its representations of not smoking constitute a desire campaign that seeks to activate or form the desire to practice hygiene in replacement of the desire to smoke.

We have seen that the fear campaign is a response to the desire campaign, and the desire campaign a response to the fear campaign. Whether through the rhetoric of fear or the rhetoric of desire, the emotional campaign seeks to manage agents' fear and desire in order to achieve certain ends. In the final chapter, I explore the manner in which the form of emotion management—whether self-discipline or self-realization—can itself be the object of an emotional campaign.

C H A P T E R   8

Analyzing Self-Discipline and Self-Realization

From the Fear of Desire to the Fear of Fear

So far I have argued that moral forces can prompt subjects to experience relational threats, thereby motivating them to look for solutions to these threats by way of the experience of relational promise. The hedonic power deployed in emotion management efforts achieves its effects of emotional socialization through making use of individuals' propensity to avoid pain and seek pleasure. But if we follow this logic, how might we explain situations where subjects choose to experience relational threats, and therefore seek out the experience of pain rather than its avoidance?

The efficiency of emotional campaigns relies on their arousal of the threat of pain as caused by a hope-based lack that one can remedy. They engender fear and desire and provide the moral means through which danger can be overcome and security implemented. They also produce what appears to be a simple choice between pain and pleasure. But what if the moral means through which security is implemented and pleasure achieved are painful, to the extent that they involve the painful problematization of an existing desire? How might we explain individuals' deliberate involvement in experiences of relational threat? More concretely, how might we understand that an individual who enjoys smoking might choose to experience the relational threat produced by smoking cessation?

It may simply be that the power exercised by smoking as an object of fear becomes greater than that exercised by it as an object of desire. Smoking, in other words, becomes a greater moral source of problems than of solutions, of moral pain than of moral pleasure, such that not smoking becomes a pleasurable solution to the problem of smoking, bearing in mind that normative forces, including biographical ones, help determine whether or not smoking is experienced as more of a solution or more of a problem.

The desire to smoke or not to smoke is therefore based on individuals' capacity to exercise two forms of desire: one that is governed by the anticipation of pleasure and one that is governed by the anticipation of the anticipation of pleasure. The form taken by one or the other of these desires does not pertain to the immediate or delayed nature of the pleasure one anticipates, since desire is by its very nature a pleasurable anticipation of pleasure, and since the pleasure involved in the anticipation of a pleasure that might be realized in the distant future can in principle be just as intense as a pleasure that might be realized in a more immediate one. The quality of this distinction must therefore lie elsewhere, and I suggest that it lies in individuals' capacity to manage experiences of moral pain and of moral pleasure through the exercise of self-objectification, which forms the basis of moral autonomy.

The absence or presence of the ability to objectify one's emotional experiences corresponds to the distinction I made earlier between self-involved and other-directed forms of autonomy, with the latter entailing the ability to experience patterns of pain and pleasure. The more a desire impedes a subject's ability to avoid objectified experiences of pain or to increase objectified experiences of pleasure, the more it becomes morally compelling for this subject to transform this desire in favor of another through an emotion management effort directed toward its self (i.e., through emotional self-control). Emotional campaigns are one among other forces that can contribute to subjects' view of a particular desire as dangerous, thereby promoting the exercise of moral self-control as a means to exercise power over it.

While discipline-based and realization-based orientations to the self both involve the experience of pain and pleasure and of fear and of desire, there is an important difference between them. Like self-realization, self-discipline involves the moral self's exercise of power over the subjective self as a means of moving from pain to pleasure. However, where self-activation and self-formation allow for the expression of the subjective self's will to act through the activation or formation of a new desire, self-repression and self-correction do not.

In self-realization there is a solution to the subjective self's inability to express its initial desire in the form of an alternative emotional experience, such that it is able to experience the freedom of having access to means through which to move away from pain and toward pleasure. On the other hand, in self-discipline there is no solution to the subjective self's inability to express its initial desire since it is denied through either its repression or its correction, such that it is caught in unfreedom. In Freudian terms, self-realization allows for the sublimation of the subjective self's desire—its expression in a manner that is acceptable to the moral self—whereas self-discipline does not.

While the moral self's self-repression and self-correction efforts require energy in order to keep the subjective self's panic/excitement-driven desire to exercise power in check, self-activation and self-formation require energy in the moral self's search for an alternative emotional experience for the subjective self. It is likely that whether or not the stick or the carrot is of greater appeal will depend on the self's greater facility of access to the one or the other of these approaches—partly as a result of habit, but also as a consequence of other normative factors, such as the cultural saliency of certain means in the exercise of power and the degree to which social forces promote or demote discipline-based or realization-based approaches. However, all things being equal, which they can only be in theory, the self-realization approach is probably a more effective means of exercising power over the self in the long term, since it is associated with pleasure rather than with pain, and since, once self-realization measures have been implemented, no further energy is required in keeping the subjective self's desire in check.

To go back to an example used earlier involving angry responses to angry clients (in Chapter 6), while both self-discipline and self-realization morally resolve the problem of responding through angry behavior to angry clients, they do not do so in the same manner. On the one hand, self-repression and self-correction involve a change in the subjective self's means of expressing anger (i.e., its means of implementing assertiveness-driven security), through either the repression or the correction of grimacing and shouting, such that the subjective self's spontaneous or habitual desire to implement security through grimacing or shouting is denied. On the other hand, self-activation and self-formation involve a change in the emotional-norm pair being experienced by the subjective self, through either the activation or the formation of an alternative desire, such as relaxation or patience, such that the subjective self's initial desire to implement security through grimacing or shouting is no longer relevant and need not be denied. Thus one might say that in self-discipline, the moral self is satisfied while the subjective self remains frustrated, whereas in self-realization, both the subjective and the moral self are ultimately satisfied. In the first case pain lingers while in the second it is effaced.

Of course, responding through self-realization to anger does not change the fact that one will have other opportunities for getting angry and will continue to have to deploy moral self-control efforts in the face of this dangerous anger (i.e., unless a new panic/excitement-driven means of dealing with anger develops that no longer produces the need to exercise moral self-control). However, whether one responds through self-realization or through self-discipline does change the dynamics of pain and pleasure involved in one's dealings with anger, should the manner in which one implements assertiveness-driven security constitute a problem.

Discipline-based and realization-based emotional economies each constitute a distinct approach to threat and promise resolution. The first entails a form of sadomasochistic self-care, where moral self-punishment or going against one's subjective self is a means of reducing one's moral pain and of increasing one's moral pleasure. The second entails a form of epicurean self-care, where moral self-gratification or going with one's subjective self is a means of reducing one's moral pain and of increasing one's moral pleasure.

In self-discipline, the subjective self's lingering pain acts as a solution to the moral self's pain and therefore comes to signify pleasure through its promise. In self-realization, the subjective self's effaced pain acts as a solution to the moral self's pain and therefore comes to signify pleasure through its promise.

The discipline-based emotion structure corresponds to the "no pain, no gain" principle, where the painful repression or correction of immoral desire is the means to engender the pleasurable anticipation of the resolution of the problem it poses, or where short-term pain and deprivation are believed to bring on long-term pleasure and fulfillment. Disciplinary modes of emotion management produce fear in the goal of repressing or correcting the desires that lead to normatively threatening, transgressive forms of agency. The transformation of subjectivity produced through discipline is based on the notion that desires that conflict with dominant social and cultural norms result from a lack of repression and correction, and perhaps also from an excess of activation and formation. Subjects in whom these desires are shown to be present are conceived of as dangerous, thereby prompting their repression and correction as a condition of the redirection of their agency in a normatively appropriate direction. Dangerous capacities must be transformed into incapacities for security to arise.

The realization-based emotion structure corresponds to the "no pleasure, no gain" principle, where the pleasurable activation or formation of moral desire is the means to engender the pleasurable anticipation of the problem it resolves, or where short-term pleasure and fulfillment are believed to bring on long-term pleasure and fulfillment. Realization modes of emotion management produce fear in the goal of activating or forming the desires that lead to normatively promising, ideal forms of agency. The transformation of subjectivity produced through realization is based upon the notion that desires that conflict with dominant social and cultural norms result from an excess of repression and correction, and perhaps also from a lack of activation and formation. Subjects in whom these desires are shown to be absent are conceived of as dangerous, thereby prompting their activation and formation as a condition of the redirection of their agency in a normatively appropriate direction. Dangerous incapacities must be transformed into capacities for security to arise.

The discipline-based fear and desire structure is one in which immoral desire is the cause of danger. The *fear of desire*—the relational threat produced by the perception that one lacks the ability to repress or correct immoral desires—is deployed in the formation of dominant emotional norms. For instance, this fear is expressed in the being emotional/rational emotional-norm pair, which names the felt in/capacity to prevent the hold that one's illegitimate or incorrect desires have over one's reason.[1] Its main effect is to promote emotional norms that contain or become attached to self-discipline as a solution to danger. We might call the type of capacity that grows out of this desire *moral self-discipline*, where the solution to one's moral pain involves the repression or correction of immoral, irrational desire.

Emotion management efforts that follow this logic might involve the painful and abrupt curtailment of urges that are perceived as immoral and as dangerous forms of agency. As such, the fear of desire is also a fear of the self's excessive freedom, gratification, and activity. In spite of the increasing dominance of the logic of the fear of fear that is tied to an emotional economy of self-realization, the fear of desire that informs emotion management efforts is still so common in contemporary Western culture that it is not difficult to come up with examples. For instance, one might deny oneself foods one enjoys as a means of achieving a healthy weight, or cease to smoke based on the method described as "quitting cold turkey." In both instances, subjects are motivated by the perception that their illegitimate or erroneous desires increase their moral pain and decrease their moral pleasure, such that their painful repression or correction is warranted.

Alongside the fear of desire, a fear that informs a number of emotional-norm pairs in liberal societies' discipline-based fear and desire structure is the *fear of pleasure*. This is the relational threat produced by the perception that one lacks the ability to discipline one's immoral desires as a result of the pleasure they generate. One must therefore produce the desire to repress or correct one's immoral desires in spite of the dangerous pleasure they engender. We might call the type of capacity that grows out of this desire *moral weaning*, where the implementation of security involves the graduated repression or correction of immoral desire as a counteraction to the directional force exerted by the promise of pleasure.

The progressive disciplining of urges that are perceived as immoral through moral weaning is based on the principle that the desirability of pleasure must be counteracted through a reduction in the undesirability of pain. The idea, according to which too much pain is counterproductive, is rendered in the expressions "don't be so hard on yourself" and "give yourself a chance." An example of moral weaning is the practice of smoking cessation based on the perspective that it is a dangerously pleasurable addiction from which one should be progressively released through the use of nicotine gums or patches.

Unlike the transformation of subjectivity engendered by the disciplining of the self, and while it can by no means be said to supplant disciplinary processes in the advanced liberal context, the transformation of the self produced through the realization of the self does not involve the repression or correction of immoral desire in an effort to negate existing desire. It does not revolve around a fear of immoral desire—a fear of threatening populations' capacity for directive action that must be squashed. Rather, it revolves around a fear of the absence of moral desire—a fear of threatening populations' incapacity for directive action (for the exercise of power) that must be produced. Realization-based means in the exercise of power involve a *fear of fear* rather than a *fear of desire*.

The realization-based fear and desire structure is one in which the absence of moral desire is the cause of danger. The *fear of fear*—the relational threat produced by the perception that one lacks the ability to activate or form moral desires—is deployed in the formation of dominant emotional norms. For instance, this fear is expressed in the feelings of being repressed/liberated, which name the in/capacity to prevent one's healthy impulses from being blocked or impaired by unhealthy forces.[2] Its main effect is to promote emotional norms that contain or become attached to self-realization as a solution to danger. We might call the type of capacity that grows out of this desire *moral self-realization*, where the solution to one's moral pain involves the activation or formation of moral, healthy desire.

Emotion management efforts that follow this logic often involve the pleasurable expression of urges that are perceived as moral and as security-producing forms of agency. The fear of fear is an increasingly common trigger of emotion management efforts in contemporary Western culture. For instance, one might focus on transforming one's relationship to eating or smoking through feelings associated with the practice of a healthy lifestyle. This perspective is rendered in expressions such as "feel the fear and do it anyway"[3] and "think positive." Here subjects believe that their latent or immature desires increase their moral pain and decrease their moral pleasure, such that their pleasurable activation or formation is warranted.

The adventure therapy workshops discussed by Lori Holyfield (1997) in her ethnography of such meetings constitute another interesting example of the manner in which emotion management can be achieved through moral self-realization. The workshops aim to improve such things as self-esteem, cooperation, personal responsibility, and trust through the production of structured experiences of danger. Facilitators suggest new, positive means of interpreting the unpleasant sensations associated with risk taking such that the individuals may appropriate them in their self-realization after the fear experience takes place. In other words, the unpleasant sensations that accompany the relational threats generated by the workshops are transformed through later recall and associated with a pleasurable sense of accomplishment, honesty, courage, and fun. Emotional transformation is achieved by soliciting the experience of painful emotions and by encouraging participants to reinterpret these positively, in a process of self-formation within which they become desirable.

Alongside the fear of fear, a fear that informs a number of emotional-norm pairs in late liberal societies' realization-based fear and desire structure is the *fear of pain*. This is the relational threat produced by the perception that one lacks the ability to realize one's moral desires as a result of the dangerous pain this process generates. One must therefore produce the desire to activate or form one's moral desires in spite of the dangerous pain this effort engenders. We might call the type of capacity that grows out of this desire *moral compensation*, where the implementation of security involves the facilitated activation or formation of moral desire to counteract the directional force exerted by the promise of pain.

Compensating for the pain produced by the realization of moral desire is based on the principle that the desirability of pleasure is a means to offset the undesirability of pain. The idea according to which pain can be erased if it is counterbalanced by pleasure is rendered in numerous contemporary forms of amusement or entertainment-based learning and is at the heart of the "infotainment" industry. An example of moral compensation is the practice of smoking cessation based on the perspective that it is a pleasurable habit for whose loss one must compensate with rewards such as gifts, money, food indulgences, and trips.

A recent advertisement for Cadbury's Moments[4] is a good example of the enactment of moral compensation. A young woman is seen to be enjoying a chocolate bar to the sound of soothing spa music when she is violently interrupted by an older authoritative woman's obviously painful removal of the hair on her legs by waxing. The discomfort quickly moves to the background as our victim is seen to make up for the pain through her enjoyment of the chocolate. The following words accompany the visuals, confirming the compensatory nature of the pleasure produced by the chocolate: "Introducing new Cadbury Moments. It doesn't have to be a perfect moment...[sound of stripping and cries of pain]...to indulge in new Cadbury Moments."

We now better understand how it is that we might take pleasure in and desire fear experiences like those brought on by bungee jumping, horror movie watching, or painful beauty rituals, or how we might feel pained by and fear desire experiences like those brought on by cigarette smoking, having sex, or eating chocolate cake. These can constitute means through which forms of agency that have been previously construed as painful or pleasurable are morally acted upon in the resolution of some problem, in a self-controlled effort to move away from pain and toward pleasure.

Social groups can be differentiated on the basis of whether they predominantly promote self-discipline or self-realization in the resolution of moral problems. I have suggested that some emotional economies are characterized by the greater promotion of opportunities for exercising self-discipline, where subjects' relationship to norms is governed by a logic of compliance with a command (a logic of transgression, of law and order, and of immoral powerfulness), while others are characterized by the greater promotion of opportunities for exercising self-realization, where subjects' relationship to norms is governed by a logic of favorable measurement to an ideal (a logic of inadequacy, of grades and examinations, and of immoral powerlessness).

Discipline-based societies tend to vilify desire as a solution to the problem of excessive power or as a form of immoral capacity, while realization-based societies tend to vilify fear as a solution to the problem of a lack of power or as a form of immoral incapacity. The first will promote forms of moral autonomy that are based on the notion that one lacks the capacity to repress or correct one's irrational desires, whereas the second will promote forms of moral autonomy that are based on the notion that one lacks the capacity to activate or form one's healthy desires.

However, even though the specific modalities of agency that are produced through the transformation of subjectivity should be carefully considered and differentiated, the manner in which they are embodied is probably not so neatly defined. In practice, many desires—such as the desire that governs nonsmoking in former smokers—are probably structured by a mixture of the sustained self-repression of a desire (in this example, to smoke) and of the self-formation of a desire (to practice a healthy lifestyle). Agential change may be achieved through either one measure or a combination of measures that belong to moral self-discipline or to moral self-realization.

Emotion management is not simply something that is done to subjects, but rather something that is achieved through subjects' agency or emotion-based capacity for action, on the basis of a hedonic exercise of power that acts upon this capacity. Whether they are engendered by way of emotional norms tied to self-discipline or to self-realization, the power effects of emotion management are accomplished through the directional effects of subjectivity rather than through physical force. Subjects are enlisted in the subjective regulation and moral management of their selves through the embodiment of objects of fear and desire and of the emotional norms, signs of danger and security, and means of power to which they are attached.

The transformation of subjectivity through emotion management is by no means a practice that is unique to liberal and late liberal societies. However, the increasing call for the use of emotion management during various periods in the development of liberal societies testifies to the growing awareness of their utility in the exercise of power (de Courville Nicol, 2004). Highly rationalized forms of emotion management are without a doubt a central means through which agency is acted upon today. As such, particular attention should be paid to the mass media as a privileged means in popular culture's contemporary exercise of hedonic power. I now consider a contemporary body of analyses that have in common a fear of irrational fear.

CULTURE-OF-FEAR CRITICS

The distinction between rational and irrational fear is a central concern of contemporary culture-of-fear analysts, who focus on the misalignment between lay agents' fears and the probability of harmful consequences as objectively determined by risk experts, on the causes of this misalignment, and on the harmful consequences of this misalignment. In the exemplar *American Fear*, Peter N. Stearns (2006) examines some of the ways in which fear causes Americans to worsen their quality of life, distort facts, trump rational decision making, and focus on the insignificant. Stearns argues that Americans' attempt to bypass fear increases their fearfulness and their vulnerability to agencies that seek to profit from their anxieties about fear. Stearns worries that fear will get the better of reason.

Like many other culture-of-fear analysts, Stearns seeks to explain why individuals in a society that is more secure than ever in terms of reduced rates of disease and of premature mortality are so afraid. Factors he invokes in order to explain Americans' generalized anxiety include an overprotective approach to childrearing promoted by contemporary experts' view that exposing children to fearful experiences is traumatizing, the media's increased use of and promotion of fear, and an increased sensitivity to foreign threats. According to Stearns, Americans fear excessively because their culture is one in which fear is unfamiliar and cause for resentment. As the evolution of the popular children's series *Curious George* demonstrates, children are no longer taught to react with nonchalance to fear, but rather to seek reassurance and support when experiencing an emotion that is not only painful but also perceived as illegitimate. As a consequence, maintains Stearns, children are taught to remove or punish the sources of fear. In essence, Stearns argues that children's lack of exposure to experiences of fear produces the inability to cope with fearful situations once they become adults and also makes them feel resentful when they experience these.

In a chapter titled "Fearing Fear: A New Socialization," Stearns explains how a contemporary fear of fear came into being through major transformations in American culture from the 1920s onward, propelled by psychological forms of expertise. These include a shift from the concern for physical well-being to a concern for emotional well-being in childrearing, and the concern that fear is bad for the body and inhibits reason. Thus Stearns contrasts a Victorian approach to fear, seen as an opportunity for virtuous self-mastery and courage, with its post-Victorian counterpart, in which fear is a damaging emotion that ought to be prevented if possible, and if not, expressed rather than repressed and diminished through reassurance. Stearns notes both the lifting of a taboo in the acknowledgment that one is fearful as well as social transformations in (particularly male) subjects' moral relationship to fear: "Indeed, current standards are particularly striking in their contrast with nineteenth-century norms, which quite explicitly called on Americans, or at least American men, to face fear directly and stare it down" (63).

Stearns's approach is common in a wide body of literature on irrational fear and its morally or ideologically suspect effects.[5] My aim is not to dismiss all the literature or the nuances within it that we might brand as "culture-of-fear critique." However, in what follows I make two key points in an effort to get beyond some of the shortcomings of this approach. First, I argue that fear's role in the exercise of subjectively and morally embodied autonomy, as well as its tie to social norms, is not adequately accounted for in this perspective due to an overly narrow understanding of danger as the risk of physical harm that is objectively determined by experts. Second, I argue that the culture-of-fear perspective is itself a powerful rhetoric that ought to be situated within a larger socially normative context.

The pool of potential dangers on whose basis we might feel threatened is infinite, since there are an infinite number of ways in which various forces can be associated with a painful outcome to constitute problems, or objects of fear. Similarly, the pool of potential emotional orientations to those dangers, of potential signs that trigger their experience, and of potential means of power through which to implement security, is also endless. It does not follow that the forces that we consider to be dangerous emerge arbitrarily. Morally normative, socially produced, culturally coherent, and politically motivated understandings of what constitutes danger are among the forces that have a significant impact on agents' experiences of danger, whether subjective (where the cause is felt to be external) or moral (where the cause is felt to be internal, or the agent's responsibility).

Culture-of-fear theorists urge subjects to consider the irrational basis of their desire to act in various ways based on their incorrect assessment of risk. Danger is equated with the risk of physical harm as determined by experts with little consideration for local and biographical context, or for underlying moral concerns. The culture-of-fear approach to danger can be contrasted with the social constructionist approach, which emphasizes that laypeople and experts do not necessarily share the same criteria for measuring risk or for determining what is harmful. In explaining the social constructionist approach to risk, Deborah Lupton (1999) writes, "If a 'risk' is understood as a product of perception and cultural understanding, then to draw a distinction between 'real' risks (as measured and identified by 'experts') and 'false' risks (as perceived by members of the public) is irrelevant. Both perspectives are describing forms of risk, and both lead to certain actions" (33).

As Lupton further argues, technico-scientific approaches to risk fail to consider their own biases in the construction of danger. She points to the work of Mary Douglas (1992), who deplores the condescension with which the cognitive sciences make sense of individuals' risk taking, as well as its pathologization of individual behavior through a failure to consider the sociological, cultural, and ethical considerations that govern perception. As Douglas argues, the cognitive-science approach to risk is based on an atomistic model in which individuals, governed by their brains and irrespective of the cultural forces that shape their perception, foolishly miscalculate harm outcomes. I have defined risk/precaution as the felt in/capacity to prevent a harmful outcome based on a calculation of its probabilities, whatever the form taken by this estimation, in order to include within the experience of risk all estimations of danger (i.e., not just those expert-based anticipations of physical harm), and all the actions that might serve in the precaution-driven implementation of security (i.e., not just those expert-determined means of preventing physical harm).

With this in mind, I suggest an alternative reading of the social transformation identified by Stearns: as a shift from the prevention-based fear of desire, in an emotional economy centered on discipline, where the object of fear is the immoral capacity to transgress and disobey, to the prevention-based fear of fear, in an emotional economy centered on realization, where the object of fear is the immoral incapacity to perform and compete. In the former, the emotion management of self (and therefore the emotion management of others, including children) involves the repression or correction of illegitimate or erroneous desires through the worry/safety-based prevention of the hold that one's illegitimate or incorrect desires have over one's reason (i.e., being emotional/being rational), while in the latter, it involves the activation or formation of latent or immature desires through the worry/safety-based prevention of the blocking or impairing of healthy impulses (i.e., being repressed/being liberated). Thus the objects of fear and the emotional orientation through which they are feared have changed, with the modern fear of irrational desire that ought to be prevented giving way to the late modern fear of unhealthy fear that ought to be prevented.

The culture of fear, then, can be thought of as the expression of a social order in which the prevention-based worries of the self-realization society have replaced the prevention-based worries of the self-discipline society. In late modern society, the quest for the implementation of safety through health has replaced (or at the very least is in serious competition with) the quest for the implementation of safety through reason.

Inasmuch as emotions ground our ability to exercise embodied autonomy, we must historicize and place in their larger normative contexts the various ways in which and for whom fear and desire form moral problems. Culture-of-fear critics' problem with fear is best understood as a campaign of fear based on a fear of desire—as a problem with illegitimate or incorrect desires and capable outcomes. Irrational fears promote irrational desires that must be repressed or corrected through self-discipline in order to prevent immoral capacity. The modern perspective of culture-of-fear critics was dominant in the self-discipline society and is the basis of a nostalgic critique of the society that follows it (i.e., where nostalgia/utopia is the felt in/ capacity to confront one's failure to move beyond one's longing for past circumstances through the longing for new ones) and that forms its antithesis. As such, it can be distinguished from and constitutes a critique of the late modern normative context.

In contrast with the modern perspective of culture-of-fear critics, the late modern contemporary culture's problem with fear is best understood as a fear of fear[6]—as a problem with unactivated or unformed desires and incapable outcomes. Unhealthy fears promote unhealthy desires that must be activated or formed through self-realization to prevent immoral incapacity. The late modern perspective of healthism[7] is dominant in the self-realization society and is the basis of a dystopian critique of the society that precedes it (i.e., where dystopia/revolution is the felt in/capacity to confront one's failure to move beyond one's rejection of past circumstances through the creation of new ones) and that forms its antithesis. As such, it can be distinguished from and constitutes a critique of the modern normative context.

Thus while, in the modern emotional economy, illegitimate or incorrect forms of desire are emotionally managed through experiences that include being emotional/being rational (the felt in/ability to prevent the hold that one's illegitimate or incorrect desires have over one's reason), incivility/civility (the felt in/capacity to confront the primitive, animalistic, or bodily impulses that hold one's reason hostage through self-discipline), and impulsivity/self-restraint (the felt in/capacity to confront one's irrational failure to delay gratification), in the late modern emotional economy, blocked or impaired forms of desire are emotionally managed through experiences that include being repressed/being liberated (the felt in/ability to prevent one's healthy impulses from being blocked or impaired by unhealthy forces), disempowerment/empowerment (the felt in/ability to confront the personal shortcomings that compromise one's healthy desire through self-realization), and passivity/proactivity (the felt in/ability to confront one's unhealthy failure to take command of one's life).

Culture-of-fear theorists express a desire for a discipline-based emotional economy and its fear of desire, in which transgressive forms of agency should be repressed or corrected, and express a fear of a realization-based emotional economy and its fear of fear, in which adequate forms of agency should be activated or formed. Contemporary healthism expresses a desire for a realization-based emotional economy and its fear of fear, in which inadequate forms of agency should be activated or formed, and a fear of a discipline-based emotional economy and its fear of desire, in which transgressive forms of agency should be repressed or corrected.

In a word, two logics—the one modern, the other late modern—may be said to conflict in contemporary culture. The first is oriented toward the disciplining of irrational desire, and the other toward the realization of healthy desire. One's response to contemporary anxieties is likely to shift depending on whether one follows one or the other of these logics (e.g., Is it irrational or unhealthy to fear global warming or is it healthy or rational to do so? Is it irrational or unhealthy to fear one's inability to speak in public or is it rational or healthy to do so? Is it irrational or unhealthy to fear one's consumption of red meat or is it rational or healthy to do so?).

Whether one tends to follow one or the other of these logics is likely to be tied to one's social position (e.g., age, gender, economic status, health status) and to the cultural forces with which one interacts. If one were to adopt a disciplinary approach in the attempt to produce a moral or satisfactory answer to these questions, one would be likely to invoke scientifically established facts in order to separate subjective, imaginary dangers from objective, real ones. One would also be likely to associate danger with the risk of physical harm. If, on the other hand, one were to adopt a realization approach, one would be likely to invoke ideals or standards in order to separate unacceptable, abnormal dangers from acceptable, normal ones. One would also be likely to associate danger with the risk of psychological harm.

The experience of danger is the quality of an embodied relation to forces that is not based on the inherent dangerousness of these forces, even though these may be experienced as such. In this way, the distinction that is sometimes made between subjective or imaginary danger and objective or real danger must be thought of as a moral distinction carried by social norms that has emotion management effects. In other words, this distinction determines what subjects ought to or ought not to fear and therefore promotes agents' moral responsibility toward the transformation of irrational fears into non-fears, or of the absence of rational fears into their existence.

Subjective danger is a concept that is generally used to designate a perception of danger that is governed by subjective impressions or moral convictions rather than by scientific facts. By contrast, objective danger is a concept that is used to designate a perception of danger that is governed by scientific facts rather than by subjective impressions or moral convictions. The notion of objective danger usually involves a further commitment to the principle that a force is dangerous because it is likely to bring about physical harm. The determination of "objective danger" therefore rests upon a value commitment to scientifically established truth and statistical information concerning the probability of physical harm outcomes. As such, it is based on morally normative social expectations.

While it is usual to view the anticipated pain caused by physical harm as a legitimate form of danger, it has become increasingly common to view the anticipated pain caused by psychological harm as an equally legitimate form of danger. In the contemporary context, these competing forms in morally normative understandings of danger respectively correspond to a reason-based commitment to self-discipline and a health-based commitment to self-realization.

Within the disciplinary emotional economy, the distinction between subjective and objective danger is made as a means of differentiating between inaccurate and accurate, or irrational and irrational evaluations of anticipated pain. Subjective or imaginary dangers designate expressions of danger that fail to conform to morally normative social expectations regarding the accurate nature of danger, while objective or real dangers designate their conformity to moral norms regarding the accurate nature of danger. Subjective dangers are construed as those dangers that result from an inaccurate understanding of reality (i.e., dangers that result from irrational fears) and that induce immoral consequences, whereas objective dangers are construed as those dangers that result from an accurate understanding of reality (i.e., dangers that result from rational fears) and that induce moral consequences through moral capacity.

Here, dangers are understood as harmful physical consequences. The solution to one's inability to form a moral, rational understanding of danger is self-discipline (e.g., If I fear flying where flying is associated with a low risk of physical harm, I ought to repress or correct my desire not to fly; if I am a child who fears the loss of my teddy bear where this loss is associated with a low risk of physical harm, I ought to repress or correct my desire not to part with my teddy bear; if I am someone who fears nuclear disaster where the statistical unlikelihood of such a disaster is associated with a low risk of physical harm, I ought to repress or correct my desire to reject the use of nuclear energy).

Within the realization emotional economy, the distinction between unacceptable and acceptable danger is made as a means of differentiating between nonstandard and standard, or unhealthy and healthy, forms of anticipated pain. Unacceptable or abnormal dangers designate expressions of danger that fail to conform to morally normative social expectations regarding the standard forms of danger, while acceptable or normal dangers designate their conformity to moral norms regarding the standard forms of danger. Unacceptable dangers are construed as those dangers that result from nonstandard forms of anticipated pain (i.e., dangers that result from unhealthy fears) and that induce immoral consequences, whereas acceptable dangers are construed as those dangers that result from standard forms of anticipated pain (i.e., dangers that result from healthy fears) and that induce moral consequences through moral capacity.

Here, dangers are understood as harmful psychological consequences. The solution to one's inability to form a moral, healthy understanding of danger is self-realization (e.g., If I fear flying where flying is associated with a high degree of psychological distress, I ought not to repress or correct my desire not to fly, but I may activate or form my desire to fly, should cultural standards deem this fear to be unhealthy and this danger acceptable or normal; if I am a child who fears the loss of my teddy bear where this loss is associated with a high risk of psychological harm, I ought not to repress or correct my desire to hang on to my teddy bear, but I may activate or form my desire to part with my teddy bear if the standards of my culture deem this fear to be unhealthy; if I am someone who fears nuclear disaster where the slightest possibility of such as a disaster is associated with psychological distress, I ought not to repress or correct my desire to reject the use of nuclear energy, but rather acknowledge my fear to be a healthy one, should the standards of my culture deem this danger to be unacceptable or abnormal).

It is useful, in the course of exercising one's autonomy, to fear some forces and not others, and it is also useful to be able to question which forces ought to or ought not to be feared. In many ways, political struggle is a struggle over who ought to fear what and on what grounds. In the terms of embodied in/capacity theory, moral perceptions of danger emerge through agents' interactions with social norms, such that the matter of their accuracy or acceptability is ultimately value driven and tied to particular emotional economies. In a word, since the experience of both danger and moral danger is affected by subjects' interactions with morally normative social expectations, it matters that some perceptions of danger are promoted while others are discouraged.

Culture-of-fear critics' focus on the irrational conditions and effects of fear is based on a narrow view of fear and danger as governed by a logic of objectively determinable risks and physical harms. This leads to a neglect of the manner in which a whole range of emotions are constituted, triggered, and resolved in ways that are tied to culturally coherent, socially expected, and politically motivated forms of agency in the exercise of both subjective and moral forms of autonomy. And while the health-based orientation to fear can be shown to have various problematic conditions and effects, this is also true of the reason-based orientation. It is not as if one's rational dealings with objects of fear cannot also rest upon and produce morally dubious or ideologically suspect conditions and effects. There is certainly no shortage of atrocities committed in the name of science, or of social injustices big and small provided legitimacy with facts.

Moreover, inasmuch as there is a long tradition of associating irrational emotions or emotions as irrational forces with the body and femininity (Petersen, 2004; Lutz, 1996; Hochschild, 1983), we should also attend to the gender politics of culture-of-fear theorizing. When considering the social norms that govern emotional expression, being emotional is a felt incapacity that has been traditionally associated with the feminine, while being rational is a felt capacity that has been traditionally associated with the masculine (more precisely, being rational is not usually understood as an emotional state). It is also worth highlighting that being afraid—being terrified, being phobic,[8] being worried[9]—is a felt incapacity that often designates the feminine, whereas being unafraid—being courageous, being able to escape, being safe—is a felt capacity that often designates the masculine.

On the other hand, in contemporary culture, being repressed is a felt incapacity that connotes the masculine, whereas its pair, being liberated, connotes the feminine. In her report on the findings of her ethnography of dominant perceptions of emotions, Lupton (1998) notes that emotional expression (as opposed to repression) is evaluated positively by participants and is associated with health, with women, and with subjects of "Latin, Mediterranean or Middle Eastern descent" (55). Men under the age of forty viewed being more emotional as a form of capacity and also viewed emotional expression as pleasurable. Also included in the findings of Lupton's ethnography of contemporary subjects (1998, 56) is participants' view that anger is more likely to produce shame in women, whereas weeping is more likely to produce shame in men. If we take it that anger connotes aggression and masculine capacity, whereas weeping connotes worry and feminine incapacity, these results suggest that confrontation-oriented emotions signify the masculine, whereas prevention-oriented emotions signify the feminine, and that the latter, as well as a certain notion of emotional expression, have gained in cultural favor.

In this sense, inasmuch as it is the rise in irrational worry (i.e., the irrational desire for safety from subjective or imaginary dangers) in its opposition to the decline of rational courage (i.e., the rational fear of objective or real dangers that produce terror) that forms the object of Stearns's and other culture-of-fear analysts' worry, part of what is being feared by these theorists may be the feminization of agency, or feminine forms of desire and capacity. The culture of fear that culture-of-fear analysts fear involves more than a fear of the spread of fear; it involves the fear of the spread of particular forms of fear as the grounds for desire forms tied to actions they perceive as immoral.

While we cannot and would not want to get rid of the experience of fear in general, we can and might want to get rid of or transform some of its specific modalities. To this end, we must increase our understanding of the embodied, relational, and interactive particular-ities of fear and desire experiences: what we fear and desire, how we fear and desire, how we come to fear and desire, how we overcome danger and implement security, and when and why we are sometimes unable do so. Gaining a better understanding of how mass medi-atized forces of emotion management interact with contemporary selves in ways that promote or challenge the exercise of embodied autonomy is absolutely central to this endeavor.

SITUATION ASSIMILATION AND THE MASS MEDIA

Culture-of-fear critics[10] share a fear of the mass media's emotion man-agement of its public, which they view as both a means of manipula-tion[11] and an important force in the spread of irrational fear. We can understand contemporary-fear critics' fear of emotional manipulation as a fear of the desires that are activated or formed by contemporary experts and the mass media. This fear is present in the work of David L. Altheide (1997), who argues that the contemporary news media's use of a problem frame, merged with the entertainment format of commercial media, has contributed to the pervasive presence of fear in American society. The entertainment format used by the contemporary news media provides information in a dramatic and exciting way, while the problem frame with which it shares many affinities is a familiar narrative through which undesirable and relevant events with known solutions are simplistically and misleadingly presented. Like other culture-of-fear theorists, Altheide is interested in explaining why Americans are more fearful than their forebears, in spite of "comparative advantage in terms of diseases, accidents, nutrition, medical care, and life expectancy" (649). He argues that popular culture and the mass media distort the public's view of reality and causes it to be more fearful than necessary.

Culture-of-fear critics are certainly right in pointing to mass media as an important site of subjectivity formation. Mass media are a particularly powerful means through which desire is activated and formed in the realization-based emotional economy—through which selves are emotionally socialized. It is important that we attend to the political effects of this emotion management. In closing, I use Noël Carroll's notion of "situation assimilation" in cinematic horror (1990) as a point of departure in thinking about how mass mediatized representations form subjectivity by way of agents' interactions with objects of fear and desire.

In a problematization of the concept of character identification, Carroll (88–96) emphasizes that identification can have several connotations, including the idea that one likes a character, that one sees similarities between the character and oneself, that one has values in common with the character, and that one has sympathy for a character. However, the concept of character identification is also sometimes deployed to mean that the audience member becomes one with the character. There are many problems with this meaning of the concept, according to Carroll. For instance, because the viewer has more information than the character, there is a difference between what the character can be said to feel and what the viewer feels (e.g., the character can be enjoying a swim while the viewer can feel concern for the character who is about to be attacked by sharks). Moreover, while the character can be said to experience concern for their self in situations that compel such concern, the viewer might be said to experience concern for the character rather than for himself or herself.

Carroll notes that protagonists and audience members can have parallel emotional evaluations of the monster since the latter are cued by the former, but this does not mean that the two are fused or that the two share the same emotional state. In particular, the audience is located outside the situation and responds to the monster through the entertained thought of a monster (art-horror) as opposed to through belief in a monster (horror). In sum, Carroll argues that rather than identify with characters, we assimilate their situations (this requires that we have a culturally governed understanding of the protagonist's internal evaluation of their situation) and see their situation from the outside as well.

To translate some of these insights into the terms of embodied in/ capacity theory, we can usefully posit that through situation assimilation (rather than through character identification), audiences can experience the same objects of fear and desire as the characters do. For example, if a protagonist feels terrified by an oversized shark, guilty about having harmed a defenseless child, or happy about a declaration of eternal love, audiences can be said to experience terror, guilt, or happiness not so much because they identify with the character as because they assimilate the character's situation and already share or newly take on the character's objects of fear and desire, to which particular emotional orientations are attached.

In the process of situation assimilation, characters' verbal and bodily emotives[12] might be said to help shape audiences' interactions with objects of fear and desire. Moreover, because audiences are positioned outside the frame of events and therefore have more information than the protagonists, they can experience objects of fear and desire that the protagonists are not aware of but that are suggested by their larger situation. For example, the audience can feel sad about a loss a protagonist is about to suffer where the protagonist has no knowledge of the upcoming loss. Moreover, the audience's knowledge of the narrative's genre also means that they can assimilate the situation in ways that differ from the characters' capacity to do so. For example, the audience watching a romantic comedy can experience the happiness of reconciliation that structures the happy ending even while the characters are in the throes of romantic alienation and conflict.

One might also add that audiences can experience the characters themselves as objects of fear and desire. Villains and heroes are just such objects of fear and desire, and may also act as signs of danger and security. Thus audiences may experience villains' actions as danger producing and those of heroes as security producing. Interacting with villains and heroes as signs of danger and security might also trigger specific emotional experiences and the desire to implement security in particular ways.

For example, if a given type of character, such as the transgressive drug addict or the inadequate seducer of women, is represented as painfully incapable, it will constitute an object of fear to which the audience is likely to relate through an emotional orientation already attached to it or suggested by the narrative, on whose basis an opportunity for the pleasurable exercise of capacity is likely to be presented as well. Thus the transgressive drug addict might be shown to move from regret to self-forgiveness by undergoing therapy in a rehabilitation facility, or the inadequate seducer of women might be shown to move from artificiality to authenticity by being enlightened about his true self. Or if a given type of character, such as the law-abiding citizen or the competent law-enforcement agent, is represented as pleasurably capable, it will constitute an object of desire to which the audience is likely to relate through an emotional orientation already attached to it or suggested by the narrative, on whose basis an opportunity for the pleasurable exercise of capacity is also likely to be presented. Thus perhaps the law-abiding citizen shows how one can move from corruption to virtue by refusing to give in to temptation, or perhaps the competent law-enforcement agent helps us move from injustice to justice by being resourceful.

It should be emphasized that the emotional effects of situation assimilation do not require that we believe in the reality or plausibility of a situation, only that we interact with objects of fear and desire through "thoughts entertained" (i.e., through imagining a painful or a pleasurable outcome). As I argued in an earlier chapter, this is because emotional experience is governed by the anticipation of pain and pleasure, or by the perception of danger and security, rather than by the actuality of pain and pleasure outcomes.

The situation assimilation through which audiences experience the objects of fear and desire produced by the narratives they consume, on whose basis existing emotional orientations to these objects may be reinforced or new ones suggested, and on whose basis existing means of implementing security may be reinforced or new ones suggested, is an approach that may be useful in making sense of audiences' emotional interaction with various mass media outputs, such as advertising, reality television, newscasts, web forums, self-help literature, and online gaming.

While Carroll developed the notion of situation assimilation to replace that of character identification, in light of the various shortcomings of the latter concept in explaining audiences' feelings, the notion of situation assimilation might also be said to be preferable to that of identification to make sense of emotional experience in the process of interpersonal, face-to-face interaction. An agent cannot be said to actually feel what another person feels in the course of face-to-face interactions. They can only be said to relate to what the other is imagined to feel, based on various cues that include emotives (Reddy, 1999, 1997). Moreover, what one feels in the course of one's proximate interactions with others may include an assimilation of their situation from the outside, as well as one's disapproving or approving concern for them (as opposed to the concern they experience for their self), and one's felt perception of them as an object of fear or desire. As such, the concept of situation assimilation is able to account for dimensions of emotional interaction that escape the concept of identification.

Subjects who are emotionally managed through mass mediated means may in some instances be prompted to manage their selves, and in others simply experience the emotional regulatory effects of these emotion management efforts. Their agency is acted upon through emotional means of which they are often unaware. We have seen that these effects may include the development of various objects of fear and desire, the emotional orientation and the means of dealing with them, and the signs of danger and security that trigger their experience. For instance, we can see how wrinkles have been culturally constituted as an object of fear (especially for women) and as a sign of danger through their association with painful outcomes that are attached to felt forms of in/capacity (e.g., stigmatization/attractiveness) and to particular means of exercising power (e.g., various beauty regimens, cosmetic surgery). Or we can see how particular ideals of selfhood (e.g., being productive, outgoing, entrepreneurial) have been culturally constituted as objects of desire and signs of security through their association with pleasurable outcomes that are attached to felt forms of in/capacity (e.g., feeling clinically depressed/feeling oneself) and to particular means of exercising power (e.g., antidepressants, psychotherapy).

Increasing our knowledge of the particularities of fear and desire experiences includes historicizing the contemporary understanding of fear as a moral danger by identifying some of the co-constitutive forces that have prompted the perception of fear as an object that is itself to be feared. The contemporary moral compulsion to overcome the danger of fear (i.e., of immoral powerlessness) and to implement the security of freedom from fear (i.e., of moral powerfulness) is tied to advanced liberal ways of making sense of and of governing selves and others; it feeds powerful therapeutic industries and fuels consumption more generally; and it is tied to dominant forms of subjective and moral experience and to particular patterns in social relations, forms both of inclusion and of exclusion.

All societies engage in the emotional socialization of their members, on whose basis individuals adopt similar forms of emotional orientation to objects of fear and desire, acquire the signs of danger and security that trigger emotional experience, and develop embodied means of power through which to implement security. Distinct social groups may be said to promote distinct emotional orientations, objects of fear and desire, signs of danger and security, and means of implementing security. The extent to which individuals are emotionally managed or prompted to emotionally manage themselves—the extent to which individuals exercise moral autonomy—is also a feature that may serve to distinguish between social economies of fear and desire.

Late modern societies promote a high degree of individual responsibilization. These are societies in which members experience a great deal of internal conflict—societies in which individuals habitually experience anxiety/interest (a dissatisfaction with existing means of resolving problems and the moral desire to improve these means) and distress/relief (a persistent incapacity to resolve problems and the moral desire to create these means). These are societies in which individuals are required to engage in frequent emotion management efforts in order to conform to social expectations for which they are ill equipped or not equipped as they currently are. In other words, these are societies in which individuals are relentlessly prompted to morally transform themselves in order to experience the social approval and other felt capacities required to feel secure. This emotional socialization of the self by the self takes place alongside and often as a result of the emotional socialization of the self by ubiquitous mass mediatized emotional regulation effects and appeals for emotional self-transformation. As such, we need to remain attentive to the ways in which actions that are socially rewarding and freely engaged in may produce heteronomy.

Afterword

I initially planned to write about post-1960s self-help books dealing with disorders of fear such as stress, anxiety, panic, and phobia. While I plan to return to this project, in the course of attempting to produce it I came to realize that I did not simply wish to contribute a discourse analysis of the cultural features of the subjectivity made manifest by these books. I wanted to shed light on the embodied nature of subjects' experiences of fear as they pertain to morally normative social forces, while also accounting for subjects' agency in this process. However, I not only lacked the conceptual tools that might allow me to make sense of the embodied nature of individual and collective forms of emotional and emotionally driven agency, but I felt that existing approaches to fear, and to emotions more generally, would not allow me to carry out the type of analysis I felt I should produce.

I faced many challenges in writing this book, not the least of which was my desire to produce an approach to emotional life that would appeal to analysts across disciplinary thresholds and with a wide range of research interests. I felt it important to propose an alternative to the view that it is in emotions' nature, and in fear's nature more particularly, to produce irrational effects, and that emotions can be analyzed without consideration for what they feel like. I also felt there was much that was taken for granted or left unspecified about the various identities and effects of fear emotions in contemporary morally and politically engaged sociocultural analyses of these emotions in everyday life, as well as a tendency to view the use of fear to achieve various ends as inherently immoral. I felt it important to think through with greater care the ways in which emotions are triggered by emotion management efforts in the moral attempt to direct the course of agents' actions, whatever the corresponding motives (economic, political, governmental, artistic, personal, and the like), while placing on hold the question of the potentially morally problematic nature of these motives or of their effects.

Having been greatly influenced by and having myself contributed to the "governmentality" approach to contemporary selfhood as the outcome of liberal strategies that enlist the self in its own government as means of increasing the reach and depth of power effects, in this book I have sought to contribute tools for analyzing the place of feeling in the exercise of power. More precisely, I have sought to understand the exercise of power in its relation to embodied agents, such that we might begin to unpack the complicated web of interactions between the exercise of power through emotional means and subjects' exercise of individual responsibility and of autonomy more broadly by way of a better understanding of the power effects of emotions.

While numerous analysts have touched upon or emphasized the ways in which contemporary subjects are governed through the production of feelings of personal responsibility for problems or painful outcomes,[2] greater attention ought to be paid to the forms and modalities taken by these feelings as felt structures of experience that prompt particular kinds of actions. Moreover, we ought to be able to distinguish between forms of capacity that promote the exercise of embodied autonomy and forms of capacity that threaten this exercise. In other words, there is a difference between getting agents to freely engage in courses of action that promote their ability to exercise power, and getting agents to freely engage in courses of action that lessen their ability to exercise power, especially where this lesser ability promotes the greater ability of others. As I have sought to argue in this book, socially rewarding actions—actions of social conformity that may very well feel good—can produce heteronomy. In short, some capacities promote incapacity.

My goal became that of producing a coherent, accessible, and nuanced theoretical approach to emotional life that is empirically relevant and that has interdisciplinary scope. I shift the terms through which we think of emotional agency in a number of ways and insist upon the need to ground this agency in a perspective that accounts for its affectively structured, interactive, and relational features. Concepts of use in contemporary social, cultural, and political analysis are rendered more precise (e.g., fear, desire, hope, emotional pain, emotional pleasure, moral pain, moral pleasure, danger, security, embodied autonomy) or are redefined (e.g., force, action, agency, power, domination, resistance, freedom) in an effort to make sense of agency's embodied dimensions, and new ones are introduced or expanded upon (e.g., relational threat and promise; objects of fear and desire; signs of danger and security; emotional-norm pairs; affective, agential, and symbolic attunement; emotional differentiation and blending; emotional regulation; hedonic power; emotion management; emotional socialization; responsibilization; emotional economies).

In initially preparing a book on self-help approaches to contemporary disorders of fear, it was my intention to analyze the cultural promotion of specific categories of disorder through their action as forms of lack in the capacities that are in alignment with the neoliberal norms of individual autonomy, entrepreneurship, flexibility, and productivity—as expressions of governing at a distance and of politico-economic imperatives. But stress, anxiety, panic, and phobia should also be thought of as collective forms of incapacity that express subjects' emotional experience of the failure to achieve the agential expectations of the advanced liberal order, the fulfillment of which individuals are held to be responsible for through the moralizing effects of self-help philosophy and practice.[3] Self-help's naming of contemporary forms of collective emotional pain as manifestations of individual suffering or pathology (together with the DSM[4] and numerous other cultural agents) and the massive appropriation of this naming by the public should tell us something about the extent to which these constitute forms in embodied agents' attempts to exercise power, or of their failure to do so. In retrospect I see that this laid the groundwork for the development of the idea of emotional-norm pairs as embodied means of moving from incapacity to capacity that develop interactively and in relational context.

As a result of my desire to account for the exercise of power through emotional means, which required an understanding of the differentiated expressions of fear in their relation to agency, I set this first book project aside because I felt that my approach as it stood at the time left unrecognized actual suffering and the forms it takes in those who consult self-help manuals. The question of the complex forces through which this suffering came into being also remained unanswered. I was failing to account for self-help consumers' agency, by which I do not simply mean their capacity to resist or subvert social forms of oppression, but rather their capacity to exercise power, and the challenges they face in its exercise, as conditioned by a co-constitutive exchange between their selves as embodied forces and the other forces that surround them.

In other words, I realized I had to begin thinking about what I might mean by "the pathological." I also wanted to be able to account for biological forces in the exercise of agency. This is rugged terrain, not only because of the suspicion with which talk of biology[5] is treated by many cultural analysts, but because of the suspicion with which hermeneutic and ontological accounts of agency have come to be regarded, alongside concepts that include autonomy, freedom, human nature, normality, and pathology (more particularly subjective or moral pathology). For instance, autonomy has been problematically understood as an expression of individuals' "free will," of the supremacy of the rational and cognitive masculine mind over the irrational and emotional feminine body, and of individuals' impermeability to the forces that surround them (Blackman 2008). Autonomy is also understood by governmentality theorists like Nikolas Rose as a means through which subjects are enlisted in the potentially oppressive government of their selves in alignment with a variety of sociopolitical goals.

These worries are legitimate. The case should continue to be made that humanist discourses of biological nature and of its pathological and substandard expressions have contributed to and continue to contribute to the perpetration of grave forms of social injustice and to collective experiences of suffering, much as we need to reflect upon the various ways in which the biological has become the site of various technologies of the self through which individuals aim to and are prompted to increase their autonomy and freedom (Rose, 2007). Biology is a force we must contend with and with which we interact in making our way through the world. This does not mean we should not continue to be concerned about the morally aberrant forms taken by the instrumentalization of biological forces, or to be critical of some of the ways in which their meaning is produced. While the detailed consideration of the features and dynamics of biological forces in emotional experience and human agency was not the focus of this book, I do think it important to be open to and engage with the work of those who are involved in this task.[6]

Cultural pathologization has become code for the medicalization, psychologization, and individualization of social problems—processes that trump the acknowledgment of the social injustices that produce collective forms of suffering and that thwart the type of change that it is believed would alleviate them. The massive expansion of psychiatric disorders can alternatively be understood as an effect of the contemporary imperative of autonomous agency and freedom, which is the vehicle for invisible and potentially oppressive forms of power.[7] It does not follow, however, that we should do away with the concept of the pathological as a destructive force that causes suffering, or with the concept of the therapeutic as a counterdestructive force. In spite of the contribution of these concepts, by way of biomedical and psychological discourses and practices, to the extended reach and depth of normalizing power, to the individualization of social problems, and to the phenomenal expansion of the pharmaceutical industry—and in spite also of the destructive effects of a number of practices implemented with a therapeutic intent—it is my goal, in a subsequent work, to explore the ways in which refashioned notions of the pathological and of the therapeutic remain useful as forces of counterdestruction.

The pathological, which designates a diseased state or a process of autodestruction, has "pathos" as its etymological root. As such, it also connotes the experience of suffering, which I understand as the experience of the subjective or moral inability to overcome emotional pain—an inability that can be conceived of collectively as well as individually. As such, the pathological state is a self-destroying state that causes suffering. But it can also be understood as a self-destroying state of suffering, if the suffering is a cause of self-destruction.

Cultural pathologization is a process through which existing forms of suffering become culturally visible. When a form of suffering becomes a cultural preoccupation, it also likely becomes the object of social remedies—of therapeutic or humanist practices that seek to alleviate it. In becoming the object of collective efforts at moral transformation, emotional pain is also transformed into moral suffering through responsibilization. It seems that an increasing number of forms of suffering have become subject to cultural pathologization in contemporary society, as well as to responsibilization. However, while this explanation helps us understand our growing awareness of various collective forms of suffering and of the desire to transform these through biomedical, psychological, and other means, it does not tell us why some forms of emotional pain become culturally interesting while others go unnoticed (many of the forces over which various agents are compelled to act subjectively or morally do not form the object of cultural interest). Nor does it tell us about the social and political forces involved in the production of collective forms of suffering, or about what this emotional pain feels like.[8] As Lauren Berlant (2004) argues, compassion can be understood as a social relation, and the acknowledgment of some forms of suffering and not others, as well as the strategies put forth to help those who suffer, as political technologies.

Collective forms of suffering—such as the particular kinds of suffering of the exploited and alienated industrial workers identified by Marx (1996) and Engels, or the particular kinds of suffering of the contemporary belabored selves identified by Micki McGee (2005)—can take on numerous identities. We ought to be attentive to the structured emotional dynamics at work in the groups that experience chronic forms of emotional pain. The notion of social justice does not make much sense if it fails to take into account what it feels like to be treated unjustly, or at the very least what if feels like to experience the self-destructive effects of the exercise of power, should one not experience these effects as an injustice. As such, in the absence of the feeling of the illegitimacy of one's suffering, a better understanding of the emotional experiences that may betray destructive circumstances and signal the need for social change are needed (e.g., being overwhelmed/coping, torment/resignation, doom/fate, weariness/entertainment, addiction/abstinence, dysfunction/adaptation), alongside a better understanding of the emotional experiences that may be most effective in bringing about positive social change (e.g., outrage/vindication, resentment/fairness, oppression/emancipation, injustice/justice).[9]

If, as I have argued in this book, emotional pain is a necessary component of subjective and moral emotional experience, why do some of its forms and not others become subject to collective moral control efforts? Why do some forms of suffering acquire a special status? Why do others go unnoticed? We need to ask about how social forces promote collective experiences of emotional pain and pleasure, of suffering and well-being, such as the dysfunction/adaptation of those with lesser capacity to exercise power, or the heartlessness/compassion of the more powerful, as well as the channeling of these felt in/capacities in ways that reproduce and reinforce distinct ways of suffering and of being well. In short, we need to make sense of the coming into being of collective forms of emotional pain and pleasure—those forms that are the object of notice as well as those that are not—so that we can begin to grasp the dynamics of autonomy and of heteronomy.

Emotional experience necessarily involves suffering, and emotional experience is a condition of the exercise of embodied autonomy, therefore suffering is not indicative of heteronomy. By contrast, emotional pleasure can promote forms of agency that compromise the integrity and vitality of embodied selves, therefore emotional pleasure is not indicative of autonomy. As such, we need to be able to make a distinction between forms of suffering and of well-being that promote agents' embodied autonomy and forms of suffering and of well-being that are detrimental to this capacity. In other words, we need to differentiate between autonomy-enhancing, beneficial forms of emotional pain and pleasure—forms of suffering and of well-being that promote the integrity and vitality of embodied selves—and their autonomy-destroying, harmful forms—forms of suffering and of well-being that compromise the integrity (i.e., soundness, wholeness) and vitality (i.e., powerfulness, directional energy) of embodied selves. To achieve this, we probably need a new paradigm—one that is neither governed by reason nor governed by health, at least not in their exist-ing, antagonistic forms (i.e., reason in its opposition to emotion, the body, and the lack of boundaries, or health in its opposition to collec-tive being, control, and an excess of boundaries). This new paradigm may be a conception of reason as grounded in the integrity and vitality of each embodied self, and also a conception of health where the vital-ity and integrity of each self is produced through its co-constitutive exchanges with collective being.

Notes

Introduction

1. For an overview of the main trends in or of the increasing variety of stimulating scholarship in the analysis of emotional and social life and embodiment, useful references in getting started are Bendelow (2009); Blackman (2008b), Greco and Stenner (2008); Stets and Turner (2007a); Fraser and Greco (2005), Turner and Stets (2005); Petersen (2004); Barbalet (2002a, 2001); Goodwin, Jasper, and Polletta (2001); Williams (2001); Katz (1999); Lupton (1999, 1998); Harré and Parrott (1996); Harré (1986), and Hochschild (1983).
2. The opposition between reason and emotion popularized by René Descartes during the Enlightenment has been much discussed in feminist, postmodernist, and psychoanalytic writings. For a brief discussion of this in relation to the sociology of emotions, see Shilling (2002). Williams's (2001) and Barbalet's (2001) books on emotions and social theory are also very useful for mapping the implications of this opposition for analysis, as is Petersen's (2004) book on emotions and gender.
3. For instance, see Ahmed (2010, 2004), Lafrance (2009), Blackman (2008b), Reuter (2007), Freund (1991, 1990), Lupton (1998, 1999), Williams (2000, 2001), Bendelow (2009), Probyn (2005), Miller (1997), and Barbalet (2001, 2002a).
4. I am referring to the gothic literary genre that characterizes the work of authors like Horace Walpole (*The Castle of Otranto*, 1764), Ann Radcliffe (*The Mysteries of Udolpho*, 1794; *The Italian: or, The Confessional of the Black Penitents*, 1797), Matthew Gregory Lewis (*The Monk*, 1795), and Mary Wollstonecraft Shelley (*Frankenstein; or, the Modern Prometheus*, 1818).

Chapter 1

1. Cf. Campbell (2004, 45), Freud (1959, 1965, chapter 4), and Hall (1954).
2. Alfred Hitchcock is reported to have said, "There is no terror in the bang, only in the anticipation of it."

3. Lupton (1999) reports on the findings of psychometric research-ers, who show that individuals are more likely to perceive situations about which information is accessible as risky, and to overestimate risk when they readily identify with a risk-related outcome.

4. I later discuss anxiety as a modality of fear, rather than as an experi-ence that is distinct from it.

5. I am committed to Bendelow (1993) and Bendelow and Williams's (1995) call for increased attention to the emotional dimensions of pain, which should not be reduced to sensation conceived of as a system of biological signals impervious to the socially mediated embodied experience of individuals. The same observation should be made about pleasure.

6. As such, it is important not to confound the object of desire with the solution. The solution to the object of fear is the means of power that brings the object of desire to life.

7. For a discussion of the manner in which emotions become attached to or stick to objects, see Ahmed (2004).

8. See Hunt (1999) for a critical account of social explanations of anxiety-driven displacements and for some of the challenges involved in the tracking of their referents. See Glassner (1999) and Stearns (2006) for analyses of contemporary displacements in the American context.

9. Freud meant something along these lines with the concept of trans-ference or of affective cathexis. Cf. Campbell (2004, 108, 191). Ahmed (2010, 245) makes a parallel point when she argues, fol-lowing Nietzsche, that objects can lag behind feelings and feelings behind objects, where one experiences pain and looks for an object to determine its cause, or where one comes into contact with an object and experiences the feeling with which it has become associated.

10. The concept of "emotional norms" that I seek to develop shares important traits with that of "emotion norms." The latter refer to the social feeling rules or conventions that govern the experi-ence and expression of emotions, as found in the work of Elias (1978, 1982) and Hochschild (1983). While emotional norms are highly interactive with social feeling rules or conventions, or emo-tion norms, they cannot be reduced to these. Emotional norms are normative structures of emotion, or normative structures of felt in/capacity. Emotional norms are also distinct from what Reddy (1999, 1997) calls emotives, which I discuss later on, and the two can be said to interact.

11. Freund (1990, 461) similarly makes the argument that emotional experience is grounded in feelings of powerlessness and of powerful-ness. In a paper that seeks to draw connections between health and illness and the sociology of emotions, he writes that emotional expe-rience pertains to the "different felt ways of feeling empowered or

disempowered...related to the conditions of existence encountered throughout one's biography. 'External' social structural factors such as one's position in different systems of hierarchy or various forms of social control can influence the conditions of our existence, how we respond and apprehend these conditions and our sense of embodied self. These conditions can also affect our physical functioning."

12. See my later discussion of the three modalities of fear and desire: panic/excitement, anxiety/interest, and distress/relief.

13. On the issue of subjective autonomy, see my later discussion of biological, subjective, and moral autonomy.

14. See my later discussion of subjective, moral, and social emotional experiences and emotions.

15. In her plea for greater open-mindedness toward the possibility that there are universal emotions, Probyn (2005, 29) argues that universal human features can be thought of as the grounds for the development of differences rather than as a closing off of difference.

16. Examples of anthropological work on cross-historical and cross-cultural emotional diversity that in some cases also emphasize the cultural specificity of Western conceptions of emotion and of ways of talking about emotions include Abu-Lughod (1986), Harré and Finlay-Jones (1986), Heelas (1986), Lutz (1986, 1988), and Morsbach and Tyler (1986).

17. This tentative definition was inspired by Barbalet's commentary (2001) on William James's "The Sentiment of Rationality" (1897). Barbalet remarks that James's unusual approach is one in which reason and emotion exist on a continuum rather than in opposition to one another. According to James, we recognize that which is rational through the feeling of rationality, where the feeling of rationality is based on "the absence of any feeling of irrationality" (cited in Barbalet 2001, 45). The intensity of the feeling of rationality is, for James, governed by the intensity of the forces that impede upon the fluidity of cognitive action. And the content of the feeling of rationality is "a feeling of the sufficiency of the present moment, of its absoluteness—this absence of all need to explain it, account for it, or justify it" (cited in Barbalet 2001, 46). One could argue, following James, that the feeling of irrationality is the feeling that promotes the exercise of cognition as a means to implement the security of rationality. We might in this way account for the deployment of thinking as a means of power in the implementation of security that can be tied to various experiences of felt in/capacity, and perhaps especially those that involve the exercise of moral autonomy—in other words, those that involve forms of internal conflict and are experienced through the modalities of anxiety/interest or of distress/relief, which I discuss later on.

18. Katz's ethnographic analysis of Los Angeles drivers' accounts of their hostile interactions with other drivers (1999) can be taken to illustrate the manner in which drivers' anger/assertiveness at being cut off by other drivers is morally transformed into outrage/vindication and rage/revenge as emotional orientations that are tied to particular means of implementing security (i.e., making the other driver realize they were in the wrong, punishing the other driver, or hoping the other driver will be punished for his or her transgression). Katz also produces an interesting account of the embodied self's interaction with vehicles as extensions of their selves in the experience of these emotions.

19. Barbalet's discussion of class and resentment (2001, 62–81) inspired this definition.

20. While there are dissimilarities between our treatment of shame, I wish to acknowledge the influence of Elias' work (1982, 1978) on my definition of this emotion. For Elias, shame is a type of anxiety based on the fear of social degradation and disapproval, and more precisely on a feeling of inferiority that may have its origins in the child's feelings of physical inferiority, but whose adult expression is based on the feeling that one has violated internalized social expectations (the superego). Shame is the result of the violation of both social prohibitions and self-prohibitions whose origins are social.

21. Misery/joy, exclusion/inclusion, and isolation/connection are among the emotional-norm pairs that structure Mary Shelley's *Frankenstein* (1818).

22. Denial/acknowledgment, backwardness/progress, degeneration/evolution, and disenchantment/transcendence are among the emotional-norm pairs that structure Bram Stoker's *Dracula* (1897).

23. See Berlant's discussion (2004) of the ways in which compassion can act as a political technology through which some forms of suffering are acknowledged while others go unrecognized.

24. Disgusting objects are categorically abnormal, or are out of place, as Douglas (1966) so aptly puts it, and are therefore undesirable. Carroll (1990) uses Douglas's approach to explain some of the ways in which boundary violations or disruptions and ambiguous boundaries produce horror.

25. This emotional-norm pair could alternatively be referred to as the fear of abandonment/the desire to be taken care of. It may be said to structure all the emotional-norm pairs that imply attachment.

26. On the central place of power effects of and forms of resistance to the quest for happiness in contemporary culture, see Ahmed (2010).

27. Lupton (1999) and Beck (1992) are among those whose work helped inspire this definition.

28. I borrow the idea of emotional blending from Prinz (2004) and, to a certain extent, that of emotional differentiation as well. I engage with his work in this and the following section.

29. Anger may also make the unfaithful partner feel guilt/innocence and become blended with remorse/atonement and promote reparation. See my discussion of the relationship between anger/assertiveness and guilt/innocence and of their role in social conformity in Chapter 5.

CHAPTER 2

1. William Reddy's concept of emotives (1999, 1997) has similar implications.

2. I earlier defined displacement as the coming into being of signs of danger or of security that lack an obvious relationship to the objects of fear and of desire they represent. See my discussion of this concept in the section titled "Relational Threat and Relational Promise: The Anticipation of Pain and Pleasure" in Chapter 1.

3. Noël Carroll (1990, 60–88) rejects the illusion theory of fiction, which is based on the proposition that we do not know that what is happening is not actual while we are engaging with the work because we are under the illusion that it is real. He also rejects the pretend theory of fiction, which is based on the idea that when engaging with works of fiction, we are under the illusion that what is happening is real, but the emotions we experience are not authentic. Carroll supports the thought theory of fiction, which is based on the premise that we can be genuinely moved by what we do not believe to be real, or by "thoughts entertained." In other words, we do not need to believe a thing to be true to be moved by it. I suggest that this is because emotional experience is governed by the anticipation of an outcome, not by the likelihood of its realization.

4. Jesse J. Prinz (2004) notes that the basic emotions listed by a number of analysts contain distinct states we usually associate with fear, such as panic and anxiety (Panksepp), anxiety and fright (Lazarus), conditioned stimuli fear and unconditioned stimuli fear (Gray) and chronic worry disorders and panic attack disorders (Heller, Nitschke, Etienne, and Miller). I am suggesting that distinct states of fear may be thought of as modalities governed by subjects' perception of their relation to means of overcoming danger and of implementing security. As such, they also need to be understood in terms of their relationship to desire.

5. See my discussion of situation assimilation, social positioning, and objects of fear and desire in Chapter 8.

6. See Lori Holyfield (1997) for an analysis of the transformation of the painful sensations associated with risk taking into pleasurable ones

through adventure therapy. In his classic "Becoming a Marihuana User," Howard Becker (1953) makes a similar argument.

7. In these examples, I am working with the assumption that being reunited with the lost glasses is the subject's goal.

8. One could make the argument that the more an emotion is attuned to specific demands, the more the means of power through which these demands can be met are restricted.

9. On the issue of the clock-bound time discipline of the industrial era and its central role in the flourishing of capitalism, see Thompson (1967).

10. There is a vast literature in which the case is made for the existence of various primary emotions. For a survey of some of these approaches, see Prinz (2004).

CHAPTER 3

1. I insist on the fact that these are fluid distinctions. The boundaries between fleshy and nonfleshy forces are not or ought not to be clear as cyborg theorizing suggests (Haraway, 1991), and the boundaries between biologically embodied, subjectively embodied, and morally embodied beings are also porous. For instance, while the extent of horses' capacity for moral consciousness certainly seems to be more limited than that of human beings in general, horses seem to be able to exercise a certain degree of moral autonomy (i.e., they are capable of understanding others' emotions, and empathy, I argue, has self-awareness as a condition), and they can be thought of as being morally affected by their interactions with humans (cf. Blackman's (2008b) discussion of the process of attunement in horse–human relations). In short, the application of the notion of "kinds" to categories of embodied being suggests that one is one type of force and not another, and does not allow us to account for variations in degrees of subjective or moral awareness among embodied beings.

2. I am grateful to the physicist David Sean for our conversations on these matters, although this should in no way be taken to reflect his views.

3. For Foucault (1983), the exercise of power involves action upon action. In the terms of embodied in/capacity theory, the exercise of power involves directive action upon directed action, where at least one of the two actions is driven by purpose and involves affect.

4. This emphasizes the idea that the boundaries between embodied beings are porous.

5. See my discussion of social change through political protest in the section titled "Moral Actions of Social Conformity" in Chapter 5.

6. Parallels can be drawn here with Elias's concept of social habitus, which Wouters (1989b, 103) explains in the following manner:

"compared with other animals, human beings are born with very little natural self-regulation. Their natural or unlearned forms of steering conduct are—or better, have become—subordinated to learned forms, developed in earlier generations. They *do* have a natural disposition to learn to regulate themselves, but in order to become fully functioning human beings, they have to learn to regulate themselves according to the *social habitus*, i.e. the learned social standards of controlling one's drives and emotions. On every level, this learned self-regulation takes the form of a tension balance between emotional impulses and emotion controlling counter-impulses." For more on the distinction I draw between emotional regulation and emotion management, see the section titled "Emotional Regulation, Hedonic Power, and Emotion Management" in Chapter 5.

7. While their approach differs from my own in a number of respects, Turner and Stets (2007b) urge us to recognize the greater diversity of moral emotions. They argue that moral emotions can be inborn. I also believe that moral emotions can become biological norms, but insist upon the distinction between the moral emotional experience and moral emotions.

8. Unlike the concept of identification, which may be said to imply the merging of agents' emotional states, the concept of situation assimilation as I develop it is based on the notion that one reads other agents' emotional cues in order to make emotional sense of a situation and thereby acquire similar objects of fear and desire, the emotional orientations through which these are experienced, the means of power to which these are associated, and the signs of danger and security that trigger emotional experience. Situation assimilation may also be said to involve the ability to understand affective objects once their emotional sense has been acquired. For a further discussion of this concept, which I borrow from Carroll (1990) and develop in relation to my own concerns, see the section titled "Situation Assimilation and the Mass Media" in Chapter 8.

9. See Blackman (2008a) for an interesting discussion of the work of William James on suggestibility and for ideas about how to move beyond the problematic conceptions of human agents either as fully bounded and separate from others, or as fully porous and constructed by social interaction.

CHAPTER 4

1. Elias's work has been criticized for making a number of overgeneralizations about the features of premodern and modern societies that he discusses on the basis of his paradigm of the civilization process. Among others, see Delzescaux (2003) and Rosenwein (2002).

My goal here is not that of developing an alternative, all-encompassing theory of societal emotional development.

2. I elaborate on these issues in the last section of this chapter.

3. For instance, see Ehrenberg (2010), McGee (2005), Blackman (2004), Berlant (2004), Otero (2003), Rimke (2000), O'Malley (1998), Nettleton (1997), Petersen (1997), and Castel (1981).

4. See my discussion of this issue in the section titled "Subjective, Moral, and Social Emotional Experiences and Emotions."

5. For an account of a neoliberal process of responsibilization in the American context, see Berlant's (2004) analysis of the Republican Party's promotion of "compassionate conservatism," on whose basis tax cuts and welfare-to-work programs are legitimized, and where compassion constitutes a political practice of recognizing some forms of suffering and not others.

6. The intensity of self-fear experiences could also be intensified through agents' conflicts with other forces, such as in responding to a natural disaster, for instance.

7. See the section titled "Emotional Regulation, Hedonic Power, and Emotion Management" in Chapter 5 for more on this issue.

8. Since it may be argued that obedience can be painful and disobedience pleasurable, or competence painful and incompetence pleasurable, the act of conformity that is emotionally painful can be thought of as resulting from the painful transgression of or failure to measure up to embodied rules that differ from those that are being conformed to, while the act of transgression or of failure that is pleasurable can be thought of as resulting from the pleasurable conformity with embodied rules that differ from those that are being broken or fallen short of. In short, acts of nonconformity can be understood as pleasurable implementations of security, while acts of conformity can be understood as painful causes of danger. Whether an experience is mainly painful or pleasurable depends on the intensity of the danger that is being produced or on the intensity of the security that is being implemented through conformity and nonconformity with whatever rules are of embodied relevance. For more on the issue of pain and pleasure in their relation to self-control, see the section titled "From the Fear of Desire to the Fear of Fear" in Chapter 8. See also Ahmed's (2010) discussion of "affect aliens."

9. Altheide (1997, 656) argues that the contemporary news media and information technology systematically make use of a problem frame and entertainment format to produce a culture of fear. He draws a distinction between an earlier logic of acceptance of problems as a matter of the difficult nature of life and a more contemporary logic of problems as having a source of blame and a solution in moral agents. This distinction resonates with the one I am suggesting we might make between fear- and desire-based and self-fear- and

self-desire-based emotional economies, provided we do not under-stand the logic of acceptance of problems as one that involves a lack of subjective response to these problems.

10. However, I would reword Beck's catchphrase to qualify contempo-rary postindustrial risk societies, "solidarity through anxiety," with "solidarity through worry." The modality through which this worry (i.e., the felt incapacity to overcome danger through prevention) is experienced varies, depending on whether subjects feel compelled to implement security through habitual responses corresponding to panic/excitement (e.g., recycling), or on whether they feel morally impelled to implement security through more satisfactory or novel responses corresponding to anxiety/interest or distress/relief.

11. Examples of scholars whose work represents some form of culture-of-fear theorizing include Peter N. Stearns (2006), David Altheide (1997), Barry Glassner (1999), Marc K. Siegel (2005), and Frank Furedi (1997). For a documentary that uses the culture-of-fear per-spective, see Michael Moore's *Bowling for Columbine* (2002).

12. See my discussion of culture-of-fear theorizing in Chapter 8.

13. Examples of scholars working in this tradition include Nikolas Rose (1989), Patrick O'Malley (1998), Monica Greco (1993), Alan Petersen (1997), and Sarah Nettleton (1997). For work in a simi-lar tradition in the francophone world see Alain Ehrenberg (2010), Marcelo Otero (2003), and Robert Castel (1981).

14. I am not yet able to properly account for the role of defense mecha-nisms in the exercise of autonomy. For instance, are defense mecha-nisms a way for agents to bypass moral emotional experience and the self's responsibilization, or are they embodied means of exercising moral power that exist as alternatives or as complements to emo-tional differentiation and emotional blending? Or perhaps emotional differentiation and emotional blending ought to be thought of as defense mechanisms?

15. Lutz (1996) argues that the language of control that is used to discuss emotions reinforces a view of them as universal and natural impulses, and is also tied to a cultural association of women with emotionality and the loss of control. I use the language of control in discussing emotions in order to account for the ways in which moral selfhood involves the attempt to direct the self's forces in the production of moral security. I conceive of those forces that moral selves seek to control, as well as the means through which moral selves seek to control them, as the highly interactive outcome of their embodied interactions with social forces, while being irreduc-ible to these forces.

16. For instance, see Hochschild (1983), Illouz (2008), Barbalet (2001), and Williams (2001), as well as the analysts and approaches discussed in the previous section.

17. On this issue, see French novelist Alexandre Jardin's (2011) auto-biographical account of his grandfather Jean Jardin's direct involvement in the massive deportation of Jews, as cabinet minister for the French head of state and collaborator Pierre Laval, which had been covered up until the publication of his book. Jardin denounces the failure of his family, and of French authorities and historians more generally, to publicly acknowledge the role of French citizens with morals ("les gens très bien") in mass extermination.

18. See my discussion of submission/domination as a master emotional-norm pair for the Middle Ages in Chapter 7.

CHAPTER 5

1. The authors of the Baumeister et al. (2007) study use the concept of "hedonic power" to designate the effects of individuals' propensity to seek pleasure and to avoid pain. I appropriate this concept in order to develop an approach to emotional regulation and emotion management.

2. See Leys (2010) and Leys and Goldman (2010) for critiques of nonintentional approaches to emotional experience such as those of Sylvan S. Tomkins, Paul Ekman, and Antonio Damasio. Leys argues that in these approaches, it is as if danger was contained in objects, since encounters with certain objects are said to trigger emotional responses without the intervention of intention, meaning, or cognition. Embodied in/capacity suggests that there very well may be nonintentional emotional experiences, in particular those experiences that are or that come to be experienced through the panic/excitement modality of fear and desire (i.e., that are driven by will-based subjective autonomy), but that these are subject to intentionality through emotion management—through the anxiety/interest and the distress/relief modalities of fear and desire (i.e., that are driven by intention-based moral autonomy), and that some of these are the result of earlier intention-driven emotion management efforts that have become embodied. Leys worries about the political implications of what she understands as a shift from a view of emotional experience as grounded in guilt, which is seen to involve questions of meaning and agency, to a view of emotional experience as grounded in shame, which is seen to circumvent such questions because it is understood by thinkers who work in the noncognitivist tradition of Tomkins and others to be a response that is divorced from intentionality. My understanding of shame differs from both Leys' and the noncognitivists', inasmuch as it designates the intention-driven morality-based experience of self-disapproval, whose forms are self-dislike/self-like, self-disgust/self-purging, and self-hate/self-love (I explain in the last section of Chapter 3 that

these moral social emotions can be experienced subjectively or morally). I also make a distinction between the subjective and the moral experience of guilt. While guilt is a moral emotion (i.e., its object is the unsuccessful resolution of an objectified emotional problem [cf. Chapter 3]), the actions to which it is tied are not necessarily deliberate. In other words, they do not necessarily entail moral self-transformation efforts.

3. Objects of fear and desire (i.e., the content of problems and solutions) can be thought of as the embodied product of an agent's experience, but they may also be thought of as inborn. I have not yet become properly acquainted with the literature that argues for or against such a direct, inborn connection between emotional experiences and the signs of danger and security that trigger them. I do believe that we should be open to exploring the implications of such a connection. It is possible, for instance, that inborn objects of fear and desire, or their signs, if they are shown to exist, are more likely to become the object of morally normative social fears and desires. In other words, a problem or its sign that one already fears, or a solved problem or its sign that one already desires, might be more susceptible of becoming attached to morally normative social fears and desires.

4. As Leys emphasizes (Leys and Goldman 2010), intentions are not necessarily conscious.

5. I understand guilt/innocence as a differentiated expression of the more basic socially governed emotions of self-disapproval that include self-dislike/self-like, self-disgust/self-purging, and self-hate/self-love. Shame/pride and personal insecurity/self-esteem are the names I use to explicitly designate the moral experience of the emotions of self-disapproval. For more on this issue see the section that follows as well as the last section of Chapter 3.

6. Displacement should not be confused with emotional blending, even though emotional blending can cause displacement. Displacement is the process through which a sign of danger or security dissimulates the relational threats and promises for which they stand by having no obvious connection to them. Emotional blending involves the move into a secondary emotional-norm pair as a means of resolving the incapacities associated with the primary pair.

7. For some of the political implications (especially in terms of gender and race relations) of the social production of objects of fear and desire, see the work of Ahmed (2010, 2004).

8. There are obviously circumstances in which individuals will seek out pain. For a discussion of this issue, see the section titled "From the Fear of Desire to the Fear of Fear" in Chapter 8.

9. As with all emotions, there are different intensities of shame and personal insecurity that likely have to do with the pain effects of the

relational threat with which these are associated (e.g., if it is really important for me that I wear the right kind of clothes, my shame will be more intense if I violate this imperative then if it is only mildly important; and if it is really important for me that I earn a lot of money, my personal insecurity will be more intense if I fail to measure up to this ideal). The intensity of an emotion may also have to do with our incapacity to deal with it, as Ahmed (2010, 43) also argues following Hochschild (1983). The incapacity to move from fear to desire can be very painful—for instance, the incapacity to give the form of guilt, anger, or sadness to a pain I am feeling—much as the incapacity to move from desire to the implementation of security can be very painful—for instance, the incapacity to confront another's hurting of oneself through the assertiveness-driven implementation of security. In both cases, I will remain caught in the pain of emotional incapacity unless a new means of exercising power is made available to me, or unless I engage in moral self-transformation.

10. These principles have been applied to the analysis of literary and cinematic horror by Carroll (1990), who argues that monstrosity is an effect that is produced through the representation of the categorically interstitial or contradictory (e.g., creatures who are both living and dead such as ghosts and vampires), the incomplete (e.g., the lack of skin or of other body parts, the disintegrated), or the formless (e.g., the vaporous and the gelatinous). Pinedo (1997) draws on similar principles in her analysis of recreational terror.

11. Leys argues (Leys and Goldman 2010) that guilt differs from shame in being tied to one's actions rather than to one's sense of self. She maintains that guilt and not shame can be triggered by one's virtual (fantasized) or actual actions, "since for Freud the unconscious does not distinguish between the intention and the deed" (670). Unlike Leys, I consider that shame (as well as personal insecurity) is like guilt, an emotion that can concern both the self's identity and the self's actions, whether virtual or actual. I see these emotions as having to do with the self's feeling of responsibility for what it is or what it does. Where shame and personal insecurity refer to the moral self's feeling of responsibility for failing to conform to social expectations through what it is or what it does virtually or actually, guilt refers to the moral self's feeling of responsibility for failing to conform to social expectations by causing hurt to another through what it is or what it does virtually or actually. Thus it is possible to have a shameful or personally insecure identity, where one's identity transgresses or falls short of social expectations (e.g., the queer or the introvert), much as it is possible to have a guilty identity, where one's identity transgresses or falls short of social expectations by causing hurt to another (e.g., the exploiter of children or the tax evader).

12. Contemporary child rearing approaches often insist upon the importance of telling children that their behavior is inappropriate or inadequate (as opposed to telling them that they are bad or inadequate persons), presumably to counteract what are viewed as the negative effects of shame and low self-esteem on the developing sense of self, or of the problematic effects of labeling on one's identity. See, for instance, the very popular *How to Talk So Kids Will Listen and Listen So Kids Will Talk*, where it is recommended that one should "express strong disapproval (without attacking character")" (Faber and Mazlish 1980, 94). It is probable that the practice of separating self and behavior favored in current child rearing trends promotes an increased awareness of emotion management as a means of exercising power over self and other in both the parents and the children who are exposed to this approach. The experience of pride or of self-esteem nevertheless rests upon the self's prior, painful feeling of its badness or inadequacy—a feeling of shame or of personal insecurity—from which it is motivated to move away through moral self-transformation, whether this feeling has as an object the self's identity or its actions. From this it does not follow that shame or personal insecurity are emotions that should in themselves be condemned, although I can certainly think of instances in which the shaming or rendering insecure of a person can be deemed morally problematic. For instance, if it is the self-worth of a child or of any other person that one feels one ought to protect, then it is not so much the self's feeling of itself or of its actions as out of place through the experience of shame or of personal insecurity that is a problem, but rather the methods of shaming or of rendering personally insecure that degrade the person of the child. A distinction should therefore be drawn between the shame experienced by a person who feels responsible for having broken a law such as an antipollution law, or the personal insecurity experienced by a person who feels responsible for having fallen short of an ideal such as looking out for those in need, and the shame or personal insecurity experienced by a person who feels humiliated as a consequence of the external or internalized contempt practiced by another. Other relevant considerations include the legitimacy or adequacy of the social expectation that causes shame or personal insecurity, social expectations that can be deemed morally problematic because they are aimed at subjects who are permanently unable to meet them, and social expectations that can only be met through self-destructive means.

13. Miller (1997) emphasizes the inferiorizing outlook associated with disgust and attends to its role of promoting social hierarchies via contempt. I think it is possible and useful to distinguish between the condition of being of inferior worth, and the condition of being of

inferior capacity. A child's capacity to exercise embodied autonomy may be generally thought of as inferior to that of the adult, without this saying anything about the child's or the adult's worth. Or a student's capacity to exercise embodied autonomy may generally be thought of as inferior to that of the teacher, without this saying anything about the student's or the teacher's worth. In this sense, experiences of shame or of personal insecurity, or the triggering of these experiences in others, should not be thought of as inherently problematic, inasmuch as these emotional orientations condition the exercise of morally embodied autonomy in the fulfillment of socially normative expectations. When one tells children that they ought not to strike others or that they are capable of doing a better job of brushing their teeth, or when one tells students that they ought not misspell such and such a word or that they are capable of improving their capacity for critical thinking, one hopes to trigger experiences of shame/pride and of personal insecurity/self-esteem as conditions in the fulfillment of the socially normative imperatives and ideals that one holds to be of worth. Socially normative imperatives and ideals can obviously be subject to critique, but the very capacity to effectively criticize requires access to self-caring means of exercising power in the implementation of social security. In short, there is a difference between being of inferior worth (being less valuable and therefore exploitable) and being of inferior capacity (being less powerful but not necessarily less valuable). The practices we should be leery of are therefore ones that are conditioned by and reproduce feelings of humiliation and of inferiority through inferiority/contempt, rather than the ones that are conditioned by and reproduce feelings of pride/shame and personal insecurity/self-esteem.

14. Distinguishing between the subjective and moral experience of self-disgust/self-purging might help shed light on processes that promote healing in disorders in which a disgusting sense of self promotes self-destructive attempts to purge oneself of one's self. It might help us resolve the following paradox: Probyn (2005) writes that an affective complex involving "shame, self-loathing and tragic pride" (21) was the unacknowledged basis of her life-threatening anorexia nervosa as a young woman, which was inefficiently being treated through behavior modification. But she notes that it was also shame that caused her to eat for fear of being impolite and of disappointing her best friend's parents, whom she looked up to. One might reframe this by considering that an initial, subjective experience of self-disgust/self-purging, in which Probyn moved from the one to the other through the panic/excitement-driven purging of herself through the expulsion of food, gave way to shame/pride when she developed a moral relationship to her eating—when the relational

threat produced by not eating became her own responsibility—which allowed her to correct her desire not to eat.

15. The reader ought to be reminded here of the distinct ways in which I designate the feeling of moral responsibility (i.e., immorality/morality) when it pertains to self-disciplinary efforts (i.e., evil/righteousness) and when it pertains to self-realization efforts (i.e., irresponsibility/responsibility). It should also be noted that while the individual feeling of moral responsibility toward imperatives and ideals is highly interactive with morally normative social expectations (i.e., with dominant, socially produced moral norms), the two remain distinct. This means that the feelings that pertain to one's sense of being socially disruptive, such as self-dislike/self-like and pride/shame, for instance, are differentiated and blended descendants of immorality/morality that involve the additional component of social disapproval. This also means that agents' embodied imperatives and ideals can deviate to a greater or lesser extent from socially dominant moral norms, whether these are moral commands or moral standards.

16. Stress researcher Sonia Lupien (2010) holds that there are four subjective triggers of stress: ego threats, the unexpected, the unknown, and lack of control. I am suggesting that these can be understood to correspond to contemporary experiences of rivalry/advantage, surprise/predictability, unfamiliarity/familiarity, and oppression/emancipation, which make up the contemporary emotional-norm pair that is emotional stress/resilience.

17. See Armon-Jones (1988a, 37–38) for a discussion of the differences between the strong and the weak social constructionist thesis.

18. Constructionists' approach to emotional experience tends to be overly cognitive, and tends to downplay that cognition, not just emotion, is embodied. It cannot properly account for the co-constitutive relationship between emotion and cognition in subjective and moral experience, which I seek to render in the notion of embodied knowledge, or of felt perception. The radical separation between emotion and cognition, and the association of the first with the material body and of the second with the immaterial mind, is increasingly being problematized in contemporary theorizations of emotional experience. For instance, see Blackman (2008a, 2008b), Lupton (1998), Probyn (2005), and Williams (2001).

19. Rose (2008) notes the rising concern voiced by organizations like the World Health Organization toward increasing rates of mental illness.

20. As Rose writes (2008, 254): "we can think of a term such as depression...as a 'problem/solution' complex: it simultaneously judges mood against certain desired standards, frames discontents in a certain way, renders them as a problem in need of attention, establishes

a classification framework to name and delineate them, scripts a pattern of affects, cognitions, desires and judgements, writes a narrative for its origins and destiny, attributes it meaning, identifies some authorities who can speak and act wisely in relation to it and prescribes some responses to it."

21.   What we might mean by "actual" cases of depression poses another set of interesting questions I do not mean to address here.

22.   Stearns and Stearns (1986, 7) object to anthropologists' claim that anger may not be a universal emotion. This objection is based on the Stearns' understanding of anger in very general terms. They do not define anger beyond the fact that it is an emotion related to the fight response and to the perception of antagonism (15). As such, there are important parallels between what the Stearns understand as anger and what I understand as the confrontational orientation to danger and security, whose basic fear and desire form I have called terror/courage. The narrower understanding of anger that I propose, which entails the perception of another's denial of one's desires, presumes a particular type of social order (i.e., one in which individuals relate to one another as individually contained, freestanding beings). As such, anger and guilt as I define them here are probably not grounds for action in all societies.

23.   Stearns and Stearns (1986) argue that not only the behaviors associated with anger, but the emotion of anger itself, have been the object of social condemnation during various periods of American history. Yet, given the overly vague nature of their understanding of anger (i.e., as the perception of antagonisms and the fight response), in the terms of embodied in/capacity theory it is difficult to imagine a society in which some forms in the perception of antagonisms, and some manifestations of the fight response, would not be subject to moral control efforts, whether through their repression, correction, activation, or formation. See also the previous note.

24.   See also the collection of essays on emotions and social movements in Goodwin, Jasper, and Polletta (2001).

25.   Of course, social change is a complex process that does not solely involve moral agency, but it is uninteresting to belittle the importance of intentionality, both conscious and unconscious, in social change, in favor of a view that ends up promoting collective forms of heteronomy and a problematic form of relativism by emphasizing the absence of intentionality. Such, for instance, are the implications of Elias's (1978, 1982) position, who, in asking readers to suspend their feelings and moralizing judgment toward "uncivilized" modes of being (1978, 58–59), does so in the spirit that social processes are the outcome of a social order of which no individual rational agent is in control (1982, 230–32)—as if social changes were not at least in part propelled by the intention-driven actions, whether conscious

or not, of embodied subjects—thereby making them beyond our approval or disapproval. It seems to me that we can and should move beyond this view by exploring the ways in which rational agency is not necessarily deliberate (i.e., biological being, subjective being, and moral being have their own rationalities or purposes), as well as the ways in which deliberate action is not necessarily conscious (i.e., the moral self's actions are often driven by unconscious forces). Irrationality may be thought of as resulting from the conflict between the competing logics of these forces, rather than as the consequence of the conscious, intentional self's lack of control over its irrational self (i.e., usually conceived of as the emotional, bodily self) and other irrational forces (i.e., all forces that escape the conscious self's rational control). I explore this in more detail elsewhere in this book. See Rosenwein (2002) for a useful critique of the assumption that emotions are irrational as well as for a deconstructive reading of Elias. See Reddy (1999, 1997) for compelling arguments against social constructionism's moral relativism.

26. See Ahmed (2010) for an analysis of some of the culturally dominant ways in which conformity is achieved through the promise of happiness in the contemporary West. There is of course a dual sense in which happiness can be thought of as a promise in the terms of embodied in/capacity theory. The first is the sense in which I take Ahmed to intend it: happiness as a coveted state of pleasurable being that becomes attached to various culturally promoted goals (or objects of desire that may form signs of security in the language I develop here) that include happiness as such, and to means of achieving these goals. The second is the sense that stems from an understanding of happiness as a felt from of capacity through which one overcomes the feeling of incapacity that is sadness based on a prevention orientation. In other words, as a form of desire, happiness can be understood as a relational promise in the same way as any other form of desire. This means that numerous other felt forms of capacity can be used as objects of desire and form signs of security in the promotion of social conformity, not all of which are necessarily derived from or blended with sadness/happiness.

27. For parallel discussions of emotional suffering see Ahmed (2010) on the notion of the "affect alien," and Reddy (1999) on "intense ambivalence."

Chapter 6

1. Wharton (1993) emphasizes the importance of specifying that jobs like flight attendance or bill collecting are frontline service jobs rather than merely service industry jobs.

2. While my conception of embodied autonomy is based on the principle that embodied selves are fashioned through their interactions with other forces that include other selves, such that we are affected by and affect other forces and should not be thought of as wholly discrete entities, I remain committed to the notion of each human being's individual vitality and integrity. I conceive of the ability to exercise power in the subversion of harm to oneself as a basic human need—as a key feature of the exercise of embodied autonomy. On the issue of the compromised ability to listen to one's embodied self, see Hochschild's parallel discussion (1983, 194–198) of the altruist self, which she contrasts with the narcissistic self.

3. See my brief discussion of emotional stress in the section titled "Moral Actions of Social Conformity" in Chapter 5.

4. Some of the other key points of Wouters' (1989b) critique of Hochschild's approach *in The Managed Heart* are that Hochschild fails to consider noncommercial constraints; that she focuses exclusively on the costs of emotion management; that she ignores evidence that contradicts her thesis that flight attendants feel estranged from their selves or that they enjoy their work (Wouters's own smaller study of flight attendants showed that these workers were troubled by the social instability that came with the job rather than by the requirement to act, and that some found their work pleasurable and rewarding); that she accords flight attendants too little agency and sets them in an exaggerated opposition of interests with bosses and clients; that she problematically limits emotional labor to those jobs with supervisors, thereby excluding the emotional labor performed by professionals who include doctors, teachers, therapists, and numerous others; that she downplays the importance of the emotion management performed by men; that she idealizes a fictional past in which emotion management was done freely, thereby ignoring the role of state, church, and family; and that the control of emotion management is by no means a phenomenon that is restricted to advanced capitalism.

5. Both Rose (1989) and Illouz (2008) have written books that include chapters dealing explicitly with the issue of psychology-inspired emotion management in the workplace.

6. As such, I share Reddy's (1999) interest in ways of conceptualizing individual autonomy that account for the power of social forces in the constitution of selfhood, without discounting the unique nature of the embodied being that founds this relationship, as well as his interest in producing grounds for social critique that move beyond the problematic relativism of social constructionism, while circumventing the problems associated with essentialism.

7. See also Carroll's (1990) critique of the illusion and pretend theories of fiction, which I discuss in endnote 2 in Chapter 2.

8. It is not difficult to come up with such examples, but for a concrete illustration, see Tait's (2007) analysis of cosmetic surgery as a socially rewarding practice that is freely engaged in, but whose routinization may be argued to extend and amplify the very suffering it aims to relieve.

9. On this issue, see the section titled "Emotional Blending and Emotional Differentiation" in Chapter 2.

10. I want to emphasize a point made earlier that we are not necessarily conscious of our intentions.

11. For a more detailed discussion of the differences between self-discipline and self-realization in their relation to the resolution of conflicts between the subjective and the moral self, see the section titled "From the Fear of Desire to the Fear of Fear" in Chapter 8.

CHAPTER 7

1. One must use this idea with caution, since the subjects of modern and advanced modern societies have obviously not completely done away with the use of physical coercion to solve problems in everyday life. Moreover, their moral relationship to these means ought to be understood differently depending on the society in question (i.e., the moral concerns of Americans vis-à-vis physical violence are not necessarily those of Canadians, of Germans, of the Dutch, or of Australians) and is also governed by the more specific emotional economies to which individuals belong within these larger social configurations.

2. Health figures at the center of the advanced modern logic and of the subjectivities it promotes. See for instance Ehrenberg (2010), Bendelow (2009), Illouz (2008), Rose (2007), Collin (2007), Otero (2003), Nettleton (1997), Petersen (1997), and Greco (1993).

3. On this issue see Adam Curtis's BBC documentary series *The Century of the Self* (2002), as well as Stuart Ewen's (1996) "social history of spin," which is said to have inspired the series.

4. The work of governmentality theorists such as Nikolas Rose falls in line with this type of argument.

5. See a parallel discussion of this trend in Stearns's (2006, 6–7, 104) analysis of the evolution of the *Curious George* series.

6. See Reddy (1999, 1997) for a similar call for the development of nonessentialist approaches to embodied autonomy that help us get beyond the problematic forms of relativism associated with social constructionism.

7. Probyn (2005) similarly argues that we cannot live without shame, and that shame can be tied to positive emotions and changes. For instance, she explores the role of shame in spurring the desire for

connection in the Australian Reconciliation between nonindigenous and indigenous.

8. The emotional impact of any representation depends among other things on the way in which it is decoded or its meaning constructed (Hall 1997; Chandler 2009). I do not intend to get into the fascinating debates that have fueled reader-response criticism. Suffice it to say that my arguments here are based on the idea that any reading is an embodied reading, that it involves the felt perception of signs of danger and security, and that one's social positioning affects one's felt perception of signs, as well as the social positions we take on through situation assimilation (see my discussion of situation assimilation in Chapter 8).

9. For a view of all these images and captions, cf. "Graphic Health Warnings," Health Canada, last modified August 3, 2010, accessed June 9, 2009, http://www.hc-sc.gc.ca/hc-ps/tobac-tabac/legislation/label-etiquette/graph/index-eng.php.

10. Cultural norms may increase the subjective or moral salience of other norms, such as the biological norms invoked in this antitobacco campaign's depiction of a blackened smile as gum disease.

11. See my use and discussion of situation assimilation in chapter 8. It is a concept that I borrow from Carroll (1990) and that I favor over that of identification to explain the way in which agents are affected by others' perceived emotional states.

12. http://www.youtube.com/watch?v=VYtzSt7-ciY&feature=PlayList&p=DCC9ADAEBCA3374E&index=4&playnext=2&playnext_from=PL. Accessed June 9, 2009.

13. Ewen (1996, 3–4) reports on the American pioneer of public relations Edward L. Bernays's ability to convince women's rights activists to use Lucky Strike cigarettes as "Torches of Freedom" in one of their marches in the 1920s, thereby initiating the association between "corporate sales campaigns and popular social causes." This is precisely the relationship we find in the Colgate prohygiene campaign, where the attempt to sell toothpaste is tied to the popular social cause of smoking prevention.

CHAPTER 8

1. See Lutz (1996) for a discussion of the gendered dimensions of the perception of emotionality.

2. Lupton's ethnography of contemporary subjects' views on emotional expression (1998, 47) supports my claim that emotional expression is the new standard in emotion management. A majority of participants believed that emotions were better expressed than suppressed, while only a minority considered that emotions should be controlled. This finding is also interesting because it upholds the

dominant and misleading view that emotional expression is not the result of either or both social control and moral self-control.

3. This is also the title of a self-help classic by Susan Jeffers that continues to enjoy a great deal of popularity.

4. http://www.youtube.com/watch?v=dBPgwnp1S1s. Accessed on June 9, 2009.

5. See for instance Gardner (2008), Siegel (2005), Glassner (1999), Altheide (1997), and Furedi (1997).

6. The contemporary fear of fear is the object of frequent campaigns of desire (e.g., in government programs, reality television, self-help books, social movements).

7. Healthism rests upon and promotes one of the most important moral norms of the contemporary era—the expectation that one can and should affect the outcome of one's life course as a free individual. The master emotional-norm pair that governs this norm is disempowerment/empowerment (the felt in/capacity to confront the personal shortcomings that compromise one's healthy desire through self-realization). The 1960s constitute the beginning of a radicalization of a cultural focus on health, illness, and suffering as a matter of individual responsibility that becomes dominant in the 1970s (Otero 2003; Rose 1999). The term "healthism" has a number of related connotations, including a 1970s political ideology in which corporations' and the state's responsibility over health is turned over to individuals. The concept was first coined by the political economist Robert Crawford in the 1980s. Crawford (1980) argues that the health-conscious person is required to be constantly worried about health risks. He attributes the shift from collective to personal responsibility for health to the development of a neoliberal social order in the period from the mid-1970s to the mid-1980s. The health talk of the 1960s thus gave way to the responsibility talk of the 1970s, with the 1980s seeing the birth of middle class "healthism."

8. Reuter's (2007) genealogical study of the role of psychiatric knowledge in the embodiment and management of agoraphobia implies that disorders of fear have gendered dimensions that shift over time. For instance, she notes that up until World War I, more than 80 percent of the cases diagnosed were men, whereas women now make up the majority of cases. Moreover, the in/capacities with which the disorder is associated are also gendered. For example, women's treatment promotes the development of the capacity to shop, whereas men's treatment promotes the development of the capacity to work.

9. Lupton (1999, 23–24) cites research that might partially explain this perception. This research shows that increased social powerlessness is correlated with increased risk perception, such that white women

worry more than white men and nonwhite women more than white women, for instance. However, to explain the coding of worry (or of phobia, terror, or fear more generally) as feminine, one should also consider the emotive performance of worry as a means of conforming to particular images of femininity and of maternity (i.e., the benevolent concern of the ideal mother, the suffocating concern of the not-so-ideal mother), as well as the political conditions and effects of associating the feminine with incapacity. Moreover, inasmuch as some forms of felt incapacity are alternatively designated as masculine, one ought also to consider the gender politics and morally normative social expectations that condition the gendered nature of various forms of felt in/capacity.

10. Furedi's *Culture of Fear* (1997), Glassner's *The Culture of Fear* (1999), Siegel's *False Alarm* (2005), and Stearns's *American Fear* (2006) are all examples of culture-of-fear theorizing in which the mass media are viewed as playing a major role in the production of irrational fear. Other agents include corporations (particularly pharmaceutical corporations), experts (particularly psychological ones), politicians, the government, and activists.

11. Many of the contemporary worries over the effects of the mass media match those found in much earlier historical periods, in particular where mass entertainment is concerned. For instance, Goethe's *Faust* represents a preoccupation with the manipulative features of entertainment, with the business element, and with the divergence between the artist's needs and the audience's wishes (Lowenthal, 1961, 14–51).

12. See my discussion of this concept, which was developed by Reddy (1999, 1997), in "Emotives, Modalities of Fear and Desire, and Moral Self-Control" in Chapter 6.

AFTERWORD

1. See, for instance, de Courville Nicol (2004).
2. See, for instance, McGee (2005), Isin (2004), Rimke (2000), Rose (1999), O'Malley (1998), Nettleton (1997), Petersen (1997), Burchell (1993), and Greco (1993).
3. Ehrenberg makes similar arguments in accounting for contemporary depressive and addictive disorders in his recently translated *The Weariness of the Self: Diagnosing the History of Depression in the Contemporary Age* (2010).
4. For instance, a variety of anxiety disorder categories (panic disorder, generalized anxiety disorder, social phobia, and posttraumatic stress disorder) first appeared in the third edition of the *Diagnostic and Statistical Manual of Mental Disorders,* published in 1980.

5. In the introduction to their recently edited reader on emotions, Greco and Stenner (2008) argue that the affective turn is a move to reconsider ontological issues that pertain to emotions conditioned by the epistemological work of deconstruction accomplished earlier by social constructionists. The affective turn does not rest upon the problematic relationship with the natural sciences that this earlier deconstruction involved. On the reconsideration of the biological by social science and humanities scholars, see also Blackman and Venn (2010) and Blackman et al. (2008).

6. See, for instance, the cutting-edge work of Wilson (2008, 2004) as well Rose's (2007) latest work on the emergence of somatic ethics and the new journal *BioSocieties* for which he is a coeditor.

7. For a critical account of five dominant explanations for the massive contemporary expansion of psychiatric disorders, which consist of more mental illness, better diagnoses, psychiatrists as moral entre- preneurs, pharmaceutical power, and the psychiatrization of every- day problems, see Rose (2008). For the role of risk management in this process, see Rose (2005).

8. See Wilkinson (2005) for a compelling analysis of this issue in his *Suffering: A Sociological Introduction*.

9. See the collection of essays in Goodwin, Jasper, and Polletta (2001) for a series of interesting reflections on emotions, social movements, and social justice.

BIBLIOGRAPHY

Abu-Lughod, Lila. *Veiled Sentiments: Honor and Poetry in a Bedouin Society.* Berkeley: University of California Press, 1986.

Ahmed, Sara. *The Cultural Politics of Emotion.* Edinburgh: Edinburgh University Press, 2004.

———. *The Promise of Happiness.* Durham: Duke University Press, 2010.

Altheide, David L. "The News Media: The Problem Frame, and the Production of Fear." *The Sociological Quarterly* 38, no. 4 (1997): 647–68.

Armon-Jones, Claire. "The Thesis of Constructionism." In *The Social Construction of Emotions,* edited by Rom Harré, 32–56. Oxford: Blackwell, 1988a.

———. "The Social Functions of Emotions." In *The Social Construction of Emotions,* edited by Rom Harré, 57–92. Oxford: Blackwell, 1988b.

Barbalet, Jack. *Emotion, Social Theory and Social Structure: A Macrosociological Approach.* Cambridge: Cambridge University Press, 2001.

———. *Emotions and Sociology.* Oxford: Blackwell, 2002a.

———. "Introduction: Why Emotions Are Crucial." In *Emotions and Sociology,* edited by Jack Barbalet, 1–9. Oxford: Blackwell (Sociological Review Monograph Series, 2002b).

Baumeister, Roy F., Kathleen D. Vohs, C. Nathan DeWall, and Liqing Zhang. "How Emotion Shapes Behavior: Feedback, Anticipation, and Reflection, rather than Direct Causation." *Personality and Social Psychology Review* 11, no. 2 (May 2007): 167–203.

Beck, Ulrich. *Risk Society: Towards a New Modernity.* London: Sage, 1992.

Becker, Howard S. *The American Journal of Sociology* 59, no. 3 (1953): 235–42.

Bendelow, Gillian. *Sociology of Health and Illness* 15, no. 3 (1993): 273–94.

———. *Health, Emotion and the Body.* Cambridge: Polity Press, 2009.

Bendelow, Gillian, and Simon J. Williams. *Sociology of Health and Illness* 17, no. 2 (1995): 139–65.

Berlant, Lauren. "Introduction: Compassion (and Withholding)." In *Compassion: The Culture and Politics of an Emotion,* 1–14. New York: Routledge, 2004.

Blackman, Lisa. "Self-Help, Media Cultures and the Production of Female Psychopathology." *European Journal of Cultural Studies* 7 (2004): 219–36.

———. "The Dialogical Self, Flexibility and the Cultural Production of Psychopathology." *Theory and Psychology* 15, no. 2 (2005): 183–206.

———. "Psychiatric Culture and Bodies of Resistance." *Body and Society* 13, no. 2 (2007): 1–23.

———."Affect, Relationality and the 'Problem of Personality.'" *Theory, Culture and Society* 25, no. 1 (2008a): 23–47.

———. *The Body: Key Concepts.* New York: Berg, 2008b.

Blackman, Lisa, John Cromby, Derek Hook, Dimitris Papadopoulos, and Valerie Walkerdine. "Creating Subjectivities." *Subjectivity* 22 (2008): 1–27.

Blackman, Lisa, and Couze Venn. "Affect." *Body and Society* 16, no. 1 (2010): 7–28.

Bloomfield, Brian P., and Theo Vurdubakis. "Disrupted Boundaries: New Reproductive Technologies and the Language of Anxiety and Expectation." *Social Studies of Science* 25 (1995): 533–51.

Burchell, Graham. "Liberal Government and Techniques of the Self." *Economy and Society* 22, no. 3 (1993): 267–82.

Campbell, Robert Jean. *Campbell's Psychiatric Dictionary.* 8th Edition, Oxford: Oxford University Press, 2004.

Carroll, Noël. *The Philosophy of Horror or Paradoxes of the Heart.* New York: Routledge, 1990.

Castel, Robert. *La gestion des risques: de l'anti-psychiatrie à l'après-psychanalyse.* Paris: Les Éditions de Minuit, 1981.

Chandler, David. "Semiotics for Beginners." http://www.aber.ac.uk/media/Documents/S4B/sem08c.html.

Cloud, Dana L. *Control and Consolation in American Culture and Politics: Rhetorics of Therapy.* Thousand Oaks, CA: Sage, 1998.

Colgate Total Advertisement for Total Whitening Toothpaste. Directed by Colgate. http://www.youtube.com/watch?v=VYtzSt7-ciY&feature=PlayList&p=DCC9ADAEBCA3374E&index=4&playnext=2&playnext_from=PL.

Collin, Johanne. "Relations de sens et relations de fonction: risque et médicament." *Sociologie et sociétés* 39, no. 1 (2007): 99–122.

Crawford, Robert. "Healthism and the Medicalization of Everyday Life." *International Journal of Health Services: Planning, Administration, Evaluation* 10, no. 3 (1980): 365–88.

Curtis, Adam. *The Century of the Self.* London: BBC, 2002.

De Courville Nicol, Valérie. *Le soupçon gothique: l'intériorisation de la peur en Occident.* Québec: Presses de l'Université Laval, 2004.

Dean, Mitchell. "Sociology after Society." In *Sociology after Postermodernism*, edited by David Owen, 205–28. Thousand Oaks, CA: Sage, 1997.

Delzescaux, Sabine. *Norbert Elias: Civilisation et décivilisation.* Paris: L'Harmattan, 2003.

Douglas, Mary. *Purity and Danger: An Analysis of Concepts of Pollution and Taboo.* New York: Routledge, 1966.

————. *Risk and Blame: Essays in Cultural Theory*. New York: Routledge, 1992.

Durkheim, Émile. *L'Éducation Morale*. Paris: Presses Universitaires de France, 1963.

————. *The Rules of Sociological Method and Selected Texts on Sociology and Its Method*. New York: Free Press, 1982.

Ehrenberg, Alain. *The Weariness of the Self: Diagnosing the History of Depression in the Contemporary Age*. Kingston, Ontario: McGill-Queens University Press, 2010.

Elias, Norbert. *The Civilizing Process: The History of Manners*. Chapel Hill: University of North Carolina Press, 1978.

————. *The Civilizing Process: State Formation and Civilization*. Oxford: Basil Blackwell, 1982.

Engels, Friedrich. "The Class Nature of Morality." In *Reader in Marxist Philosophy*, edited by Howard Selsam and Harry Martel. New York: International Publishers, 1987.

Ewen, Stuart. *PR! A Social History of Spin*. New York: Basic Books, 1996.

Faber, Adele, and Elaine Mazlish. *How to Talk So Kids Will Listen and Listen So Kids Will Talk*. New York: Perennial Currents, 1980.

Foucault, Michel. *Discipline and Punish: The Birth of the Prison*. New York: Random House, 1979.

————. "The Subject and Power." In *Michel Foucault: Beyond Structuralism and Hermeneutics*, edited by Hubert L. Dreyfus and Paul Rabinow, 208–26. Chicago: University of Chicago Press, 1983.

————. *The History of Sexuality: Volume 1: An Introduction*. New York: Vintage Books, 1990.

Fraser, Mariam, and Monica Greco, eds. *The Body: A Reader*. New York: Routledge, 2005.

Freud, Sigmund. *Inhibitions, Symptoms, and Anxiety*. New York: Norton, 1959.

————. *New Introductory Lectures on Psycho-Analysis*. New York: Norton, 1965.

Freund, Peter E. S. "The Expressive Body: A Common Ground for the Sociology of Emotions and Health and Illness." *Sociology of Health and Illness* 12 (1990): 452–77.

Freund, Peter E. S., and Meredith McGuire. *Health, Illness, and the Social Body: A Critical Sociology*. Englewood Cliffs, NJ: Prentice Hall, 1991.

Furedi, Frank. *Culture of Fear: Risk-Taking and the Morality of Low Expectation*. London: Cassell, 1997.

Gardner, Dan. *Risk: The Science and Politics of Fear*. Toronto: McClelland and Stewart, 2008.

Giddens, Anthony. *The Consequences of Modernity*. Cambridge: Polity Press, 1990.

Glassner, Barry. *The Culture of Fear: Why Americans are Afraid of the Wrong Things*. New York: Basic Books, 1999.

Goodwin, Jeff, and James M. Jasper. "Emotions in Social Movements." In *Handbook of the Sociology of Emotions*, edited by Jan E. Stets and Jonathan H. Turner, 611–36. New York: Springer, 2007.

Goodwin, Jeff, James M. Jasper, and Francesca Polleta. *Passionate Politics: Emotions and Social Movements*. Chicago: University of Chicago Press, 2001.

Gould, Deborah. "Rock the Boat, Don't Rock the Boat, Baby: Ambivalence and the Emergence of Militant Aids Activism." In *Passionate Politics: Emotions and Social Movements*, edited by Jeff Goodwin, James M. Jasper, and Francesca Polletta, 135–57. Chicago: University of Chicago Press, 2001.

Greco, Monica. "Psychosomatic Subjects and the 'Duty to be Well': Personal Agency within Medical Rationality." *Economy and Society* 22, no. 3 (1993): 357–72.

Greco, Monica, and Paul Stenner, eds. *Emotions: A Social Science Reader.* New York: Routledge, 2008.

Hacking, Ian. *The Social Construction of What?* Boston: Harvard University Press, 1999.

Hall, Calvin S. *A Primer of Freudian Psychology.* New York: New American Library, 1954.

Hall, Stuart. *Representation: Cultural Representations and Signifying Practices.* London: Sage, 1997.

Haraway, Donna. *Simians, Cyborgs and Women: The Reinvention of Nature.* New York: Routledge, 1991.

Harré, Rom. *The Social Construction of Emotions.* Oxford: Basil Blackwell, 1986.

Harré, Rom, and Robert Finlay-Jones, eds. "Emotion Talk across Times." In *The Social Construction of Emotions*, edited by Rom Harré, 220–33. Oxford: Blackwell, 1986.

Harré, Rom, and W. Gerrod Parrott, eds. *The Emotions: Social, Cultural and Biological Dimensions.* London: Sage, 1996.

Healy, David. *The Antidepressant Era.* Cambridge, MA: Harvard University Press, 1997.

Heelas, Paul. "Emotion Talk across Cultures." In *The Social Construction of Emotions*, edited by Rom Harré, 234–66. Oxford: Blackwell, 1986.

Hochschild, Arlie R. *The Managed Heart: Commercialization of Human Feeling.* Berkeley: University of California Press, 1983.

———. "Reply to Cas Wouter's Review Essay on the Managed Heart." *Theory, Culture and Society* 6 (1989): 439–45.

Holyfield, Lori. "Generating Excitement: Experienced Emotion in Commercial Leisure." *Social Perspectives on Emotion* 4 (1997): 257–81.

Horwitz, Allan V. *Creating Mental Illness.* Chicago: University of Chicago Press, 2002.

Horwitz, Allan V., and Jerome Wakefield. *The Loss of Sadness: How Psychiatry Transformed Normal Sorrow into Depressive Disorder.* New York: Oxford University Press, 2007.

Hunt, Alan. "Anxiety and Social Explanation: Some Anxieties about Anxiety." *Journal of Social History* 33, no. 1 (1999): 509–28.

Illouz, Eva. *Saving the Modern Soul: Therapy, Emotions, and the Culture of Self-Help.* Berkeley: University of California Press, 2008.

Isin, Engin F. "The Neurotic Citizen." *Citizenship Studies* 8, no. 3 (2004): 217–35.

Jardin, Alexandre. *Des gens très bien.* Paris: Grasset, 2011.

Jeffers, Susan. *Feel the Fear and Do It Anyway.* New York: Fawcett Columbine, 1987.

Katz, Jack. *How Emotions Work.* Chicago: University of Chicago Press, 1999.

Kirk, Stuart A., and Herb Kutchins. *Making Us Crazy: DSM: The Psychiatric Bible and the Creation of Mental Disorders.* New York: Free Press, 1997.

Lafrance, Marc. "Skin and the Self: Cultural Theory and Anglo-American Psychoanalysis." *Body and Society* 15, no. 3 (2009): 3–24.

Leys, Ruth. "How Did Fear Become a Scientific Object and What Kind of Object Is It?" *Representations* 110, no. 1 (2010): 66–104.

Leys, Ruth, and Marlene Goldman. "Navigating the Genealogies of Trauma, Guilt and Affect: An Interview with Ruth Leys." *University of Toronto Quarterly* 79, no. 2 (2010): 656–79.

Lowenthal, Leo. *Literature, Popular Culture and Society.* Englewood Cliffs, NJ: Prentice Hall, 1961.

Lupien, Sonia. *Par amour du stress.* Montreal: Éditions au carré, 2010.

Lupton, Deborah. *The Emotional Self.* London: Sage, 1998.

———. *Risk.* New York: Routledge, 1999.

Lutz, Catherine. "The Domain of Emotion Words on Ifaluk." In *The Social Construction of Emotions,* edited by Rom Harré, 267–88. Oxford: Blackwell, 1986.

———. *Unnatural Emotion: Everyday Sentiments on a Micronesia Atoll and Their Challenge to Western Theory.* Chicago: University of Chicago Press, 1988.

———. "Engendered Emotion: Gender, Power, and the Rhetoric of Emotional Control in American Discourse." In *The Emotions: Social, Cultural and Biological Dimensions,* edited by Rom Harré and W. Gerrod Parrott, 151–70. London: Sage, 1996.

Marx, Karl. "Manifesto of the Communist Party." In *Marx: Later Political Writings,* edited by Terrell Carver, 1–30. New York: Cambridge University Press, 1996.

McGee, Micki. *Self-Help Inc.: Makeover Culture in American Life.* Oxford: Oxford University Press, 2005.

Miller, William Ian. *The Anatomy of Disgust.* Cambridge, MA: Harvard University Press, 1997.

Moore, Michael. *Bowling for Columbine,* 2002.

Morsbach, H., and W. J. Tyler. "A Japanese Emotion: Amae." In *The Social Construction of Emotions,* edited by Rom Harré, 289–307. Oxford: Blackwell, 1986.

Nettleton, Sarah. "Governing the Risky Self: How to Become Healthy, Wealthy and Wise." In *Foucault: Health and Medicine*, edited by Alan Petersen and Robin Bunton, 207–22. New York: Routledge, 1997.

O'Malley, Patrick. *Crime and the Risk Society*. Darmouth: Aldershot, 1998.

Otero, Marcelo. *Les règles de l'individualité contemporaine: Santé mentale et société*. Québec: Presses de l'Université Laval, 2003.

Petersen, Alan. "Risk, Governance and the New Public Health." In *Foucault: Health and Medicine*, edited by Alan Petersen and Robin Bunton, 189–206. New York: Routledge, 1997.

———. *Engendering Emotions*. New York: Palgrave Macmillan, 2004.

Pinedo, Isabel Cristina. *Recreational Terror: Women and the Pleasures of Horror Film Viewing*. Albany: State University of New York Press, 1997.

Prinz, Jesse J. *Gut Reactions*. Oxford: Oxford University Press, 2004.

Probyn, Elspeth. *Blush: Faces of Shame*. Minneapolis: University of Minnesota Press, 2005.

Radcliffe, Ann. "On the Supernatural in Poetry." *New Monthly Magazine* 16 (1826): 145–252.

Reddy, William M. "Emotional Liberty: Politics and History in the Anthropology of Emotions." *Cultural Anthropology* 14, no. 2 (1997): 256–88.

———. "Against Constructionism: The Historical Ethnography of Emotions." *Current Anthropology* 38, no. 3 (1999): 327–51.

Reuter, Shelley Z. *Narrating Social Order: Agoraphobia and the Politics of Classification*. Toronto: University of Toronto Press, 2007.

Rimke, Heidi Marie. "Governing Citizens through Self-Help Literature." *Cultural Studies* 14, no. 1 (2000): 61–78.

Rose, Nikolas. *Governing the Soul: The Shaping of the Private Self*. New York: Routledge, 1989.

———. "Governing 'Advanced' Liberal Democracies." In *Foucault and Political Reason: Liberalism, Neo-Liberalism and Rationalities of Government*, edited by Andrew Barry and Thomas Osbourne. Chicago: Chicago University Press, 1996a.

———. *Inventing Our Selves: Psychology, Power, and Personhood*. Cambridge: Cambridge University Press, 1996b.

———. *Powers of Freedom: Reframing Political Thought*. Cambridge: Cambridge University Press, 1999.

———. "In Search of Certainty: Risk Management in a Biological Age." *Journal of Public Mental Health* 4, no. 3 (2005): 14–21.

———. *The Politics of Life Itself: Biomedicine, Power, and Subjectivity in the Twenty-First Century*. Princeton, NJ: Princeton University Press, 2007.

———. "Disorders Without Borders? The Expanding Scope of Psychiatric Practice." In *Emotions: A Social Science Reader*, edited by Monica Greco and Paul Stenner, 246–57. New York: Routledge, 2008.

Rosenwein, Barbara H. "Worrying about Emotions in History." *The American Historical Review* 107, no. 3 (2002): 1–28.

Shilling, Chris. "Two Traditions in the Sociology of Emotions." In *Emotions in Sociology*, edited by Jack Barbalet, 10–26. Oxford: Blackwell (Sociological Review Monograph Series, 2002).

Siegel, Marc K. *False Alarm: The Truth about the Epidemic of Fear*. Hoboken, NJ: John Wiley & Sons, 2005.

Stallcup, Jackie E. "Power, Fear, and Children's Picture Books." *Children's Literature* 30 (2002): 125–58.

Stearns, Carol Z., and Peter N. Stearns. *Anger: The Struggle for Emotional Control in America's History*. Chicago: University of Chicago Press, 1986.

Stearns, Peter N. *American Fear: The Causes and Consequences of High Anxiety*. New York: Routledge, 2006.

Stets, Jan E., and Jonathan H. Turner, eds. *Handbook of the Sociology of Emotions*. New York: Springer, 2007a.

———. "Moral Emotions." In *Handbook of the Sociology of Emotions*, edited by Jan E. Stets and Jonathan H. Turner, 544–66. New York: Springer, 2007b.

Tait, Sue. "Television and the Domestication of Cosmetic Surgery." *Feminist Media Studies* 7, no. 2 (2007): 119–35.

Thompson, Edward Palmer. "Work-Discipline and Industrial Capitalism Past and Present." *Time* 38, no. 1 (1967): 56–97.

Tomes, Nancy. "Epidemic Entertainments: Disease and Popular Culture in Early-Twentieth-Century America." *American Literary History* 24, no. 4 (2002): 625–52.

Turner, Jonathan H. "Psychoanalytic Sociological Theories and Emotions." In *Handbook of the Sociology of Emotions*, edited by Jan E. Stets and Jonathan H. Turner, 276–94. New York: Springer, 2007.

Turner, Jonathan H., and Jan E. Stets. *The Sociology of Emotions*. Cambridge: Cambridge University Press, 2005.

Wharton, Amy S. "The Affective Consequences of Service Work: Managing Emotions on the Job." *Work and Occupations* 20, no. 2 (1993): 205–32.

Wilkinson, Ian. *Suffering: A Sociological Introduction*. Cambridge: Polity Press, 2005.

Williams, Simon J. "Reason, Emotion and Embodiment: Is 'Mental' Health a Contradiction in Terms?" *Sociology of Health and Illness* 22, no. 5 (2000): 559–81.

———. *Emotion and Social Theory: Corporeal Reflections on the (Ir)Rational*. London: Sage, 2001.

Williams, Simon J., and Gillian Bendelow. "Emotions, Health and Illness: The 'Missing Link.'" In *Health and the Sociology of Emotions*. Cambridge: Blackwell, 1996.

Wilson, Elizabeth A. *Psychosomatic: Feminism and the Neurological Body*. London: Duke University Press, 2004.

———. "The Work of Antidepressants: Preliminary Notes on How to Build an Alliance between Feminism and Psychopharmacology." In *Emotions: A*

Social Science Reader, edited by Monica Greco and Paul Stenner, 240–45. New York: Routledge, 2008.

Wouters, Cas. "Response to Hochschild's Reply." *Theory, Culture and Society* 6 (1989): 447–50.

———. "The Sociology of Emotions and Flight Attendants: Hochschild's Managed Heart." *Theory, Culture and Society* 6 (1989): 95–123.

Index

CPSIA information can be obtained at www.ICGtesting.com
Printed in the USA
LVOW10*1015070314

376456LV00007B/36/P